PRAISE FOR

I AM ZLATAN

SHORTLISTED FOR THE AUGUST PRIZE 2012

"The best footballer's autobiography of recent years is probably *I Am Zlatan*. . . . In fact, having sold 700,000 copies in Sweden alone and been published in fifteen countries, it's probably the bestselling European immigrant's tale since Zadie Smith's *White Teeth*. . . . Once you get past the obligatory snigger prompted by the phrase 'footballer's autobiography,' you can see that Zlatan's book strangely resembles an earlier immigrant's tale: *Portnoy's Complaint,* Philip Roth's classic novel about growing up Jewish in 1930s and 1940s Newark, New Jersey. Each man's story illuminates the other. Moreover, each illuminates the increasingly typical yet rarely heard immigrant experience. Most of the talk about immigrants comes from politicians pontificating about them. These books are wonderful first-hand accounts of what it's like to grow up in an immigrant family. Though Zlatan and Roth are separated by an ocean and four decades, the overlaps are remarkable."

—*Financial Times* (UK)

"Might well be the most compelling autobiography ever to appear under a footballer's name."

—*The Guardian* (UK)

"This is no PR fluff, nor the usual watered-down account of a pampered multi-millionaire. . . . When was the last time a footballer still playing at the peak of his powers spoke out with such devastating honesty? And the whole story is delivered like he is sitting on a bar stool next to you, telling a tale over a pint down the pub. This book must be treasured."

—*Daily Mail* (UK)

I AM ZLATAN

I AM ZLATAN

MY STORY ON AND OFF THE FIELD

ZLATAN IBRAHIMOVIĆ
with David Lagercrantz

TRANSLATED FROM THE SWEDISH BY
Ruth Urbom

RANDOM HOUSE TRADE PAPERBACKS

NEW YORK

2014 Random House Trade Paperback Edition

Copyright © 2011 by Zlatan Ibrahimović and David Lagercrantz
English translation copyright © 2012, 2013 by Ruth Urbom

Published in the United States by Random House Trade Paperbacks,
an imprint of Random House, a division of Random House LLC,
a Penguin Random House Company, New York.

RANDOM HOUSE and the HOUSE colophon are registered trademarks of
Random House LLC.

First published by Albert Bonniers Förlag, Stockholm, Sweden,
in 2011 as a Swedish hardcover edition and 2012 as a digital English edition.
This changed version of the translation was published in paperback by
Penguin Books Ltd., London, in 2013.

LIBRARY OF CONGRESS CATALOGING-IN-PUBLICATION DATA
Ibrahimovic, Zlatan.
I am Zlatan : my story on and off the field / Zlatan Ibrahimovic
with David Lagercrantz ; translated from the Swedish by Ruth Urbom.
pages   cm
ISBN 978-0-8129-8692-1
eBook ISBN 978-0-8129-8693-8
1. Ibrahimovic, Zlatan, 1981– 2. Soccer players—Sweden—Biography.
3. Milan (Soccer team). I. Lagercrantz, David. II. Title.
GV942.7.I27A3 2014
796.334092—dc23
[B]
2014006346

Printed in the United States of America on acid-free paper

www.atrandom.com

8 9

Book design by Casey Hampton

This book is dedicated to my family and my friends, to all those who have followed me through the years and been by my side, good days as well as bad. I also want to send a thought to all the kids out there, all the kids who feel different, who don't quite fit in, and who are singled out for the wrong reasons. It's okay not to be like everyone else. Keep believing in yourself. Things worked out for me, after all.

CAST OF CHARACTERS

Co Adriaanse   My first coach at Ajax.

Aleksandar,
also known as Keki   My little brother, born in 1986.

Massimo Ambrosini   AC Milan team captain. Midfielder.

Micke Andersson   My coach at Malmö FF, in the Superettan League and later in the Allsvenskan League.

Roland Andersson   Former soccer player and member of the Swedish national team. My coach when I joined Malmö FF.

Mario Balotelli   Young talent with Inter Milan. Striker. Later with Manchester City.

Marco van Basten   Striker, outstanding goal-scorer. Totally dominated at AC Milan. Named World Player of the Year in 1992.

Leo Beenhakker   Soccer boss, previously managed teams, including Real Madrid. Sports director at Ajax when I joined that team.

Txiki Begiristain   Sports director at Barcelona during my time with that club. Later resigned.

Silvio Berlusconi   Owner of AC Milan. Former Italian prime minister.

Hasse Borg   Former player and defender with the Swedish national team. Sports director at Malmö FF during my time with the club.

Fabio Cannavaro   Arrived at Juventus at the same time I did. Defender. Named World Player of the Year in 2006. Won the World Cup with Italy in 2006.

Fabio Capello   Demon manager. My coach at Juventus.

Antonio Cassano   Striker at AC Milan. Member of Italian national team.

Tony Flygare   Childhood friend. Soccer talent at Malmö FF.

Louis van Gaal   Soccer boss. Former manager. Director of Ajax during the latter part of my time there.

Italo Galbiati   Capello's right-hand man at Juventus.

Adriano Galliani   Soccer boss, vice president of AC Milan.

Gennaro Gattuso   Midfielder at AC Milan. A warrior. Won the World Cup with Italy in 2006.

Pep Guardiola   Former midfielder, played for Barcelona. My coach at that club.

Helena   My girlfriend, my partner. Mother of my children.

Thierry Henry   My friend at Barcelona. French superstar, formerly
                            with Arsenal, where he became that club's top goal-
                            scorer of all time. Won the World Cup in 1998 and
                            the European Championship in 2000 with France.

Andrés Iniesta   Brilliant midfielder and winger with Barcelona.
                            Won the World Cup in 2010 and the European
                            Championship with Spain in 2012.

Filippo Inzaghi   Striker, leading goal-scorer. Star with AC Milan. I
                            lived in his apartment in Turin. Won the World Cup
                            with Italy in 2006.

Jurka   My mom. Born in Croatia. She worked as a cleaner.

Kaká   Brazilian, attacking midfielder, global star. Named
                            World Player of the Year in 2007. Transferred from
                            AC Milan to Real Madrid.

Ronald Koeman   My coach during the latter part of my time at Ajax.

Joan Laporta   President of Barcelona for most of my time with that
                            club.

Henrik "Henke"
Larsson   Legendary Swedish striker. Played for Celtic and
                            Barcelona. Recipient of the European Golden Boot
                            award in 2001. A mentor to me at the start of my
                            career.

Bengt Madsen   Chairman of the board at Malmö FF during my time
                            there.

Daniel Majstorović   Member of the Swedish national team, has played for various teams abroad. A good friend.

Roberto Mancini   My coach during my first two years at Inter Milan.

Marco Materazzi   Rock-solid defender who won the World Cup with Italy in 2006. Played with me at Inter Milan.

Hasse Mattisson   Team captain at Malmö FF during my time with the club.

Maximilian   My eldest son, born in 2006.

Maxwell   Brazilian player. Incredibly elegant defender. My friend ever since my early days at Ajax. We also played together at Inter Milan and Barcelona.

Olof Mellberg   Friend, member of the Swedish national team, defender. Played for Aston Villa and Juventus, among other teams.

Lionel Messi   Global star. Focus of the game in Barcelona. Joined the club as a thirteen-year-old. Named World Player of the Year in 2009 and 2010.

Gudmundur Mete   A good friend. We played together at Malmö FF.

Mido   Striker. Egyptian. A good friend at Ajax.

Luciano Moggi   Soccer boss, legendary sports director at Juventus during my time with that club.

Massimo Moratti   Oil baron, owner of Inter Milan.

José Mourinho   Legendary manager. My coach at Inter Milan. Later
                         went to Real Madrid.

Pavel Nedvěd   Midfielder with me at Juventus. Named European
                         Player of the Year in 2003.

Alessandro Nesta   Star defender with AC Milan. Won the World Cup
                         with Italy in 2006.

John Steen Olsen   Agent who discovered me at Malmö FF. Managed to
                         sell me to Ajax. One of my close friends today.

Alexander Östlund   Friend, former member of the Swedish national
                         team. Played for various clubs including Southamp-
                         ton.

Alexandre Pato   Brilliant young striker at AC Milan. Brazilian.

Andrea Pirlo   Midfielder at AC Milan, later sold to Juventus. Won
                         the World Cup with Italy in 2006.

Mino Raiola   My agent, my friend, my adviser.

Robinho   Super-talent from Brazil. Second striker at AC
                         Milan, previously with Real Madrid and Manches-
                         ter City.

Ronaldinho   Brazilian. Superstar. Named World Player of the
                         Year in 2004 and 2005. We played together at AC
                         Milan.

Ronaldo   One of the greatest players of all time. Brazilian.
                         Striker. Named World Player of the Year in 1996,
                         1997, and 2002. My idol as a kid.

Cristiano Ronaldo   Striker, global star. Named World Player of the Year in 2008. Played for Manchester United. Transferred to Real Madrid for a record sum. (Usually referred to as "Cristiano" in this book to distinguish him from the player who, for me, will always be the one true Ronaldo.)

Sandro Rosell   Joan Laporta's successor as president of Barcelona.

Sanela   My older sister, born in 1979.

Sapko   My older half-brother, born in Bosnia in 1973.

Šefik   My dad. Born in Bosnia. Has worked as a bricklayer and property caretaker.

Thomas Sjöberg   Former soccer player and member of the Swedish national team. Assistant coach during my early days with Malmö FF.

Thijs Slegers   Dutch journalist and friend.

Rune Smith   Journalist who wrote the first major article about me.

Lilian Thuram   Defender. Played with me at Juventus. Won the World Cup in 1998 and the European Championship in 2000 with France.

David Trézéguet   French goal-scorer and star. We played together at Juventus. European champion in 2000 and World Cup winner in 1998 with France.

Rafael van der Vaart   Midfielder during my time at Ajax.

Patrick Vieira   Midfielder, played with me at Juventus and Inter Milan. Superstar. Friend. Brilliant player. Won the World Cup in 1998 and the European Championship in 2000 with France.

Vincent   My second son, born in 2008.

Christian Wilhelmsson
("Chippen")   Midfielder, member of the Swedish national team, friend.

Xavi   Brilliant midfielder at Barcelona. Joined the club as an eleven-year-old. Won the European Championship in 2012 and the World Cup in 2010 with Spain.

Gianluca Zambrotta   Legendary defender, played with me at both Juventus and AC Milan. Won the World Cup with Italy in 2006.

I AM ZLATAN

1

Pep Guardiola, the Barcelona manager, with his gray suits and brooding expressions, came up to me, looking a little self-conscious.

I thought he was all right in those days, not exactly another Mourinho or Capello, but an okay guy. This was long before we started to do battle with each other. It was the autumn of 2009, and I was living my boyhood dream. I was playing with the best team in the world and had been welcomed by seventy thousand people at Camp Nou. I was walking on air—well, maybe not completely. There was a certain amount of nonsense in the papers. That I was a bad boy and all that: that I was difficult to manage. Even so, I was there. Helena, my partner, and our sons liked it. We had a nice house in Esplugues de Llobregat, and I was ready. What could possibly go wrong?

"Listen," Guardiola said. "Here at Barça, we keep our feet on the ground."

"Sure," I said. "Fine!"

"So we don't turn up to training sessions in Ferraris or Porsches."

I nodded, didn't go ballistic on him and say things like What the hell business is it of yours what cars I drive? At the same time, though, I was thinking, What does he want? What kind of message is he sending here? Believe me, I don't need to make a big deal of looking tough anymore and drive up in some flash car and park it on the pavement or something. That's not what it's about. I do love cars. They're my passion, and I could sense something else behind what he was saying. It was like, Don't think you're anybody special!

I'd already gotten the impression that Barcelona was a little like school, or some sort of institution. The players were cool—nothing wrong with them—and Maxwell was there, my old friend from Ajax and Inter. To be honest, though, none of the guys acted like superstars, which was strange. Messi, Xavi, Iniesta, the whole gang—they were like schoolboys. The best soccer players in the world stood there with their heads bowed, and I didn't understand any of it. It was ridiculous. If the coaches in Italy say, "Jump," the stars will look at them and go, What are they, nuts? Why should we jump?

Here everyone did as they were told. I didn't fit in, not at all. I thought, Just enjoy the opportunity. Don't confirm their prejudices. So I started to adapt and blend in. I became way too nice. It was crazy.

Mino Raiola, my agent and good friend, said to me, "What's up with you, Zlatan? I don't recognize you."

Nobody recognized me—none of my friends, no one at all. I started to feel down, and here you have to know that, ever since my days at Malmö FF, I've had the same philosophy: I do things my way. I don't give a damn what people think, and I've never enjoyed being around uptight people. I like guys who go through red lights, if you know what I mean. Now, though, I wasn't saying what I wanted to say.

I said what I thought people wanted me to say. It was completely messed up. I drove the club's Audi and stood there and nodded my head the way I did when I was at school, or rather the way I should have done when I was at school. I hardly even yelled at my teammates anymore. I was boring. Zlatan was no longer Zlatan, and the last time that had happened was when I went to school at the ritzy Borgarskolan, where I saw girls in Ralph Lauren sweaters for the first time and nearly shit in my pants when I tried to ask them out. Even so, I started the season off brilliantly. I scored one goal after another. We won the UEFA Super Cup. I was amazing. I dominated on the pitch. Yet I was a different person. Something had happened— nothing serious, not yet, but still. I grew quiet, and that's dangerous— believe me. I need to be angry to play well. I need to shout and make some noise. Now I was keeping it inside. Maybe it had something to do with the press. I dunno.

I was the second-most-expensive transfer in history, and the papers wrote that I was a problem child and had a flawed character, all the crap you can imagine, and unfortunately I was feeling the pressure of everything—that here at Barça we don't make a show and stuff, and I guess I wanted to prove that I could do it too. That was the stupidest thing I've ever done. I was still awesome on the pitch. It just wasn't as much fun anymore.

I even thought about quitting soccer—not walking out on my contract, though: after all, I'm a professional. But I lost my enthusiasm, and then it was the Christmas break. We headed back to Sweden, to a ski resort up north, and I rented a snowmobile. Whenever life's at a standstill I need some action. I always drive like a maniac. I've done 325 km an hour in my Porsche Turbo and left the cops eating my dust. I've done so much crazy stuff I don't even want to think about it, and now in the mountains I was ripping it up on my snowmobile. I got frostbite and had the time of my life.

Finally an adrenaline rush! The old Zlatan was back, and I thought, Why should I stick it out? I've got money in the bank. I don't need to slave away with that idiot of a manager. I could just have fun instead, and look after my family. It was a great time. It didn't last long, though. When we returned to Spain, disaster hit—not right away, it was more like it crept up, but it was hanging in the air.

There was a massive blizzard. It was as if the Spaniards had never seen snow before, and in the hills where we lived there were cars stranded all over the place. Mino, that fat idiot—that wonderful, fat idiot, I should say, just to prevent any misunderstanding—was shivering like a dog in his street shoes and his summer jacket, and convinced me to take the Audi. That turned into a complete and utter shambles. We lost control on a downhill slope and crashed into a concrete wall, wrecking the car's entire right axle.

A lot of guys on the team had crashed their cars in the storm, but nobody did it quite as massively as I did. I won the crashing-your-car tournament, and we all had a good laugh about that, and I was still actually myself once in a while. I still felt pretty good. Then Messi started saying things. Lionel Messi is awesome. He's totally amazing. I don't know him all that well. We're very different people. He joined Barça when he was thirteen years old. He's been brought up in that culture and doesn't have a problem with that school crap. Within the team, the play centers on him, which is entirely natural—he's brilliant. But now I was there, and I was scoring more goals than him. He went up to Guardiola and told him, "I don't want to be on the right wing anymore. I want to play in the center."

I was the striker. Guardiola didn't give a damn about that, though. He changed the tactical formation. He swapped the 4–3–3 for a 4–5–1 with me at the front and Messi right behind me, and I ended up in the shadows. The balls passed through Messi, and I didn't get to play my game. On the pitch I've got to be as free as a bird. I'm the guy who wants to make a difference at every level. Guardiola sacrificed me. That's the truth. He locked me in up front. All right, I can understand his dilemma. Messi was the star.

Guardiola had to listen to him. But I mean, come on! I had scored loads of goals at Barça and I'd been pretty awesome as well. He couldn't change the whole team to suit one guy. I mean, why the hell had he bought me, anyway? Nobody pays that kind of money to strangle me as a player. Guardiola had to take both of us into consideration, and, of course, the atmosphere among the club's management grew tense. I was their biggest investment ever, and I wasn't happy in the new setup. I was too expensive to be left unhappy. Txiki Begiristain, the sports director, insisted that I had to go and speak to the manager:

"Sort it out!"

I didn't like that. I'm a player who accepts circumstances. "All right, fine, I'll do it."

One of my friends told me, "Zlatan, it's as if Barça had bought a Ferrari and was driving it like a Fiat," and I thought, Yeah, that's a good way of looking at it. Guardiola had turned me into a simpler player and a worse player. It's a loss for the whole team.

So I went over to him. It was on the pitch, during a practice session, and I was careful about one thing. I wasn't going to get into an argument, and I told him that.

I said, "I don't want to fight. I don't want to have a war. I just want to discuss things," and he nodded.

He might have looked a little scared, so I repeated what I'd said.

"If you think I want to have a fight, I'll drop it. I just want to have a word."

"That's fine. I like to talk to the players."

"Listen," I continued, "you're not making use of my capacity. If it was just a goal-scorer you were after, you should have bought Inzaghi or somebody else. I need space, I need to be free. I can't just run straight up and down the pitch the whole time. I weigh two hundred pounds. I'm not built for that."

He mulled it over. He always mulled everything right into the goddamned ground.

"I think you can play like this."

"No, it'd be better if you put me on the bench. With all due respect, I get where you're coming from, but you're sacrificing me in favor of other players. This isn't working. It's as if you bought a Ferrari, but you're driving it like a Fiat."

He mulled it over a bit more.

"Okay, maybe that was a mistake. This is my problem. I'll straighten it out."

I was happy. He was going to straighten it out. I left with a spring in my step, but then came the cold shoulder. He hardly looked at me, and I'm not somebody who gets worked up about that sort of thing, not really, and in spite of my new position, I carried on being brilliant. I scored goals—but not as pretty as the goals I'd scored in Italy. I was too far up front. It wasn't the same old "Ibracadabra" anymore, but even so . . . Playing against Arsenal in the Champions League over in the new Emirates Stadium, we totally outplayed them. The atmosphere was intense. The first twenty minutes were absolutely unbelievable: I scored 1–0 and 2–0, both beautiful goals again, and I thought, Who cares about Guardiola? I'm just gonna go for it!

Then I was taken out, and then Arsenal came back and made it 1–2 and 2–2, which was bullshit for us, and afterward I had an injured calf muscle. Normally, the managers are worried by something like that. An injured Zlatan is a properly serious thing for any team. But Guardiola was cold as ice. He didn't say a word, I was out for three weeks, and not once did he come up and ask me, How are you doing, Zlatan? Will you be able to play the next match?

He didn't even say good morning. Not a single word. He avoided eye contact with me. If I went into a room, he would leave. What's going on? I thought. Is it something I did? Do I look wrong? Am I talking funny? All these things were buzzing around in my head. I couldn't sleep.

I was thinking about it constantly. Not because I needed Guardiola's love, exactly. He could hate me, as far as I was concerned. Hatred and revenge get me going. Now, though, I lost my focus, and I talked things over with the players. Nobody had any idea. I asked Thierry Henry, who was on the bench then. Thierry Henry is the best goal-scorer in the history of the French national team. He's brilliant. He was still amazing then, and he was also having a tough time with Guardiola.

"He's not talking to me. He won't look me in the eye. What do you figure happened?" I asked.

"No idea," Henry replied.

We started to joke about it, saying things like Hey, Zlatan, did you make any eye contact today? Nah, but I caught a glimpse of his back. All right, you're making some progress! Silly stuff like that, and it did help a bit. It was really getting on my nerves, though, and I would ask myself every day, every hour, what did I do? What's wrong? I couldn't find any answers, nothing. Only that him giving me the cold shoulder must have had something to do with the conversation about my position. There just wasn't any other explanation. That would be ridiculous if it was true. Was he trying to psych me out ahead of a chat about my position? I tried to step up to him. Go up to the guy and look him in the eye. He was avoiding me. He seemed worked up. Sure, I could have scheduled a meeting and asked him what was going on. But there was no way I was going to do that. I had groveled enough to him. This was his problem.

Not that I knew what it was. I still don't know, or maybe I do . . . I think the guy can't handle strong personalities. He wants well-behaved schoolboys—and what's worse, he runs away from his problems. He can't cope with looking them in the eye, and that just made everything worse.

And things did get worse.

The volcanic-ash cloud came from Iceland. All flights throughout Europe were grounded, and we were supposed to face Inter Milan at San Siro. We went by bus. Some bright guy at Barça thought it was a good idea. I was free of injury then. The journey was a disaster. It took sixteen hours, and we arrived in Milan exhausted. This was our most important match so far, the semifinal in the Champions League, and I was prepared for boos and hysteria at my old home ground: no problem—quite the opposite, in fact. I feed on that kind of thing. The situation otherwise was rotten, and I think Guardiola had a hang-up about Mourinho.

José Mourinho is a big star. He'd already won the Champions League with Porto. He'd been my manager at Inter. He's nice. The first time he met Helena, he whispered to her, "Helena, you have only one mission. Feed Zlatan, let him sleep, keep him happy." That guy says whatever he wants. I like him. He's the leader of his army. But he cares too. He would text me all the time at Inter, wondering how I was doing. He's the exact opposite of Guardiola. If Mourinho lights up a room, Guardiola draws the curtains. I guessed that Guardiola was trying to match up to him.

"It's not Mourinho we're up against. It's Inter," he said, almost as if we were sitting there imagining we were going to play soccer against the manager, and then he got started on his philosophizing.

I was barely listening. Why should I? That was advanced bullshit, about blood, sweat, and tears, and all that. I had never heard a soccer manager talking like that. Absolute nonsense! Now he was actually coming up to me. This was the training session at San Siro, and people were there checking us out, and they were saying things like Ibra's back!

"Can you play from the first whistle?" Guardiola asked.

"Definitely," I replied. "I'm up for it."

"But are you ready?"

"Absolutely. I'm good."

"But are you ready?"

He was like a parrot, and I was getting some bad vibes.

"Listen, it was a terrible journey, but I'm in form. My injury's healed. I'll give a hundred percent."

Guardiola looked doubtful. I couldn't figure him out, and afterward I phoned Mino Raiola. I'm constantly on the phone to Mino. Swedish journalists always say, Mino's hurting Zlatan's image. Mino is this, Mino is that. Shall I spell it out here? Mino is a genius. So I asked him, "What's up with this guy?"

Neither of us could figure it out. We were getting pissed off. I did get to play in the starting lineup, and we were up 1–0. Then things took a turn. I was taken off after sixty minutes, and we lost 3–1. That was bullshit. I was furious. In the past, like when I was with Ajax, I used to dwell on a loss for days and weeks. But now I had Helena and the kids. They help me to forget and move on, and so I focused on our return to Camp Nou. It was important to recover, and the atmosphere kept getting ratcheted up every day.

The pressure was insane. It was as if there were rumblings in the air, and we needed a big win in order to move on. But then . . . I don't want to think about it—well, actually I do, because it made me stronger. We won 1–0. But it wasn't enough. We crashed out of the Champions League, and afterward Guardiola looked at me like it was all my fault, and I thought, That's it. I've played my last card. After that match, it felt like I was no longer welcome at the club, and I felt rotten when I drove their Audi. I felt like shit when I sat in the locker room, and Guardiola glared at me as if I was a disturbance, an alien. It was ridiculous. He was a wall—a brick wall. I didn't see any signs of life from him, and every hour with the club I wished I could be out of there.

I didn't belong anymore, and when we had an away match with Villarreal, he let me play for five minutes. Five minutes! I was seething inside, not because I was on the bench. I can deal with that, if the manager is man enough to say, You're not good enough, Zlatan. You haven't made the grade.

Guardiola didn't say a word, not a peep, and now I'd had enough. I could feel it in my whole body, and if I'd been Guardiola, I would've been scared. Not that I'm saying I'm handy with my fists! I've done all kinds of shit. I don't get into fights, though. All right, on the pitch I guess I've headbutted a few people. When I get angry, the red mist descends. You don't want to be nearby.

Now, if I'm going to go into details here, I went into the locker room after the match and I hadn't exactly planned any frenzied attack. But I was not happy, to put it mildly, and now my enemy was standing there, scratching his head. There weren't many other people there.

Touré was there, and a few others, and then there was the metal box where we put our uniform from the match, and I was staring at that box. Then I gave it a kick. I think it went flying about three meters, but I wasn't finished yet. Not by a long shot. I yelled, "You haven't got any balls!" and certainly even worse than that, and then I added, "You're shitting yourself in front of Mourinho. You can go to hell!"

I completely lost it, and you might have expected Guardiola to say a few words in response, something like Calm down, you don't talk to your manager like that. He's not the type, though. He's a spineless coward. He just picked up the metal box, like a little care-taker, and then left, never to mention it again, not a word. Of course, word got out. On the bus, everybody was beside themselves, going, "What happened? What happened?"

Nothing, I thought to myself. Just a few words of the truth. I didn't feel like talking about it. I was furious. Week after week, my manager and boss had shut me out, with no explanation why. It was completely ridiculous. I'd had massive arguments in the past. But the next day, we'd sorted things out and there were no hard feelings. Now, though, there was just silence and mind games, and I thought, I'm twenty-eight years old. I've scored twenty-two goals and fifteen assists here at Barça alone, and I'm still being treated like I don't exist. Should I sit back and take it? Should I carry on trying to adapt? No way!

When I realized I would be on the bench against Almeria, I re-membered that line: *Here in Barcelona we don't turn up to training sessions in Porsches or Ferraris.* What kind of nonsense was that, anyway? I'll take whatever car I want, at least if I can piss off idiots. I jumped in my Enzo, put my foot down on the gas, and parked right in front of the door to the training facility. Of course, it was a huge circus. The papers wrote that my car cost as much as the sum total of all the Almeria players' monthly wages. I didn't give a damn. The crap in the media was small potatoes in this context. I'd made up my mind that I was going to have my say.

I'd decided to start to fight my corner, and you should know that that's a game I know how to play. I'd been a fighter before, believe me. I couldn't neglect my preparations, though, and so I talked it over with Mino. We always plan our tricks together, both the smart ones and the dirty ones. And I ran it by my friends.

I wanted to see things from different perspectives, and, my God, I got every kind of advice. The Rosengård guys wanted to come down and smash the place up, and of course that was nice of them, but it didn't really seem like the right strategy under the circumstances, and of course I discussed things with Helena. She's from a different world. She's cool. She can be tough too. Now she came out with some encouragement: "At any rate, you've become a better father. When you haven't got a team you like, you make a team here at home," she said, and it made me happy.

I had a lot of kickabouts with the kids, and I tried to make sure everybody was doing all right, and of course I sat around with my videogames. That's a bit of an addiction with me. I get completely sucked in. Since the years with Inter when I could stay up till four or five in the morning and go to practice on just two or three hours' sleep, I've set some boundaries for myself: no Xbox or PlayStation after ten o'clock.

I couldn't just fritter my time away, and I really tried to dedicate those weeks in Spain to the family, and just cool off in the garden, even have an occasional Corona. That was the good side of things. At night, though, when I lay awake, or in training sessions when I saw Guardiola, my dark side woke up. The rage just throbbed in my head, and I clenched my fists and planned my retaliation. No, I came to realize, there was no turning back now. It was time to take a stand and become my old self again.

Because, don't forget: *You can take the boy out of the ghetto, but you can never take the ghetto out of the boy.*

2

I got a BMX bike from my brother when I was little. I named it Fido Dido.

Fido Dido was a fierce little cartoon guy with squiggly hair. I thought he was the coolest thing ever. But then my bike got stolen from outside the Rosengård swimming pool, and my dad came up there with his shirt open and his sleeves rolled up. He's the sort who's like, Nobody lays a hand on my kids! Nobody takes their stuff. Not even a tough guy like my dad could do anything about it, though. Fido Dido was gone, and I was absolutely heartbroken.

After that, I started stealing bikes. I picked the locks. I got to be an expert at it. Boom, boom—and the bike was mine. I was the bicycle thief. That was my first thing. It was quite innocent. Sometimes it did get out of hand. One time I got dressed all in black, Rambo-style, and took a massive pair of bolt-cutters and stole a military bike. I definitely got a buzz from that. I loved it. To be honest, it was more for the kicks than the bikes. I started sneaking around in the dark, and

I chucked a few eggs at windows and that sort of thing, and I only got caught a few times.

One time that was pretty embarrassing happened in Wessels department store out in Jägersro shopping center. I deserved it, to be honest. A pal and me went into a department store wearing big puffer coats in the middle of the summer—totally stupid thing to do—and under our coats we had four table-tennis paddles and some other junk we picked up. "And just how do you plan to pay for this?" the security guard asked us when we got caught. I took out six 10-öre coins—less than one krona, or equivalent to about five cents—from my pocket: "With these." But the guy had no sense of humor, and I resolved to be more professional in the future, and I guess I ended up a pretty skilled little terror in the end.

I was small as a kid. I had a big nose and a lisp and had to go to a speech therapist. A woman came to school and taught me how to say "S," which I thought was humiliating, and I guess I needed to get my revenge. Besides that, I was completely hyper. I couldn't sit still for a second and was constantly running around. It felt like nothing bad could happen to me as long as I ran fast enough. We lived in Rosengård, outside Malmö in southern Sweden, and the area was full of Somalis, Turks, Yugos, Poles—all sorts of immigrants—and Swedes. All of us played at being cocky. Anything could set us off, and things weren't easy at home—not by any stretch of the imagination.

We lived in an apartment up four flights of stairs in those days, and we didn't go in for hugs and that sort of thing. Nobody asked, How was your day today, little Zlatan? There was none of that. There was no adult around who helped with your homework or asked you about your problems. You had to deal with things yourself, and there was no whining if someone had been nasty to you. You had to grit your teeth, and there was chaos and arguing and a fair few smacks and slaps. Sure, sometimes you'd hope for a bit of sympathy. One day I fell from a roof at the child-care center. I got a black eye and ran home bawling, expecting to get a pat on the head, or at least a few kind words. I got a clip on the ear.

"What were you doing up on the roof?"

There was no Poor Zlatan. It was "Stupid idiot, climbing up on a roof, I'll give you a thrashing." I was completely shocked and ran off. Mom had no time for giving comfort, not in those days. She worked her fingers to the bone to provide for us—she really was a fighter. She couldn't cope with much else, though. She'd had it tough, and all of us had a terrible temper. There was no Swedish-style civilized conversation at home, like Darling, could you please pass the butter? It was more like Get the milk, asshole! There were doors slamming and Mom crying. She cried a lot. She's got my love. She's had to work hard her whole life. She would clean for about fourteen hours a day, and every now and then we would go along and empty wastebaskets and stuff to get a little pocket money. Sometimes, though, Mom would blow a fuse.

She'd hit us with a wooden spoon, and sometimes the spoon would break and I'd have to go out and buy a new one, as if it were my fault she'd hit me so hard. I remember one day in particular. While I was at the child-care center I'd thrown a brick and it somehow bounced and broke a window. When Mom heard about it, she went ballistic. Anything that cost money made her crazy, and she hit me with the spoon. Bang, boom! It hurt, and maybe the spoon broke again. I dunno. Sometimes there weren't any of those spoons at home, and one time Mom came after me with a rolling pin. I managed to get away, and I talked it over with Sanela.

Sanela is my only full sibling. She's two years older than me. She's a tough girl, and she thought we ought to pull Mom's leg a bit. Goddamn, hitting us over the head like that? Insane! So we went to the supermarket and bought some of those spoons, three for 10 kronor (a couple of bucks), and gave them to Mom as a Christmas present.

I don't think she got the irony. She didn't have any space for that sort of thing. There had to be food on the table. All her energies went toward that. There were a lot of us at home, including my half-sisters (who later vanished from the family and broke off contact with all of us), and then my little brother, Aleksandar, known as Keki, and there wasn't enough money. There wasn't enough of anything, and the older kids looked after us younger ones. We wouldn't have made it otherwise, and there were a lot of instant noodles with ketchup, and eating at friends' places or at my Auntie Hanife's. She lived in the same block of apartments and had been the first of all of us to come to Sweden.

I hadn't even turned two when Mom and Dad got divorced, and I don't remember any of it. That's probably just as well. It wasn't a good marriage, from what I understand. It was noisy and messy, and they'd gotten married so Dad could get a residency permit, and I assume that it was natural that all of us ended up with Mom. I missed my dad. He was better off, and there was more fun stuff going on around him. Sanela and I would meet up with Dad every other weekend. He'd often turn up in his old blue Opel Kadett, and we'd go to Pildamm Park or out to Ön, the island off the coast of Malmö, and get burgers and ice creams. One time he splurged and got us each a pair of Nike Air Max, those cool trainers that cost about a thousand kronor (over $100). Mine were green and Sanela's were pink. Nobody else in Rosengård had trainers like those, and we felt totally wicked. Things were good with Dad, and we could get 50 kronor (about $6) for a pizza and a Coke. He had a good job and only one other son, Sapko. He was our fun weekend dad.

Later, things got tougher. Sanela was brilliant at running. She was the fastest in her age group in the whole Skåne region in the 60-meter dash, and Dad was proud as a peacock and would drive her to training sessions. "Good, Sanela. But you can do better," he used to say. That was his thing. "Do better, do better, don't settle for that," and this time I was along in the car. That's how Dad remembers it, anyway, and he noticed it right away. Something wasn't right. Sanela was very quiet. She was struggling not to cry.

"What's happened?" he asked.

"Nothing," she replied. Then he asked again, and finally she told him. We don't need to go into details; it's Sanela's story. But my dad, he's like a lion. If anything happens to his kids, he goes wild—especially if it's about Sanela, his only daughter, and there was a huge to-do, with hearings and investigations by Social Services and custody disputes and shit. I didn't understand much of it. I was about to turn nine.

It was the autumn of 1990, and they shielded me from that. Even so, I knew something was up. Things weren't going smoothly at home. It wasn't the first time. One of my half-sisters was doing drugs, hard stuff, and she'd hidden some at home. There was often a lot of uproar surrounding her, and suspicious people who would phone, and a lot of fear that something serious would happen. Another time, Mom got arrested for receiving stolen goods. Some acquaintances had told her, "Look after these necklaces!" and she did what they said. She didn't realize. They turned out to be stolen goods, and the police burst in at home and arrested her. I have a vague memory of it, sort of an odd feeling of Where's Mom? Why's she gone?

Then, after this latest thing with Sanela, Mom was crying again, and I fled from it. I stayed outside, running around, or I played soccer. Not that I was the most balanced kid, or the most promising. I was just one of the snot-nosed kids who kicked a ball—worse than that, actually. I'd have incredible outbursts. I headbutted people and screamed at my teammates. Still, I had soccer. It was my thing, and I played all the time, down in the courtyard, on the pitch, during breaks. We went to the Värner Rydén School then, Sanela in Year Five and me in Year Three, and there wasn't exactly any doubt about which one of us was better behaved. Sanela had to grow up fast and become like a second mother to Keki and look after the family when our sisters took off. She took on an incredible amount of responsibility. She behaved. She was not the girl who got called into the headmaster's office to get chewed out, and that's why I got worried when the message came. We both had to go in to see the headmaster. Well, if it had been only me who got sent in, that would have been normal, absolutely routine. Now, though, it was me and Sanela. Had somebody died? What was it about?

My stomach started to hurt as we walked down the school corridor. It must have been late autumn or winter. I felt worried. When we went in, Dad was sitting there with the headmaster, and then I was happy. Dad usually meant fun times. But this was no fun. Everything was tense and formal, and I started to get the creeps. To be honest, I didn't really understand much of it, just that it was about Mom and Dad and it wasn't good, not at all. Now I know. Many years later, as I've been working on this book, the pieces of the puzzle have fallen into place.

In November 1990, Social Services had conducted their investigation, and Dad had got custody of both Sanela and me. The environment at Mom's was regarded as unsuitable—not really because of her, I've got to say. There was other stuff, but it was a major thing, being judged unfit by the world, and Mom was absolutely devastated. She was going to lose us? It was a disaster. She cried and cried, and sure, she'd hit us with wooden spoons and boxed our ears and didn't listen to us, and she'd had bad luck with men and nothing worked out, and all that, but she loved her kids. She'd just grown up with the cards stacked against her, and I think Dad realized that. He went over to her place that afternoon.

"I don't want you to lose them, Jurka," he told her.

He demanded that she shape up, though, and Dad is not one for kidding around in those kinds of situations. I'm sure he said some harsh things: If things don't improve, you'll never see those kids again, and stuff like that. I don't know exactly what happened. Sanela lived at Dad's place for a few weeks, and I stayed with Mom, in spite of everything. That wasn't a good solution. Sanela didn't like it at Dad's. She and I discovered him asleep on the floor, and there were beer cans and bottles on the table. "Dad, wake up! Wake up!" we'd shout, but he carried on sleeping. I thought it was strange—like, Why is he doing that? We didn't know what to do, but we wanted to help him. Maybe he was cold? We covered him with bath towels and blankets so he'd be warm. Otherwise, I didn't understand a lot of what was going on. Presumably, Sanela understood more. She'd noticed how his moods changed and how he would fly into a rage and howl like a bear, and I think that frightened her. And she was missing her little brother. She wanted to go back to Mom, whereas it was the opposite for me. I missed Dad, and on one of those evenings I phoned him up. I'm sure I sounded desperate. It was lonely without Sanela.

"I don't want to be here. I want to live with you."

"Come over," he said. "I'll send a taxi."

———

There were more investigations by Social Services, and in March 1991 Mom got custody of Sanela, and Dad got me. We were split up, my sister and me, but we've always stuck together—well, to put it more accurately, we've had our ups and downs. Basically, though, we're really close. Today, Sanela is a hairdresser, and sometimes people come into her salon and say, "My God, you look so much like

Zlatan!" and she always replies, "Bullshit, it's him who's like me." She's awesome. Neither one of us has had it easy. My dad, Šefik, had moved out of Rosengård to a nicer place at Värnhemstorget in Malmö, and you can tell that he's got a big heart—he'd be prepared to die for us. It's just that things didn't turn out the way I imagined. I had known him as the weekend dad who bought us burgers and ice creams.

Now we were supposed to share our everyday lives, and I noticed immediately that his apartment was bare. Something was missing—maybe a woman. There was a TV, a sofa, a bookcase, two beds. Nothing extra, nothing pleasant, and there were beer cans on the tables and trash on the floor, and on the occasions when he would get an impulse and do some wallpapering, maybe only one wall would get done. "I'll do the rest tomorrow!" It never happened, and we moved often, never managing to settle down. But things were bare in another sense too.

Dad was a property caretaker who worked terrible shifts, and when he came home in his handyman's dungarees with all the pockets for screwdrivers and stuff, he would sit down by the phone or the TV and didn't want to be disturbed. He was in his own little world, and he would often put his headphones on and listen to Yugoslavian folk music. He's crazy about Yugo music. He's recorded a few cassettes of himself performing. He's a real entertainer when he's in the mood. Most of the time, though, he remained in his own little bubble, and if my buddies phoned, he would hiss at them, "Don't phone here!"

I wasn't allowed to bring my friends home, and if they phoned me, Dad wouldn't tell me. The phone was not for me, and I didn't really have anyone to talk to there at home—well, I did: if there was something serious, Dad was there for me. Then he would do anything at all, go out into town in his cocky way and try to sort everything out.

He had a way of walking that made people go, Who the hell is that? Where ordinary things were concerned, like what had happened at school, or on the soccer pitch, or with my friends, he wasn't interested, and I had to talk to myself, or go out. Of course, Sapko, my half-brother, lived with us for a while, and I talked to him sometimes. He must have been about seventeen then. I don't remember much about it, and it wasn't long before Dad kicked him out. They'd had some terrible arguments. That's another sad thing, of course; and then it was just Dad and me left. We were each alone in our own corner, you could say, because the strange thing was that he didn't have any friends around either. He would sit on his own and drink. There was no company. Above all, there was nothing in the fridge.

I stayed out all the time, playing soccer and riding around on stolen bikes, and I'd often come home hungry as a wolf. I'd fling open the cupboard doors and think, Please, please, let there be something there. But no, nothing, just the usual: milk, butter, a loaf of bread, and, on good days, some juice—multivitamin juice drink in the 4-liter carton from the Middle Eastern shop, because it was the cheapest—and then beer of course, Pripps Blå and Carlsberg, six-packs with those plastic rings around the cans. Sometimes there was nothing but lager, and my stomach growled. That's a pain I'll never forget. Just ask Helena. The fridge should be full, I'm always telling her. I'll never shake that. Recently, my boy Vincent was crying because he wanted his pasta and it was still cooking. The kid was screaming because his food wasn't ready fast enough, and I felt like bellowing, If you only knew how good you've got it!

I could search through every drawer, every nook and cranny for a single piece of pasta or a meatball. I would fill up on toast. I could scarf an entire loaf of bread, or else I would go over to Mom's. She didn't always exactly welcome me with open arms. It was more like What the hell, is Zlatan coming as well? Doesn't Šefik feed him? And sometimes she'd give me an earful: "Do you think we're made of money? You're going to eat us out of house and home!" Still, we helped each other, and over at Dad's I started waging a little war on the beer. I poured some of it out—not all of it, because that would have been too obvious, but some.

He rarely noticed anything. There was beer everywhere, on the tables and shelves, and I would often put the empty cans in big black trash bags and take them in to get the deposit. I got 50 öre (about 5 cents) a can. Even so, sometimes I'd scrape together 50 or 100 kronor ($6 or $12). That was a lot of cans, and I was happy to have the money. Of course, it was no fun, and, like all kids in that sort of situation, I learned to notice exactly what mood he was in. I knew when it wasn't worth talking to him. The day after he'd been drinking, things would be fairly quiet. The second day, it was worse. In some cases, he could ignite like a flash. Other times, he was incredibly generous. Gave me 500 kronor (around $60), just like that. In those days, I collected soccer cards. You got a piece of chewing gum and three photo cards in a little pack. Oh boy, which guys will I get? I would wonder. Maybe Maradona? Most of the time I'd be disappointed, especially when they were just boring Swedish stars I didn't know anything about. One day, Dad came home with a whole box. That was like a big party, and I tore them all open and got a bunch of cool Brazilians, and sometimes we'd watch TV together and chat. Those times were as good as anything.

Other days, he was drunk. I have horrible images in my mind, and when I got a bit older, I'd get into it with him. I didn't back down like my brother. I'd tell him, "You drink too much, Dad," and we had huge fights, completely senseless sometimes, to be honest. I'd argue, even though I could see that he'd just scream back, "I'll kick you out," and stuff like that. I wanted to show that I could stick up for myself, and sometimes the noise was unbearable.

He never laid a hand on me, though, not once. Well, one time he picked me up six feet in the air and threw me onto the bed, but only because I'd been mean to Sanela, the apple of his eye. Basically, he was the nicest person in the world, and I understand now that he hadn't had it easy. "He drinks to drown his sorrows," my brother said, but that might not have been the whole truth. The war hit him really hard.

The war was an odd thing altogether. I was never allowed to find out anything about it. I was shielded. Everybody tried really hard. I didn't even understand why Mom and my sisters dressed in black. It was completely incomprehensible, like a sudden fad. It was Grandma who had died in a bombing raid in Croatia, and they were all in mourning—everybody but me, who wasn't allowed to know and would never care whether people were Serbs or Bosnians or whatever. But my dad had it worst.

He came from Bijeljina in Bosnia. He'd been a bricklayer down there, and his whole family and all his old friends lived in that town, and suddenly all hell had broken loose. Bijeljina was being raped, more or less, and it was no wonder he started calling himself a Muslim again, not at all. The Serbs invaded the town and executed hundreds of Muslims. I think he knew a lot of them, and his entire extended family was forced to flee. The whole population of Bijeljina was replaced, with Serbs moving into the empty houses, including into Dad's old place. Somebody else just went in and took over the house, and I can totally understand that he had no time for me, when he would sit all evening waiting for the TV news or a phone call from down there. The war consumed him, and he became obsessed with monitoring the course of events. He sat on his own and drank and mourned and listened to his Yugo music, and I made sure

I stayed outdoors or headed over to Mom's. Mom's was another world.

At Dad's, it was just me and him. At Mom's, it was a three-ring circus. People came and went, and there were loud voices and noises. Mom had moved five floors up in another block of apartments on the same street, at Cronmans Väg 5A, to the floor above Auntie Hanife, or Hanna, as I called her. Keki, Sanela, and I were really close. We made a pact. There was a load of shit going on at Mom's as well. My half-sister was getting deeper into drugs, and Mom would jump every time the phone rang or there was a knock at the door—as if to say, Please, no. Haven't we had enough disasters? What now? She grew old before her time, and was completely fanatical against any type of illegal substance. Not long ago she called me, absolutely hysterical: "There's drugs in the fridge."

"My God, drugs!" I got worked up as well. I thought, Not again. I rang Keki, really aggressive: "What the hell? There are drugs in Mom's fridge!" He didn't get what was going on, but then a light went on. It was *snus*—Swedish chewing tobacco—she was talking about.

"Take it easy, Mom, it's only *snus*."

"Same shit," she said.

Those years really left their mark on her, and I'm sure we ought to have been nicer back then. We just hadn't learned things like that. We only knew how to be tough. My half-sister with the drug problem had moved out early on, and was in and out of treatment clinics, but always went back on the shit. Finally, Mom broke off contact with her—or it was a mutual thing. I don't really know all the background information. It was really tough, anyway, but that's a character trait in our family. We're dramatic and hold grudges and say things like I never want to see you again!

Anyway, I remember one time when I was visiting my sister, the one with the drugs, in her own little apartment. It might have been my birthday. I think it was. She had bought some presents. She was kind, even with everything else. Then I was about to head to the bathroom, and she leapt up and stopped me. No, no, she yelled, running in and cleaning up in there. I could tell something was wrong, like there was some secret. There was a lot of stuff like that. Like I said, though, they kept that away from me, and I had my own stuff, my bikes and my soccer, and my dreams about Bruce Lee and Muhammad Ali. I wanted to be like them.

———

Dad had a brother back in the former Yugoslavia. His name was Sabahudin, but he was called Sapko, and my older brother was named after him. Sabahudin was a boxer— a real talent. He fought for the Radnićki boxing club in the town of Kragujevac, won the Yugoslavian championship with his club, and was selected for the national team. Then, in 1967, when he was newly married, and only twenty-three, he went swimming in the Neretva River, where there were strong currents, and I think he had a defect in his heart or lungs. He was pulled underwater and drowned, and you can just imagine. That was a hard blow for the family, and after that Dad became something of a fanatic. He had all the big matches recorded on video, and it wasn't just Sabahudin on those videocassettes, but Ali, Foreman, and Tyson, and then all the Bruce Lee and Jackie Chan movies as well.

That's what we would watch when we were hanging out in front of the TV. Swedish TV didn't exist as far as we were concerned. It just didn't register. I was twenty years old before I saw my first Swedish film, and I didn't have a clue about any Swedish heroes or sports figures, like Ingemar Stenmark or anybody. But Ali I knew. What a legend! He did things his own way, no matter what people said. He didn't make excuses, and I've never forgotten that. That guy was cool. That's the way I wanted to be, and I imitated some of his things, like I am the greatest. You needed to have a tough attitude in Rosengård, and if you heard anybody talking trash—the worst was to be called a pussy—you couldn't back down.

Most of the time, though, we didn't have any problems. You don't shit on your own doorstep, as we used to say. It was more a matter of us in Rosengård against everybody else. I was there, watching and yelling at those racists who march every year on November 30 to commemorate the death of Sweden's King Charles XII, the "warrior king." And once, at the Malmö Festival, I saw a whole mob from Rosengård, about two hundred of them, going after one guy. That didn't look too great, if I'm honest. But because they were from my housing project I went over to join in with them, and I don't think that guy was feeling too clever afterward. We were cocky and wild, all of us. Sometimes it wasn't that easy to be tough.

When Dad and I lived by the Stenkula school, I would often stay at Mom's till late, and then I would have to walk home through a dark tunnel that passes under a major road. A number of years earlier, my dad had gotten mugged and badly beaten up there, and he ended up in the hospital with a collapsed lung. I often thought about that, even though I didn't want to, of course. The more I repressed it, the more it would surface, and in the same area there was a railway line and a main road. There's also an ugly alleyway and a few bushes and two lampposts: one just before the tunnel and one right after. Otherwise, it was dark, with really bad vibes. So the lampposts became my landmarks. I would run like a madman between them with my heart pounding, thinking, I bet there're some creeps standing inside there, like the ones who attacked Dad. The whole time, I'd be thinking frantically, If I just run fast enough, it'll be all right; and I always came home out of breath, not a bit like Muhammad Ali.

Another time, Dad took Sanela and me to go swimming at Arlöv, and afterward I was at a friend's place. When I was about to leave, it started raining. It was pouring down, and I cycled home like an idiot in the rain and stumbled in, completely soaked. We were living on Zenitgatan then, some distance from Rosengård, and I was in a bad way. I was shaking and had pains in my stomach. I was in incredible pain. I couldn't move. I lay curled up in bed. I threw up. I had a seizure. I was freaking out.

Dad came in and, of course, he is the way he is, and his fridge was empty and he drank too much. When it really comes down to it, there's no one like him, and he phoned for a taxi and picked me up in the only position I could lie in, sort of like a little prawn, and he carried me down to the car. I was as light as a feather in those days. Dad was big and strong and completely beside himself. He was a lion again and he yelled at the driver—it was a woman: "He's my boy, he is everything to me, to hell with the traffic rules, I'll pay the fines, I'll fix it with the police," and the woman did as he said. She ran two red lights and we made it to the children's ward at Malmö General Hospital. The whole situation had become acute, as I understand it. I was going to have an injection in my back, and Dad had heard some crap about people who had been paralyzed by that kind of thing, and I guess he really tore into the staff. He would go on a rampage through the whole city if anything went wrong.

Eventually, he calmed down, and I lay on my stomach sobbing and got the injection in my spine. It emerged that I had meningitis, and the nurse lowered the blinds and switched off all the lights. I had to be in total darkness, and I was given medication and Dad kept a vigil by my bedside. At five o'clock the next morning, I opened my eyes and the crisis was over, and I still don't know what caused it. Maybe I wasn't looking after myself properly.

I wasn't exactly getting a balanced diet. I was small and really puny in those days. Even so, I must have been strong in some way. I forgot about it and carried on, and instead of sitting at home moping around, I looked for a buzz. I was out and about constantly. There was a fire in me and, just like Dad, I could explode, saying things like Who the hell do you think you are? Those were tough years, I understand that now. Dad was up and down, often completely absent or furious: "I want you home by such and such time" or "You're damn well not doing that."

If you were a guy in Dad's world and something bad happened to you, you had to stand up and be a man. There was never any of that New Man stuff, none of that "I've got a pain in my tummy today. I'm feeling a bit down." Nothing like that.

I learned to grit my teeth and get on with it, but also, don't forget, I learned a whole load about sacrifice as well. When we bought a new bed for me at IKEA, Dad couldn't afford the delivery charge. That would have cost an extra 500 kronor (about $60) or something. So what could we do? Simple. Dad carried the mattress on his back the whole way from IKEA—completely nuts—mile after mile, and I followed along behind with the legs. They hardly weighed anything. Even so, I couldn't keep up.

"Take it easy, Dad. Wait."

He just kept on going. He had that macho style, and sometimes he would turn up in his whole cowboy look at parents' night at school. Everybody would wonder, Who's that? People noticed him. He got respect, and the teachers didn't dare to complain about me as much as they had been planning to do. It was like, We'd better be careful with that guy!

People have asked me what I would have done if I hadn't become a soccer player. I have no idea. Maybe I would have become a criminal. There was a lot of crime in those days. Not that we went out thieving. But a lot of stuff just happened, and not just bikes. We'd be in and out of department stores as well, and sometimes I got a buzz just from doing it. I got a kick out of swiping stuff, and I've got to be happy that Dad never found out. Dad drank, sure, but there were a lot of rules as well. You've got to do the right thing, and all that. Definitely no stealing, no way. All hell would have broken loose.

The time we got caught at Wessels department store in our puffer coats, I was lucky. We'd grabbed stuff worth 1,400 kronor (about $165). It was more than just the usual candy bars. My friend's dad had to come and get us, and when the letter arrived at home saying "Zlatan Ibrahimović has been caught shoplifting . . . ," I managed to tear it up before Dad saw it. I was caught up in it and continued stealing, so yeah, things could have turned out badly.

One thing I can say for certain is that there were no drugs. I was totally against them. I didn't just pour out Dad's beer. I got rid of my mom's cigarettes. I hated all drugs and poisons, and I was seventeen or eighteen before I got drunk the first time, and puked in the stairway like any other teenager. Since then, I haven't been drunk too many times, just one episode where I passed out in the bathtub after the first Scudetto with Juventus. That was Trézéguet, that snake, who egged me on to drink shots.

Sanela and I were also strict with Keki. He wasn't allowed to smoke or drink, or else we'd go after him. That was a special thing, with my little bro.

We looked after him. For more delicate things, he'd go to Sanela. With tougher stuff, he'd come to me. I stood up for him. I took responsibility. Otherwise, I wasn't exactly a saint, and I wasn't always that nice to my friends and teammates. I did aggressive stuff, the kind of thing that would make me go ape today if anybody did the same to Maxi and Vincent. But it's true. Let's not forget that. I had two sides even then.

I was both disciplined and wild, and I came up with entire philosophies about that. My thing was that I had to both talk the talk and walk the walk. Not just going, I'm awesome, who are you? Of course not—there's nothing quite as lame—but I also didn't want to just perform and say mealymouthed stuff like the Swedish stars did. I wanted to be great and give it some swagger as well. Not that I believed I would turn out to be some kind of superstar, exactly. Jesus Christ, I was from Rosengård! Maybe I turned out a bit differently because of that.

I was rowdy. I was wild. But I had character as well. I didn't always get to school on time. I had a hard time getting up in the mornings—still do—but I did my homework, at least some of the time. Math was dead easy. Just bam, bam! and I could see the answer. It was a bit like on the soccer pitch. Images and solutions came to me in a flash. I was bad at showing my work, though, so the teachers thought I was cheating. I wasn't exactly a pupil they expected to get good exam results. I was more the kid who got kicked out of class. I did actually study. I would cram before exams, and then forget everything the day after. I wasn't exactly a bad kid. I just had a hard time sitting still, and I would fling erasers and that kind of thing. I had ants in my pants.

Those were difficult years. We moved constantly; I don't know why. We rarely lived at any one place for more than a year, and the teachers took advantage of that. You have to transfer to the school in the area where you live, they said, not because they were sticklers for the rules but because they saw an opportunity to get rid of me. I changed schools often and had a hard time making friends. Dad had his on-call shifts and his war and his drinking, and really bad tinnitus in his ears, a ringing noise inside him, and I was looking after myself more and more and trying not to worry about the chaos in our family. There was always something. People from the Balkans are a tough bunch. My sister with the drugs had broken off contact with Mom and the rest of us, and I suppose it wasn't entirely unexpected after all the arguments about drugs and the treatment centers. Even my other half-sister was cut off from the family. Mom just kind of erased her, and I don't even know what it was about. There was some to-do about a boyfriend, a guy from Yugoslavia. He and my sister had had a fight and for some reason Mom took the guy's side, and so my sister flipped out and she and Mom had a terrible shouting match, and that wasn't good. Still, it shouldn't have been such a big deal.

That wasn't exactly the first time we had a blowout in our family. Mom had her pride, and I'm sure both she and my sister got into some sort of deadlock. I recognize that in me. I don't forget things either. I'll remember a nasty tackle for years. I remember shit that people have done to me, and I can bear incredible grudges. This time, it went too far.

There had been five of us kids at Mom's, and now suddenly there were only three: me, Sanela, and Aleksandar, and there was no going back. It was like it was carved in stone. Our half-sister was no longer one of us, and the years passed. She was gone. Then, fifteen years later, her son phoned my mom. My half-sister had had a son—a grandson for my mom, in other words.

"Hi, Grandma," he said, but Mom didn't want any part of it.

"Sorry," she said, and hung up.

I couldn't believe it when I heard. I got a pain in my stomach. I can't describe the feeling. I wanted to sink into the floor. You shouldn't do that. Never, ever! There's so much pride in my family that messes things up for us, and I'm just glad I had soccer.

3

In Rosengård, we had different housing project neighborhoods, and no project was worse than any other—well, the one we called the Gypsy was looked down upon. It wasn't as if all the Albanians or Turks stayed together in one spot, though. It was your project that counted, not the country your parents had come from. You stuck with your project, and the neighborhood where Mom lived was called Törnrosen, which means Briar Rose. There were swings, a playground, a flagpole, and a soccer pitch where we played every day. Sometimes I didn't get to join in. I was too small. Then I'd blow up in an instant.

I hated being left out. I hated losing. Even so, winning wasn't the most important thing. The most important thing was the nice moves. There was a lot of "Hey, wow! Check that out!" You were supposed to impress the kids with tricks and moves, and you had to practice and practice until you were the best at them. Often, mothers would shout from the windows:

"It's late. Dinner's ready. Time to come in."

"In a minute," we'd say, and continue playing, and it could get late and start raining and all hell could break loose, but we just kept playing.

We were completely tireless, and the pitch was small. You had to be quick with your head and your feet, especially with me being little and puny and easy to tackle, and I learned wicked new stuff all the time. I had to. Otherwise I didn't get any Wow!'s; nobody would get me going. Often I'd sleep with my soccer ball and think of the tricks I was going to do the next day. It was like a film that was rolling constantly.

My first club was called MBI, Malmö Ball and Sporting Association. I was just six years old when I started. We played on a gravel pitch behind some green shacks, and I would ride to training sessions on stolen bikes and probably wasn't all that well behaved. The coaches sent me home a couple of times, and I would shout and swear back at them. I constantly heard, "Pass the ball, Zlatan!" That annoyed me, and I felt like a fish out of water. At MBI there were immigrant kids as well as Swedes, and many of the parents would grumble about my tricks from the projects. I told them to go to hell and changed clubs many times before I ended up at the FBK Balkan club. That was something else.

At MBI, the Swedish dads would stand around and call out, "Come on, guys. Good work!"

At Balkan, it was more like "I'll do your mom up the ass." They were psycho Yugoslavs who smoked like chimneys and flung their boots about, and I thought, Great, just like at home. I love it here! The coach was a Bosnian. He'd played at a pretty high level down in Yugoslavia, and he became a sort of father figure to us. Sometimes he'd drive us home, and he'd give me a few kronor for an ice cream or something to take care of my hunger.

I stood in goal for a while. I don't know why. Maybe I had flown into a rage at the old goalkeeper and said something like You're useless, I could do it better myself. I'm sure it was something like that. There was one match where I let in a load of goals, and I went berserk. I roared that everyone was shit. That soccer was shit. That the whole world was useless, and I was going to take up ice hockey instead:

"Hockey is way better, you assholes! I'm gonna be a hockey pro. Get fucked!"

That was it. I looked into all that stuff about ice hockey and thought, Shit! All the stuff you needed. A protective suit! It cost a ton. So the only thing to do was knuckle down and carry on with that crap, soccer. I stopped being the goalkeeper and came up into the forward line, and I got to be pretty awesome.

One day, we had a match, and I wasn't there. Everybody was shouting, "Where's Zlatan? Where's Zlatan?" It was just a few minutes before kickoff, and I bet the coach and my teammates wanted to strangle me. "Where is he? How the hell can he not turn up for such an important match?" Then they caught sight of a character who was pedaling like mad on a stolen bike, heading straight for the coach. Was that nut job going to crash into him? No, I skidded to a stop in the gravel right in front of the coach and ran straight onto the pitch. I gather the coach was absolutely furious.

He got gravel in his eyes. He got completely splattered. But he let me play, and I assume we won. We were a good gang. One time I got pulled out for some crap or other, and I was put on the bench for the first half. Our team was down 4–0 against a bunch of snobs from Vellinge; it was the brown kids versus the fancy kids, and there was loads of aggression in the air. I was so mad I was about to explode. How could that idiot put me on the bench?

"Are you stupid?" I asked the coach.

"Calm down. You'll come on soon."

I came on in the second half and scored eight goals. We won 8–5 and taunted the rich kids, and sure, I was good. I was technical and could see chances all the time. On the pitch at Mom's I had become a little master at coming up with unexpected moves in tight spaces. Even so, I'm sick of all the people who go around quacking, "I saw right away that Zlatan would turn into something special, blah blah blah. I practically taught him everything he knows. He was my best bud." That's bullshit.

Nobody said anything. Not as much as they said afterward, anyway. No big clubs came knocking on the door. I was a snot-nosed kid. There was no, Oh, we've got to be nice to this little talent. It was more like Who let the brown kid in?, and even then I was really inconsistent. I could score eight goals in one match and then fail to come up with anything in the next.

I hung out a lot with a guy called Tony Flygare. We had the same teacher for our community language lessons. His mom and dad are from the Balkans too, and he was something of a tough guy as well. He didn't live in Rosengård, but nearby on a street called Vitemöllegatan. We were both born in the same year, but his birthday is in January and mine is in October, and that did make a difference. He was bigger and stronger, and he was seen as a bigger soccer talent than me. There was a lot of attention on Tony—"Check him out, what a player!"—and I ended up being overshadowed by him a bit. Maybe that was a good thing, I dunno. I had to grit my teeth and fight as the underdog. Like I said, in those days I was no big name.

I was a wild kid, a terror, and I really had no control over my temper. I continued blowing my stack at players and referees, and I kept changing clubs the whole time. I played for Balkan. I came back to MBI and then to Balkan again and then to the BK Flagg club. It was all a mess, and nobody exactly gave me a ride to training sessions, and sometimes I'd look over at the parents on the sidelines.

My dad was never there, either among the Yugos or the Swedes, and I don't really know how that made me feel. That's just how it was. I looked after myself. I'd gotten used to it. Maybe it did hurt. I can't really tell. You just get used to the circumstances in your life, and I didn't think too much about that. Dad was the way he was. He was hopeless. He was amazing. He was up and down. I didn't count on him, not the way other people count on their parents. Sure, I did hope sometimes. I'd think, Goddamn it, imagine if he'd seen that wicked move, that awesome Brazilian piece? I mean, Dad had periods when he was totally committed. He wanted me to become a lawyer.

I can't claim I thought very much of that idea. In my circles, people didn't exactly go on to become lawyers. We did crazy stuff and dreamed of becoming tough guys, and we didn't get much parental support—there was no, Shall I explain the history of Sweden to you? There were beer cans and Yugo music and empty fridges and the Balkan War. Sometimes, though, Dad'd take the time and chat about soccer with me, and I was over the moon every time. I mean, he was my dad, and one day he came up to me—I'll never forget this, there was something formal in the air:

"Zlatan, it's time you started playing for a big club."

"What do you mean, a big club? What's a big club?"

"A good team, Zlatan. A top squad, like Malmö FF." I don't think I really understood.

What was so special about Malmö FF? I didn't know anything about that kind of thing, about what was worthwhile and what wasn't. I did know of the club. I'd played against them with Balkan, so I thought, Why not? If Dad says so. I had no idea where the soccer stadium was—or anything else in the city, for that matter. Malmö might not have been far away, but it was another world. I would turn seventeen before I went into the city center, and I knew nothing of life there. So I learned the way to the practice sessions, and I rode there in about thirty minutes with my gear in a supermarket bag, and of course I was nervous. At Malmö FF it was serious. No more of the usual, Come on and play, dudes! Here you had to go through tryouts and qualify, and I noticed right away that I wasn't like the rest of them. I got ready to pack up my stuff and head home.

Already on the second day, though, I heard these words from a coach called Nils: "Welcome to the team."

"Are you serious?" I was thirteen then, and there were a couple of other foreigners there already, including Tony. Otherwise, it was just regular Swedes, including the kind from the ritzy suburbs. I felt like I was from Mars. Not just because my dad didn't have a big, fancy house and never turned up at matches. I talked differently. I dribbled the ball. I would go off like a bomb, and I took a beating on the pitch. Once I got a yellow card because I bawled out my teammates.

"You can't do that!" the referee said.

"You can go to hell too," I roared, and took off.

Things started smoldering among the Swedes. Their parents wanted me out of there, and I thought, for the thousandth time, I don't give a damn about them. I'll change to another team again. Or I'll start doing tae kwon do instead. That's cooler. Soccer is shit. Some idiot father of somebody on the team went around with a petition. "Zlatan must leave the club," it said, and all kinds of people signed that thing. They smuggled it around, saying, "Zlatan doesn't belong here. He needs to be gotten rid of. Sign here, blah blah blah."

It was nuts. Okay, I'd been in a fight with that dad's son. I'd taken a load of nasty tackles, and I lost it on one. I'd headbutted him, if I'm honest. I was filled with regret afterward. I cycled over to the hospital and begged forgiveness. It was a stupid thing to do, really, but a petition! Give me a break. The manager, Åke Kallenberg, just stared at the paper and went, "What kind of ridiculous crap is this?"

He tore it into pieces. He was a good guy, Åke. Well, up to a point. He put me on the bench for almost a whole year on the junior squad and, like everybody else, he thought I dribbled too much and yelled at my teammates too much and had a bad attitude and the wrong mind-set and all the rest. I learned one important thing in those years. If a guy like me was going to get respect, he had to be five times better than Leffe Persson and whatever their names were. He had to train ten times harder. Otherwise, he didn't have a chance. Not on this earth. Especially not if he was a bike thief.

Of course, I should have shaped up after that business. I definitely wanted to. I wasn't completely hopeless. It was a long way to the training pitch, though—over four miles—and I often had to walk the whole way. Sometimes the temptation was too great, especially if I saw a cool bike. One time I caught sight of a yellow bike with a load of massive baskets on it, and I thought, Why not? I hopped on and rode off—nice, smooth ride. After a while, though, I started to wonder. There was something peculiar about those baskets, and it suddenly dawned on me: it was a mailman's bike. I was pedaling around with the neighborhood's mail, so I hopped off and left the bike a little distance away. Didn't want to swipe people's mail as well.

Another time, the most recent bike I had swiped got pinched, and I was left standing there outside the stadium. It was a long way home and I was hungry and impatient, and so I pinched another bike from outside the locker room. I popped the lock as usual, and I remember liking it. It was a nice bike, and I was careful to park it a little way away so the former owner wouldn't happen across it. Three days later, the team was summoned into a meeting. I already had an issue with stuff like that. Meetings usually meant hassle and getting a talking-to, and I started coming up with some clever explanations. Things like It wasn't me. It was my brother. I was right to do that, because the meeting concerned the assistant coach's bicycle.

"Has anybody seen it?"

Nobody had seen it. Me neither! I mean, in that sort of situation, you don't say anything. That's how it works. You play dumb: Oh, that's a shame. Poor you, I had a bike stolen once too.

Even so, I got worried. What had I done? And what bad luck—the assistant coach's bike! You're supposed to respect the coaches. That's what I figured. Or, more accurately, I mean, you're supposed to listen to them and learn their stuff, zone game, tactics, all that stuff. Yet, at the same time, don't listen. Just dribble the ball and do the tricks. Listen/Don't listen. That was my attitude. But stealing their bikes? I didn't really think that was part of the picture. I got nervous and went up to the assistant coach.

"Erm, here's the thing," I said. "I borrowed your bike for a little while. It was kind of an emergency. A one-time thing! You'll get it back tomorrow."

I gave him my best sheepish grin, and I think it sort of worked. My smile helped me a lot in those years, and I could come up with a joke when I was in a tight spot. It wasn't easy, though. I wasn't just the black sheep. If any warmups went missing, everybody blamed me. With good reason, as it happened. I was flat broke as well. While the others always had the latest soccer shoes from Adidas and Puma in kangaroo leather, I'd bought my first ones at the discount supermarket for 59.90 kronor (about $7)—they were stocked alongside the tomatoes and vegetables—and that's how it was. I never had anything to parade around in like that.

When the team went abroad, a lot of the others had two grand with them for spending money. I had about 20 kronor ($2), and that was even after Dad hadn't paid the rent one month in order to be able to send me off. He would rather get evicted than make me stay at home. That was real nice of him. Even so, I still couldn't keep up with the others.

"Come with us, Zlatan, we'll get a pizza, a burger, we'll go and buy this and that," the guys would say.

"Nah, later. I'm not hungry. I'll just chill out instead."

I tried to be evasive and still remain cool. It wasn't much fun. It wasn't a big deal. But it was something new, and I was entering into a period where I wasn't confident. Not that I wanted to be like the others. Well, maybe a bit. I wanted to learn their things, like etiquette and stuff like that. Most of the time I did my own thing. That was my weapon, you could say. I saw the guys from the housing projects on the edge of the city like mine who would try to pretend to be classy. It never worked, no matter how hard they tried, and I thought, I'll do the opposite, I'll do my own thing that much more. Instead of saying, I've only got 20 kronor, I'd say, I haven't got any cash, not a penny. That was cooler. More out there. I was a tough kid from Rosengård. I was different. That became my identity, and I enjoyed it more and more and didn't care that I didn't have a clue about the Swedish guys' idols.

Sometimes we were the ball boys for the first team's matches. One time, Malmö FF was playing against IFK Göteborg—that is to say, a really big match—and my teammates went nuts and wanted to get autographs from the stars, particularly one called Thomas Ravelli, who clearly was the greatest hero after some penalty kicks in the World Cup. I'd never heard of the guy—not that I admitted it. I didn't want to make a fool of myself. Sure, I'd seen the World Cup. But, I mean, I was from Rosengård. I didn't give a damn about the Swedes. I'd been following the Brazilians, like Romário and Bebeto and that bunch, and the only thing about Ravelli that interested me was his shorts. I wondered where I could swipe a pair like that for myself.

We were supposed to sell BingoLotto game cards to earn money for the club. I had no idea what BingoLotto was. Had never heard of guys like Loket, the guy who presented the lottery program on TV. I went around knocking on doors in our neighborhood, saying, "Hi there, my name's Zlatan. Sorry to bother you. Would you like to buy a lottery ticket?"

I was useless at that, to be honest. I sold approximately one ticket, and even fewer of the Advent calendars they saddled us with. That is to say, basically zero, and, in the end, Dad had to buy the whole lot. That wasn't fair. We couldn't afford it, and we didn't really need more junk at home. It didn't exactly make me overjoyed to be able to open every door in every calendar in November already. It was ridiculous, and I don't understand how people can send kids out like that, basically, to beg.

We played soccer, and we were an awesome year group, the ones at Malmö born in '80 and '81. There was Tony Flygare, Gudmunder Mete, Matias Concha, Jimmy Tamandi, Markus Rosenberg. There was me. There were all kinds of sharp guys, and I kept on improving, but the grumbling continued. It was mostly the parents. They just wouldn't give in. "Here he goes," they'd say.

"Now he's dribbling again!" "He's not right for the team." It made me nuts. Who the hell were they to stand there and judge me? People have said I was considering quitting soccer around that time. That's not true. For a while I was really serious about going to a different club. I didn't have a father nearby to defend me or buy me expensive clothes. I had to look after myself, and those Swedish dads with their snobby sons were everywhere, explaining why I was wrong. Of course, I felt rotten. And I was restless. I wanted action, more action. I needed something new.

Johnny Gyllensjö, the youth-team coach, got wind of this and took it up with the club. "Come on," he said. "Not everybody can turn up with their hair all slicked down. We're about to lose a major talent!" They drew up a youth contract for me, which Dad signed. I got

1,500 kronor (around $175) a month, and that was a buzz, of course, and I made more and more of an effort. I wasn't completely impossible, like I said. It wasn't all, Don't listen to them! It was also, Listen.

I practiced hard at taking the ball down with as few touches as possible. I still didn't really shine, I have to say. It was still all about Tony, and I soaked up knowledge in order to get at least as good as him. My whole generation at Malmö was into Brazilian stuff and tricks. We spurred one another on there. It was a bit like Mom's housing project again, and when we got access to computers we'd download all kinds of feints, stuff that Ronaldo and Romário were doing, and then we'd practice until the trick took hold. There was lots of rewinding and fast-forwarding. How do they actually do that? How do they do that little thing?

We were all used to touching the ball. But the Brazilians would sort of nudge it with their foot, and we'd practice over and over again until the thing worked, and finally we'd try it out in matches. There were a lot of us who did that. I took it a step further. I went deeper into it. I was more precise in the details. I became completely obsessed.

Those tricks had always been my way of getting noticed, and I continued dribbling, no matter how much the dads and coaches grumbled. No, I didn't adapt. Or, more accurately, I did and I didn't. I wanted to be different. I wanted to do the coaches' stuff too, and it kept getting better. Sometimes it wasn't that easy. Sometimes it hurt, and I'm sure the situation with Mom and Dad affected me. There was a lot of shit that needed to come out.

At school, they hired special teachers just for my sake. I got really angry. Sure, I was rowdy. Maybe the worst one. But a special teacher! Give me a break! I got an A in art, and Bs in English, chemistry, and physics. I wasn't a druggie. I'd hardly even taken a puff on a cigarette. I was just restless and did a load of stupid stuff, yet people were talking about putting me in a special school. They wanted to set me apart, and I felt like I was from Mars. It was as if a time bomb started ticking inside me. Do I need to mention that I was good at PE? I might have been a bit unfocused in the classroom and had a hard time sitting still with a book. But I could concentrate too if we're talking about moving a ball or an egg around.

One day we were playing floorball. That special teacher came and stared. Every little thing I did, she was there, like a barnacle. I was really fuming. I lined up a world-class shot and hit her square in the head. She was completely stunned, and just stared at me. Afterward, they phoned Dad and wanted to talk about psychiatric help and a special school and that kind of shit, and you know that was not the right stuff to talk to my dad about. Nobody says bad things about his kids, especially teachers who are persecuting them. He went ballistic and charged into the school with his whole cowboy attitude: "Who the hell are you, coming and talking about psychiatric help? You're the ones who ought to be in the nuthouse, all of you. There's nothing wrong with my son, he's a fine kid, you can all go to hell!"

He was a crazy Yugo and completely in his element. Not long after that, the teacher quit. No wonder, really, and things did get a bit better. I got my self-confidence back. Even so, the whole idea! A special teacher, just for me! It makes me furious. Sure, maybe I wasn't an angel. You can't single out kids like that, though—you just can't!

If anybody ever treated Maxi or Vincent as if they were different, I would flip out. I promise you. I'd be worse than Dad. That special treatment is still with me. I didn't feel good about it. Okay, in the long run, maybe it made me stronger. I dunno. I became even more of a fighter. In the short term, though, it really ruined me. One day, I was supposed to go on a date with a girl, and I wasn't particularly confident around girls in those days. The kid with the special teacher following him around—how cool does that sound? Just asking for her phone number made me break into a sweat.

There was a good-looking girl standing in front of me, and I barely managed to stammer out, "D'you want to meet up sometime after school?"

"Sure," she said.

"How about Gustav, on such-and-such day?"

"Gustav" is Gustav Adolf Square, which is between the Triangeln shopping center and Stortorget Square in central Malmö, and she seemed to like the idea. When I got there, though, she wasn't there. I got really nervous. It wasn't exactly my home turf, and I felt awkward. Why wasn't she there? Didn't she like me anymore? A minute passed, two, three, ten minutes, and finally I couldn't stick it out any longer. It was the ultimate humiliation.

I've been stood up, I thought to myself. Who would want to go on a date with me? And so I left. Who cares about her? I thought, I'm going to be a soccer star, anyway. That was the stupidest thing to do. The girl's bus had just been a bit late. The driver had been on a cigarette break or something, and she got there just after I'd left and was just as upset as I had been.

4

I started secondary school at Borgarskolan, doing the social sciences curriculum with a special focus on soccer, and I was hoping for great things. Everything was going to be different now. Now I'd be really cool. But the whole thing was a shock. Well, okay, I suppose I'd had some preparation for what it would be like.

There were some guys from the fancy suburb of Limhamn on the team. Now there were girls as well, and other sorts of guys, standoffish types in trendy clothes who stood around in the corners, smoking. I rolled up in my sweats and jogging suits covered in Adidas or Nike logos. That was the coolest thing, I thought, and I went around like that all the time. What I didn't realize was that it all just screamed Rosengård. It was like a billboard. As if that special teacher was still clinging on to me.

At Borgarskolan, kids had Ralph Lauren sweaters, Timberland boots, and shirts with collars. Imagine! I'd hardly ever seen a guy wearing a button-front shirt with a collar before, and I realized immediately that I needed to take drastic action. There were loads of sharp girls in the school. It wouldn't do to go and chat them up while looking like a guy from the projects. I talked it over with my dad, and we had an argument. We got a study grant from the government in those days. It was 795 kronor (about $95) a month, and it was obvious to my dad that he would take care of that, because he was responsible for the cost of my upkeep, as he put it. I put it a different way: "I can't be the biggest clown in the school!"

Somehow, he swallowed it. I got the study grant and a bank account, and a bank card with a picture of a tree on it. My grant came through on the twentieth of each month, and a lot of my friends would stand there by the cash machine at 11:59 p.m. the night before, just waiting, going completely nuts. Is it almost midnight? Ten, nine, eight . . . I was a little cooler, but the next morning I had certainly taken out quite a bit and gone and bought a pair of Davis jeans.

They were the cheapest. They cost 299 kronor (about $35), and then I picked out some polo shirts, three for 99 kronor ($12). I tried out a few styles. Nothing worked. My appearance still screamed Rosengård. I didn't fit in. That's how I felt. Also, I'd been small all my life. Suddenly, that summer, I'd grown a massive amount, five inches in just a few months, and I guess I must have looked really lanky. I needed to sort myself out, plain and simple, and for the first time in my life I started hanging out in the city center, at Burger King, in the shopping malls, in the Lilla Torg square.

I carried on with some worse things too, not just for the buzz. I needed some cool stuff. Otherwise, I'd have no chance in the schoolyard. So I pinched one guy's music player, a wicked MiniDisc. We had lockers outside the classroom. They had combination locks, and I found out one kid's secret combination from a friend. When he wasn't around, I went over and sort of went, Right five, left three, and then rode off with that MiniDisc player, digging his tunes and feeling totally cool. Of course, it wasn't enough.

I still didn't have a lot to bring to the table. I was still the kid from the projects. My friend was smarter. He got himself a girlfriend from an upper-class family and talked his way in with her brother, and started borrowing his clothes. That's a good trick, for sure, even if it only worked up to a point. Those of us from the projects never really fit in. We were different. Still, this friend of mine started turning up with wicked brands, and he had a cool girl and was as cocky as anything. As for me, I felt worse than nothing. I just carried on with my soccer.

That wasn't going so well either. I had made it onto the junior team and was playing with guys who were a year older, and that was an achievement in itself. We were a brilliant gang, one of the better teams in the country in our age group. But I was on the bench. That was Åke Kallenberg's decision. Of course, a coach can put whoever he wants on the bench. In my case, though, I don't think it was just about soccer. When I came off the bench, I scored goals pretty often. I wasn't bad. They thought I was wrong in other ways.

People were saying that I didn't contribute enough to the team: "Your dribbling doesn't drive the play forward"—I heard that kind of thing hundreds of times, and I sensed the vibes. It was like, That Zlatan! Isn't he too unbalanced? There weren't any more petitions, but it wasn't far off that, and it's true, I did mix it up with my teammates. I shouted and talked too much on the pitch. I could get into arguments with spectators. Nothing too serious. But I had my temper and my playing style. I was a different type of player, and I would fly into a rage. I didn't really belong at Malmö FF: that's the view many people took. I remember the Swedish junior championship. We made it into the final, and of course that was a huge deal.

Åke Kallenberg didn't put me on the team. I wasn't even going to sit on the bench. "Zlatan is injured," he told everyone, and I leapt up. What do you mean, injured? What was he talking about?

I said to him, "What are you talking about? How can you say something like that?"

"You're injured," he repeated, and I couldn't believe it. Why was he coming out with that kind of crap when we were going to be in the final?

"You're just saying that because you don't want to deal with me." But, no, he *perceived* me as injured, and it drove me mad. There was something strange in the air. Nobody was saying what it was. Nobody was man enough. That year, Malmö FF won the Swedish junior championship title without me, and that didn't exactly reinforce my self-confidence. Sure, of course, I'd said a load of cocky stuff. For example, when my Italian teacher kicked me out of class and I said, "I don't give a damn about you. I'll learn it when I become a pro in Italy," that might be a bit of fun once you knew how things turned out. Back then, it was just big talk. I didn't believe it. How could I, when I wasn't even a regular on the junior team?

Their first team was having problems in those days. Malmö FF's first team is pretty much the best in the country. When my dad came to Sweden in the seventies, they totally dominated the league. They even made it to the final in the Champions League (the European Cup, as it was called in those days), and hardly anybody from the junior squad got taken up. The management recruited players from other teams instead. That year, the team had changed. Although nobody really understood why, things were going really badly for the club. Malmö FF, which had always been at the top of the Allsvenskan League, was in danger of being relegated. They were playing miserably. Their finances were down the toilet. They couldn't afford to buy any players, so a lot of young players got a chance instead, and you can imagine how we talked about it on the junior squad. Who are they going to call up? Will it be him? Or him?

So it was Tony Flygare of course, as well as Gudmundur Mete, who was a player from Iceland, and Jimmy Tamandi, also from Malmö. I wasn't even considered. I was the last one on the team who would get picked up. That's what I thought. That's what most people thought. So, to be honest, there was nothing to hope for. Even the junior coach was putting me on the bench. Why would the first team take me on? That wasn't even on the map. Even so, I was no worse than Tony, Mete, or Jimmy. I'd shown that in my substitutions. What was the problem? What were they up to? All these thoughts were buzzing around in my head, and I became more and more convinced that there was a load of politics involved.

As a kid, it might have been cool to be different and a little cockier than the others, but in the long run it was just a disadvantage. When it really comes down to it, they didn't want any brown kids or hotheads who did showy Brazilian moves all the time. Malmö FF was a refined, proud club. In its glory days, all the players had been blond and well behaved, with typically Swedish names like Bosse Larsson, who said nice, refined things, and since then they hadn't taken on many players with immigrant backgrounds. Okay, Yksel Osmanovski had been there; his parents were Macedonian.

He was from Rosengård as well. He was a pro with Bari then. He was better behaved than me. No, there wouldn't be any first-team games for me. I had my youth team contract. I would have to be satisfied with that and the under-twenty-ones. The under-twenty-one squad was a thing they had set up together with the soccer academy at Borgarskolan, since the junior team was for kids up to eighteen. There weren't all that many of us who got picked up there, not enough to make a team yet. The idea was to prevent us from leaving the club, and we would often play with guys from the second team against

division-three teams and stuff. It was nothing great, but I had an opportunity to get myself noticed.

Sometimes we would train with the first team, and I refused to fit
in. Normally, in those situations, a junior doesn't go in for wicked
dribbling. He doesn't make strong tackles or start screaming, "Fucking sweep it!" He behaves. I thought, Why not? I've got nothing to
lose. I gave it everything I had. I just went for it, and, of course, I
noticed they were talking about me, "Who does he think he is?" and
stuff, and I would mutter, "Go to hell!" and just keep it up. I kept at
my tricks. I played the tough guy, and sometimes Roland Andersson,
the first-team coach, was watching.

At first I was filled with hope, thinking, I wonder if he thinks I'm
good? But that changed with all the crap that was happening around
me. When I saw him again one day on the sideline, my only thought
was, I bet he's heard some grumbling. Some complaints. Around that
time, I was feeling even more disappointed in soccer, and I wasn't
having much success in other areas either, especially in school. I was
still shy and lacking in confidence, and I often only went to school to
have lunch. I ate like a horse. I basically didn't care about the rest. I
was doing less and less schoolwork and, finally, I dropped out of
school altogether, and there was a load of hassle and arguing at home.

It was like a minefield, and I kept out of the way and continued
with my tricks in the yard. I put up photos of Ronaldo in my room.
Ronaldo was the man. Not only because of his step-overs and goals
in the World Cup. Ronaldo was brilliant on every level. He was what
I wanted to be, a guy who made a difference. The players on the
Swedish national side—who were they? There was no superstar, nobody who was talked about around the world. Ronaldo was my hero
and I studied him online and tried to take in his movements, and I
thought I was getting to be an awesome player. I danced down the
pitch with the ball.

What did I have to show for it? Nothing, I thought. The world was unfair. Guys like me didn't have a chance, and I wasn't going to be a star, no matter what I could do. That's how it looked. I was finished. I wasn't right, and I tried to find other paths. I just didn't have the energy to go for it. I just kept on playing. The day when Roland Andersson stood there glowering, I was playing with the under-twenty-ones on pitch no. 1. Pitch no. 1 no longer exists. It was a grass pitch, right next to Malmö Stadium, and afterward I heard that Roland Andersson wanted to speak to me. That was all I knew. I started to panic a little and started thinking: Have I swiped a bike? Have I headbutted someone? In my mind, I went over all the stupid stuff I'd done, and there was plenty of it. I couldn't figure out how any of it could have reached him, and I thought up about a thousand explanations.

Roland is a pretty loud guy, with a deep voice. He's nice, but strict. He dominates a room, and I think my heart was pounding a little.

Roland Andersson—I'd heard he played in the World Cup in Argentina. He wasn't just one of the old Malmö FF stars from the glory days. He had been on the national squad as well. A guy with respect, and there he was at his desk, not cracking a hint of a smile. He looked serious, as if to say, Get ready for the ultimate bawling out.

"All right, Roland. How are things? Is there something you wanted?"

I always tried to play it cocky like that. It's something that had stayed with me since I was little. You couldn't show any weakness.

"Sit down."

"Okay, take it easy. Nobody died. I promise."

"Zlatan, it's time for you to stop playing with the little kids." With the little kids? What's he talking about, I thought, and what on earth have I done to the little kids?

"What do you mean?" I asked. "Are you talking about anybody in particular?"

"It's time for you to start playing with the big boys." I still didn't get it.

"Huh?"

"Welcome to the first team, lad," he continued, and honestly, I cannot describe the feeling, not in a million years.

It was as if I'd been lifted up ten meters in the air, and I'm guessing I went out and stole a new bike and felt like the coolest dude in the city.

5

At Malmö, we had a thing called the Mile.

The Mile was a goddamn long course. We would run from the stadium out to the Water Tower, down along Limhamnsvägen, past all the millionaires' piles there with views out toward the sea—especially one house I remember that was pink, and we'd all go, "Wow, what kind of people live there? How many million must they have in the bank?"

We'd continue toward Kungsparken, through a tunnel, and then up to the school I used to go to, in full view of all the girls and the rich kids. Man, what a buzz that gave me! That was my revenge. Me, the loser from Rosengård who'd hardly dared to speak to a girl, and there I was running with all the top dudes from Malmö FF, like Mats Lilienberg and the rest. It was the greatest thing, and I really made the most of it.

At the start, I followed the crowd. I was new on the first team and wanted to show that I was up to the task. But then I realized: the key thing was to impress the girls. So Tony, Mete, and I employed some little tricks. We ran the first four kilometers. Then, when we reached Limhamnsvägen, we turned off by the bus stop. Nobody saw us. We had been bringing up the rear, so we could calmly wait around for the bus and climb aboard. Of course, we were laughing our heads off. It was outrageous. Then we had to duck down like crazy when we rode past the rest of the team. I mean, that business with the bus didn't really indicate the right attitude. At the end of the road we got off, completely rested and far ahead of the others, and hid in a corner. When the rest of the team ran past, we dashed off and had plenty of power to show off in front of the school. Wow, the girls must have been thinking, those guys look like they could take anything.

Another day on the Mile, I said to Tony and Mete, "This is ridiculous. Let's pinch a bike instead." I think they were a bit skeptical. They didn't have my level of experience in this area. I managed to convince them, and so I grabbed a bike and rode off with them on the rear rack. Other times, things went completely off the rails. I wasn't exactly the most mature guy in town, and Tony was an idiot as well. That fool had gotten into porn movies. He went into a shop and rented a video and bought some chocolate instead of going on the run, and we sat and ate the chocolate while the others on the team jogged their Mile.

I suppose I should be glad Roland Andersson believed our explanations. Or maybe he didn't. He was nice. He understood us young guys. He had a sense of humor. Of course, there were rumblings elsewhere: What's with that guy, Zlatan? Where's his humility? I kept hearing the old crap: "He dribbles the ball too much. He doesn't think of the team." Some of it was perfectly true. Definitely! I had a lot to learn. The rest was jealousy. The players sensed the competition, and I wasn't really just a cheater.

I put my all into it and wasn't satisfied with just going to Malmö

FF's training sessions. I also spent hours playing on the pitch at my mom's as well. I had a trick. I'd head out to Rosengård and shout to the kids, "You'll get a ten spot if you can get the ball away from me!" It wasn't just a game. It polished my technique. It taught me to use my body to shield the ball.

When I wasn't goofing around with the little kids, I'd play soccer videogames. I could go ten hours at a stretch, and I'd often spot solutions in the games that I parlayed into real life. It was soccer 24/7, you could say. It wasn't all smooth sailing in training sessions at Malmö FF, though, and I might have messed about a bit too much. It was as if they'd brought a completely irrational factor into the club, a guy they couldn't comprehend. I mean, any bastard will make a pass in this or that scenario and will say a given thing in a particular situation. But me . . . I came from another planet. I just kept laying it on with all the crazy Rosengård stuff.

It was often the older players against the younger ones on the club. We younger ones were supposed to haul trunks and stuff and wait on the others. It was ridiculous, and the atmosphere was rotten right from the beginning. At the start of the season, Tommy Söderberg, the club's captain, had predicted that Malmö FF would win the league, but since then one thing after another had gone wrong, and now the club was in danger of being relegated to the second division. It was the first time in about sixty years, and the supporters were up in arms, and all the older players on the team had the world on their shoulders.

They all knew what it would mean for the city if they didn't remain in the Allsvenskan League—nothing short of a disaster. It was no time for partying or Brazilian footwork. I was still elated at having been brought up to the first team and wanted to show them who I was. That might not have been the right attitude to take.

It was in my blood, though. I was in a new gang. I wanted to make people sit up and take notice, and I refused to bow and scrape. When Jonnie Fedel, the goalkeeper, asked, "Where the hell are the balls?" on the first day of practice, I gave a little jump, especially when I noticed that everybody was looking at me and appeared to be waiting for me to go and fetch them. There was no way I was going to, especially when he put it like that.

"If you want them, you can go and get 'em yourself," I spat, and that was not the way people usually spoke at Malmö FF.

That was the projects talking again, and it didn't go down well. I had support from Roland and the assistant coach, Thomas Sjöberg— I knew that, even if they mostly believed in Tony, of course. He got to play and scored a goal in his debut. I was on the bench, and tried to go for it even more in practice. That didn't help, though, and I swore. Maybe I should have been satisfied and not in such a hurry. That's just not how I work. I want to get in there and show what I can do right away. It looked like I wouldn't get a chance. On September 19, we were going to be away against Halmstad at the Örjans Vall Stadium.

It was a make-or-break match. If we won or played to a draw, we would remain in the Allsvenskan League. Otherwise, we would have to battle it out in the relegation playoffs, and everyone on the club was nervous and jittery. The teams were deadlocked. At the start of the second half, Niklas Gudmundsson, our striker, was taken off on a stretcher, and I was hoping to get brought in. But no, Roland didn't so much as glance at me, and time passed. Nothing happened. It was 1–1, and that would have to do. Then, with only fifteen minutes remaining, our team captain, Hasse Mattisson, was also injured, and Halmstad made it 2–1 right after that, and I watched as the entire team went pale.

That was when Roland sent me in. While all the rest were having a nervous breakdown, I got kicking with a massive adrenaline rush. I was seventeen. It was the Allsvenskan League, with ten thousand people in the stands. It said Ibrahimović on my shirt. I thought, Wow, this is big—nothing can stop me now; and right away I had a shot that grazed the crossbar. Then something happened. We were awarded a penalty in the final minutes, and you know what that meant. There was a sense of life and death. If we converted the penalty, the club's honor would be secure; otherwise, we risked disaster—and all the big guys hesitated. They weren't willing to take the kick. There was too much at stake, so Tony, that cocky bastard, stepped up.

"I'll take it."

That took some balls. A Balkan thing to do—don't back down! Now, in hindsight, I think somebody should have stopped him. He was too young to take on something like that, and I remember how he took up his position and the whole team held their breath or looked away. It was horrible. The goalkeeper saved it. I think he faked him out a bit. We lost, and afterward Tony ended up in the freezer. That was a pity for him, and I know there are journalists who see that as a symbolic thing. That was the moment I overtook him. Tony never made it back into top-level soccer, and instead I got to play more. I came on off the bench six times in the Allsvenskan, and, in some interview, Roland referred to me as a "diamond in the rough." Word got around, and it wasn't long before kids started coming up after matches to ask for my autograph. Not that it was any big thing yet. But it got me pumped up, and I thought, I've got to get even sharper now. I can't disappoint these kids!

Check this out! That's what I wanted to shout to them. Check out the most awesome thing in the world! Actually, that was a bit strange, wasn't it? I hadn't done anything yet—not a lot, at any rate. Even so, young fans turned up out of nowhere, and it made me want to show off my moves even more. Those little squirts made me feel like I had a right to my game. They wouldn't have come up if I'd been some boring team player. I started to play for those kids, and right from the start I signed every autograph. Nobody was left out. I was young myself. I understood exactly what it would have felt like if my pals had gotten an autograph but I didn't.

"Everybody happy?" I asked, before I rushed off, and there was so much happening around me that I didn't worry too much about the team's setbacks.

It was bizarre, in a way. I was making a name for myself, all the while my club was going through its biggest crisis ever, pretty much. When we lost at home to Trelleborg, the fans wept in the stands and yelled "Resign!" at Roland. The police had to come in and protect him, and people threw rocks at the Trelleborg bus and there were riots and shit. Things didn't get any better a few days later, when we were humiliated by AIK—and the disaster was real.

We crashed out of the Allsvenskan League. For the first time in sixty-four years, Malmö FF would not be playing in the top division. Players sat in the locker room hiding under towels while the management tried to put a positive spin on things or whatever they were doing, and frustration and shame were bubbling to the surface everywhere. Some certainly thought I was a huge diva who'd been running around doing fancy tricks in all those serious matches. I didn't really care. I had other things to think about. Something amazing had happened.

It was right after I had been taken up onto the first team. We were out training on pitch no. 1 and, obviously, we were Malmö FF. We were—or rather, had been—the pride of the city. Even so, there weren't many people who came to watch our training sessions, especially in those days. But that afternoon, a man with dark, grayish hair turned up. I spotted him from far away. I didn't recognize him. I just noticed that he was staring at us from near a tree over there, and I felt a little strange. It was like I could sense something, and so I started to do even more tricks. It took a while before I figured it out.

I'd had to look out for myself when I was growing up: I hadn't had much, and sure, Dad had done some totally amazing things as well. He hadn't been like the other dads I'd seen, though. He hadn't watched my matches or encouraged me in my studies. He'd had his drinking and his war and his Yugo music. But now, I couldn't believe it. That man really was my dad. He had come to watch, and I was completely blown away. It was as if I was dreaming, and I started to play with incredible strength. Shit, Dad's here! This is fantastic. Look at me, Dad, I wanted to yell. Look at me! Check it out. Your son is the most amazing, awesome player!

I believe that was one of my greatest moments. I really do. I got him back. Not that I didn't have him before. If there had been a crisis, he'd come rushing up like the Incredible Hulk. This was something totally new, and afterward I ran over and chatted to him a bit, just casually, as if it was totally natural that my dad was there.

"How's it going?"

"Well played, Zlatan."

It was weird. Dad had gotten some sort of bug, I thought. I became his drug. He started following everything I did. He came to watch every practice session. His apartment became a sort of shrine to my career, and he cut out every article, every little piece, and he's kept it up. You can ask him today about any one of my matches. He'll have it recorded, and he'll have every single word that's been written about it, and all the jerseys and shoes I've worn and my trophies and Guldbollen awards for the best Swedish soccer player of the year. You name it, it's all there, and not all jumbled together either, like it used to be with his stuff. Everything is in its place. He can find anything in a second. He's got it all under control.

From that day at pitch no. 1 onward, he began to live for me and my soccer, and I believe it improved his health. He hasn't had it easy. He was alone. Sanela had broken off all contact with him because of his drinking and his temper and his harsh words about Mom, and it had been very hard on him. Sanela was his beloved daughter, and she always will be. Now she was no longer there for him. She had shut him out, and it was another of those harsh things in my family. Dad needed something new—which he now got. We started to chat every day, and all that became a new impetus for me as well. It was like, Wow, soccer can do amazing things, and I gave it even more. What was relegation into the second division, when my dad had just become my biggest fan?

I didn't know what I should do. Should I start playing in the Superettan—the "Super One," the ridiculous name given to the Swedish second division—or aim higher? There had been talk that AIK, one of the big Stockholm clubs, was after me. Was it true? I didn't have a clue. I didn't know a damn thing about how hot a property I was. I wasn't even a regular member of the Malmö squad. I was eighteen years old, and should have signed a first-team contract. I put it off. Everything felt up in the air, especially since Roland Andersson and Thomas Sjöberg had gotten fired. They were the ones who had believed in me when everybody else was complaining. Would I even get to play if I stayed? I didn't know, and I was unsure. Both Dad and I were unsure, and how good was I, really?

I had no idea. I'd given a few autographs to kids. Of course, that didn't mean anything, and my self-confidence was up and down. The first rush of elation at having been called up onto the first team was starting to fade. Then I met a guy from Trinidad and Tobago. It was the preseason. He was cool. He had a tryout with us, and afterward he came over to me.

"Hey, fella," he said.

"What?"

"If you're not a pro within three years, it's your own fault."

"What do you mean?"

"You heard me." Damn right I did!

It took a while to sink in. Could it be true? If anyone else had said it, I would hardly have believed them. But this guy, he seemed to know. He'd been around, and it hit me like a body blow. Was I seriously professional material? I started to think so. For the first time, I really did, and I buckled down even more.

Hasse Borg, the old defender for the Swedish national side, was sporting director for Malmö FF then. Hasse noticed me right from the start. I guess he understood my talent, and he put word out among the journalists. Things like, Look here, you should check out this fellow; and the following February, Rune Smith, a reporter from *Kvällsposten,* one of the tabloid papers in Malmö, came to a training session. Rune was cool. He would almost become a friend, and after he watched me practice we chatted a bit, him and me—nothing unusual, not at all.

I talked about the club and the Superettan League and about my dreams of becoming a pro in Italy, just like Ronaldo. Rune took notes and smiled, and I don't really know what I expected to happen. I had no experience with journalists in those days. It turned into a huge thing. Rune wrote something like "Practice this name, you'll be seeing it in the headlines: ZLATAN. It sounds exciting. And he is exciting. A different kind of player, a bundle of dynamite in the offensive lineup." Then he mentioned that bit about the diamond in the rough again, and I said a few things that sounded cocky and un-Swedish in the article, I dunno.

There must have been something about that piece. Now even more kids started coming up after the training sessions, and, in fact, some teenage girls as well, and even some adults. That was the launch of the whole hysteria, all that "Zlatan, Zlatan!" that would become my life, and which seemed so unreal at first—I would think, What's going on? Are they talking about me?

I'd be lying if I said it wasn't the most awesome thing in the world. I mean, what do you think? I had been trying to get attention my whole life, and now, suddenly, people were turning up, awestruck, asking for my autograph. Of course, that was cool. It was a major buzz. I was pumped up. I was full of adrenaline. I was flying. You know, I've heard people go, "Oh, I've got it so tough, there are people screaming outside my window. They want my autograph, poor me." That's bullshit.

Those things get you going, believe me—especially if you've had a life like mine, growing up as a snot-nosed kid in the projects. It's like a massive spotlight has been switched on. Of course, there were certain things I didn't understand yet—the jealousy thing, that psychological stuff about how a lot of people want to knock you down when you're up, especially if you come from the wrong side of the tracks and don't behave like a nice Swedish boy. I got some crap as well, things like You've just been lucky, and Who do you think you are?

I responded by getting even cockier. What else could I do? I hadn't been brought up to apologize. In my family, we didn't say, Oh, forgive me, I'm so sorry you're upset. We give as good as we get. We fight if we need to, and we don't rely on people in general. Everybody in my family has taken their knocks, and my dad always said, "Don't do anything too hasty. People only want to take advantage of you." I listened, and I thought it over. It wasn't easy, though. In those days, Hasse Borg was running around after me, all suited up, trying to get me to sign a contract for the first team.

He was incredibly eager, and it was flattering. I felt important. We had a new coach then—Micke Andersson—and I was still unsure how much I'd get to play. People thought Micke Andersson would want to focus on Niclas Kindvall and Mats Lilienberg up front and have me as a reserve, and I didn't want to get into the Supcrettan League and sit on the bench. I talked it over with Hasse Borg, and of course there are loads of things I could say about him. I don't think it was just by chance that he was a successful businessman. He gets straight to the point. He's a master at persuading people, and he drew on his own experiences as a player and went to town.

"This'll be good, lad. We'll invest in you, and the Superettan League will be the ideal incubator. You'll have opportunities to develop. Just sign!"

I felt like I agreed. I was starting to trust the guy. He kept phoning me and giving me advice, and I thought, Why not? He must know. He was a pro in Germany and all that, and he really seemed to care about me. "Agents are crooks," he said, and I believed him.

There was a guy after me. His name was Roger Ljung. Roger Ljung was an agent, and he wanted to sign me up. Dad was skeptical, though, and I knew nothing about agents myself. What is it they do? So I bought into Hasse Borg's line of thinking, that agents are crooks, and I signed his contract and got an apartment in the Lorensberg neighborhood in Malmö—a studio not far from the stadium—and a cell phone, which meant a lot to me, because I hadn't been allowed to use the phone at Dad's, and a salary of 16,000 kronor (around $1,900) a month.

I resolved to really give it a shot. But things started off badly. The first match of the season in the Superettan League, we were away at Gunnilse, who were a bunch of pushovers, and we should have had a big win. The old enmities were still there on our team, and I stayed on the bench for a long time. Goddamn it, was this how it was going to be? There wasn't much going on in the stands, it was windy, and when I finally went in I got a nasty elbow in my back. I gave my opponent one in the back too—bam! just like that—and then I went at it with the referee, who gave me a yellow card. There was a huge song-and-dance about it, both on the pitch and in the papers, and our team captain, Hasse Mattisson, claimed that I was spreading negative energy.

"What do you mean, negative? I'm just psyched up."

"You don't let things go." And then there was a load of crap about how I was nothing like the star I thought I was, and that others had ball skills just as good as mine. They just didn't show off all the time, thinking they were the next Maradona. I got frustrated. There's a photo of me where I was standing by the bus in Gunnilse, looking angry.

Eventually, it subsided. I started playing better, and I have to give Hasse Borg credit: the Superettan gave me playing time and opportunities to improve. I should be thankful for the relegation in a way. It wasn't long before good things started to happen.

It was crazy, really. I wasn't exactly another Ronaldo yet, and Swedish national newspapers don't generally get too worked up about second-division soccer. Now the tabloids were producing center spreads with titles like "The Super-Diva in the Superettan," and things like that, and the Malmö FF Supporters' Club suddenly got a big influx of young female members, and all the older players on the club were wondering, What's this all about? What's going on? And it really wasn't easy to understand, especially for me. People would sit in the stands waving banners that said, "Zlatan is the king" and would scream when I dribbled the ball like I was some rock star. What was happening? What was it all about? I didn't know. I still don't, really.

I guess a lot of people were just excited about my tricks and my fancy moves, and I was hearing a lot of Wow!'s and Check that out!'s now too, the way I had in Mom's neighborhood, and it got me going. I felt bigger when people recognized me around town, and girls would scream and kids would run up with their autograph books, and I did my thing even more. Sure, sometimes things went a little overboard. For the first time in my life, I had some cash. I spent my first paycheck on an intensive driving course to get my license. For a lad from Rosengård, a car is a basic requirement, you could say.

People in Rosengård don't boast about having a fancy apartment or a beachfront house. People brag about having flash cars, and if you want to show you've made something of yourself, the way to do it is with a wicked set of wheels. Everybody drives in Rosengård, whether they've got a driver's license or not, and when I got my Toyota Celica on lease, me and my pals were constantly out in it. By that time, I'd calmed down a bit. The whole uproar in the media made me want to keep a low profile, or at least a bit lower, and when my friends started stealing cars and that sort of thing, I said to them, "That stuff isn't for me anymore."

Even so, I still needed to get a little buzz once in a while, like the time I drove with a friend up along Industrigatan, the street where all the prostitutes in Malmö wait for johns. Industrigatan isn't far from Rosengård, and I'd been around there quite a bit as a kid, up to no good. One time, I even threw an egg at one of the women, hit her right in the head—not very nice, I admit. In those days, I didn't really think things through, and now when my friend and I came there in the Toyota, we saw a prostitute leaning over one car, apparently talking to a client, and we said, "Let's have some fun with the perv there," and so I slammed on the brakes right in front of him and we rushed out and yelled, "Police! Put your hands up!"

It was completely insane. I had a bottle of shampoo in my hand, like a really lame pretend handgun, and that john, some old man, got totally scared and tore out of there. We didn't think any more of it, it was just a thing we did. As we drove a little further, we heard sirens, and the old man from Industrigatan was sitting in a police car, and we thought, What's going on? What's this all about? True, we could have just floored it and got out of there. I was no stranger to things like that, after all. But we had our seat belts on and everything and we hadn't done anything, not really. So we stopped politely.

"It was just a joke," we said. "We pretended to be police. No big deal, is it? We're sorry," and the cops mostly laughed, like it was no big deal.

Just then a bastard turned up, one of those photographers who sit and listen to the police radio all the time, and he snapped a photo, and I, idiot that I was, put on a huge grin, because the whole media thing was new to me in those days. It was still great to be in the papers, regardless of whether I'd scored an awesome goal or been stopped by the police. So I grinned like a clown, and my pal took it even further. He had the newspaper story framed, and hung it on the wall. And that old codger, you know what he did? He gave some interviews and said he was an upstanding church member and was just helping the prostitutes. Give me a break. That story did stick around, and people even said that certain big clubs decided not to acquire me because of it. That was probably just gossip.

The press got even more out of control after that, and some members of the team talked behind my back: "He's got a lot to learn," "He's very rough"—and, really, I can understand them. It can't have been easy. They probably needed to put me down a bit. There I came, waltzing in from nowhere, and got more attention in one week than they'd had in their entire careers, and to cap it all, a load of men in sharp suits and bling watches turned up in the bleak stands in the provincial towns where we played that season—guys that didn't belong there at all, and everybody was staring at *me*.

Looking back, I don't know when I first grasped it, or even sat down and thought about it. People started saying that those men were soccer scouts from European clubs, and they were there to check me out. The guy from Trinidad and Tobago had certainly warned me about this, but it still felt completely unreal. I tried to talk about it with Hasse Borg. He avoided the subject. He didn't seem to like that topic of conversation at all.

"Is it true, Hasse? Are there foreign clubs checking me out?"

"Take it easy, kid."

"Which ones are they?"

"It's nothing," said Hasse Borg. "And we aren't going to sell you."

I thought, Sure, fine, there's no rush, in spite of everything, and so I tried to renegotiate my contract instead.

"Play five good matches in a row and you'll get a new deal," said Hasse Borg, and so I did. I played an awesome five, six, seven matches, and then we sat down and discussed terms.

I managed to get another 10,000 kronor (around $1,200) or so on my monthly salary, with another 10,000 a month to come later, and I thought that was all right. I didn't have a clue, and I went to visit my dad and proudly showed him my contract. He wasn't too impressed. He'd changed beyond all recognition. He was the most committed supporter now, and instead of burying himself in the war or something else, he sat at home all day and investigated things concerning soccer, and when he read the clause about sales to foreign clubs, he stopped short.

"What the hell!" he said. "There's nothing here about how much you'll get."

"How much I'll get?"

"You should get ten percent of the transfer fee if you're sold. Otherwise, they're just exploiting you," he said, and I thought I'd happily take 10 or 20 percent. I couldn't figure out how we would work it. If there had been a chance of something like that, Hasse Borg would have mentioned it, wouldn't he?

Even so, I asked him. I didn't want to look like a pushover, after all. "Um, Hasse," I said, "can't I get a percentage if I get sold?" Of course, I didn't expect anything else. "Sorry, lad," he said. "That's not how it works," and I told my dad. I assumed he would accept it. If it doesn't work, it doesn't work. That's not what happened, though. He went ballistic and asked for Hasse Borg's number. He phoned once, twice, three times, then finally got ahold of him, and he wouldn't be satisfied with a no over the phone. He demanded a meeting, so it was decided that we would meet Hasse Borg at ten o'clock the following morning in his office, and, as you can imagine, I was nervous. Dad was Dad, and I was worried things might get out of control. It wasn't the calmest meeting. Dad started sputtering and pounding his fist on the desk.

"Is my son a horse?"

No, of course I wasn't a horse, Hasse Borg said.

"So why are you treating him like one?"

"We're not treating him—"

It went like that, and finally Dad declared that Malmö FF would not see hide nor hair of me any longer. I would not play another second unless my contract was rewritten, and then Hasse Borg began to turn pale—which I could understand. My dad is not to be toyed with, like I said. He's a lion, and we got that bit about the 10 percent into the contract, and that would turn out to mean a lot. All respect to my dad for that, and that whole thing should have been a lesson, food for thought. Despite all that, agents were still crooks, and I still relied on Hasse Borg. He was my mentor, sort of another father figure. He invited me out to his place in the country, his half-timbered house in Blentarp, where I got to meet his dogs, his kids and wife, and the animals, and asked him for advice when I bought my Mercedes convertible on the installment plan.

Still, how can I put it? The situation was getting tougher. My confidence was growing, and I was becoming more daring. I scored a number of brilliant goals, and all the Brazilian skills I'd spent hour upon hour practicing were starting to take hold. All the effort with that stuff was finally paying off. On the junior squad I'd mainly gotten a load of crap for it and heard the parents moaning: Oh, he's dribbling again, he's not playing for the team, and all that. Now, though, there were cheers and applause coming from the stands, and I realized immediately that this was my chance. There might still be a lot of people complaining, but it's not nearly as easy to complain when we're winning matches and the fans love me.

The autograph seekers and the fans' roars and the banners in the stands gave me strength, and I was really vibing. Away against Västerås, I got a pass from Hasse Mattisson. It was during injury time. The match was pretty much over. Then I spotted a gap and chipped the ball over myself and a couple of opposing players, including Majstorović—that was a nice little one, and I could land the ball into the goal.

I scored twelve goals in the Superettan League, more than anyone else at Malmö FF, and we qualified for the Allsvenskan League again. I was undoubtedly a big guy on the team. I wasn't just an individualist, as some were saying. I was starting to make a difference, and the hysteria surrounding me kept growing. In those days, I didn't just say a load of boring crap.

I hadn't had any bad run-ins with the press yet. I was basically myself around journalists and would tell them what kind of cars I wanted and which videogames I played, and I said stuff like There's only one Zlatan, and Zlatan is Zlatan—not the most modest things, and I guess I was viewed as something totally new. It wasn't just the usual "The ball is round" type of thing.

It was more free, from the heart. I just talked, pretty much the same as I did at home, and even Hasse admitted that I was popular and there were soccer scouts hiding in the bushes. "You've got to keep a cool head," he cautioned.

Later on, I found out that he got about a phone call a day from agents back then. I was a hot property, and I assume he already realized that I could be the savior of the club's finances. I was his pot of gold, as the newspapers would write later on, and one day he came up to me and asked, "What do you say we go on a little trip?"

"Sure, sounds good."

It would be a little tour, he explained, around various clubs that were interested in acquiring me. I thought to myself, Shit, it's really starting to happen.

6

In a way, I couldn't keep up. Things had happened too fast. Only recently, I'd been a nuisance on the junior squad. Now, everything was buzzing around me, and Hasse Borg and I went out to Arsenal's training facility in St. Albans, and, well, you can just imagine.

It was hallowed ground, and I saw Patrick Vieira, Thierry Henry, and Dennis Bergkamp out on the pitch. The really awesome thing was that I was going to meet Arsène Wenger. Wenger hadn't been with the club for very long at that point. He was the first non-Englishman who'd been appointed as manager at Arsenal, and the newspapers had carried headlines like "Arsène Who?," saying, basically, who the hell is Arsène Wenger? Right off in his second season, he took home the double—both the league title and the FA Cup—and was hugely popular, and I felt like a little boy when we stepped into his office.

It was me, Hasse Borg, and an agent whose name I've forgotten, and I shivered a bit under Wenger's gaze. It was like he was trying to see right through me, or size me up. He's a man who draws up psychological profiles of his players—are they emotionally stable?—that sort of stuff. He is thorough, like all great coaches, and I didn't say much at first.

I just sat in silence and was bashful, but after a while I lost my patience. Something about Wenger set me off. He would leap up every so often to check who was outside his window. It seemed as if he wanted to keep an eye on everything, and he kept going on about one thing all the time.

"You can have a trial with us," he said. "You can give it a try. You can test things out." No matter how much I wanted to behave, those words set me off. I wanted to show him what I could do.

"Give me a pair of shoes. I'll have a trial. I'll do it right now," I said. Then Hasse Borg interrupted me, saying, "Stop, stop, we'll sort this out, you're not going to have a trial, not at all," and of course, I understood what he was getting at: either you're interested, or you're not. Having a trial means selling yourself short. It puts you in a weak position, so we said no: "We're sorry, Mr. Wenger, but we are not interested," and of course there was a great deal of talk about that.

I'm sure it was the right decision, though, and we went on to Monte Carlo, where Monaco was enthusiastic, but we said no to them as well, and to Verona, a sister club of Roma in Italy, and returned home. It had been an amazing trip, that's for sure. Nothing concrete came out of it, but I suppose that wasn't the intention anyway. I was mainly supposed to understand better how things worked down there on the Continent, and back in Malmö it was winter, freezing cold. I came down with the flu.

I'd been selected for the national under-twenty-one side. Unfortunately, I was forced to cancel my debut, and a number of scouts had to go home disappointed. The scouts were on my trail everywhere, although I wasn't really aware of it. There was just one guy I knew a little. He was a Dane by the name of John Steen Olsen. He'd been checking me out for Ajax for so long I started to say hello to him. I didn't make a big deal of it, though. He was just a part of the whole circus, and I didn't know what was just talk and what was really serious. Of course, the whole thing felt more real after our trip. I still couldn't quite believe it. I took it one day at a time, and I remember that I was looking forward to heading to training camp with Malmö FF.

We were going to La Manga. It was early March, and my body felt light. The sun was shining. La Manga is a little strip of land off the southeastern coast of Spain, a holiday resort with long, sandy beaches and bars. On the mainland nearby there's a sports facility where the big-name clubs train in the preseason. I shared a room with Gudmundur Mete from Iceland. We'd moved up together since the boys' team, and neither of us had been to a camp like this before. We didn't know any of the rules and, when we arrived late for dinner the first night, we got fined. We laughed about it for the most part, and the following morning we headed over to the practice session. It was no big deal.

Then I noticed a familiar figure alongside the pitch. I gave a start: it was John Steen Olsen. He was here as well? I called over, "Hi there!" Nothing more. I refused to get worked up. Those folks were everywhere. I'd gotten used to them. The following day, there was another guy there. I found out he was the chief scout from Ajax, and Hasse Borg seemed really stressed out.

"Things are starting to happen now. Things are starting to happen now!" he said, to which I replied, "Okay, that's good!"

I just played. It wasn't exactly easy. Suddenly, there were three guys from Ajax there. The assistant coach had also come, and I heard from Hasse Borg that more were on their way. It was nothing short of an invasion, and the next day we were going to face Moss, a Norwegian team, in a friendly match. The Ajax head coach, Co Adriaanse, was also there, along with Leo Beenhakker, the sports director.

I didn't know anything about Beenhakker then. I knew nothing about European soccer bosses in those days, but I could see that this guy was a big shot. He wore a hat in the sun and stood on the sideline, smoking a fat cigar. He had curly white hair and eyes that sort of glinted. People have likened him to the mad-professor guy in *Back to the Future,* but, if anything, Beenhakker is a harder version of him. Beenhakker radiated power and cool. He looked a little like a mafioso, and I like that. That's the style I grew up with, and it didn't surprise me at all that Beenhakker had coached Real Madrid, winning the league and the Cup with them. It was clear that he was the dominant figure and the decision maker, and people said he was able to see the potential in young players like nobody else, and I thought, Wow, this is the real thing! Of course, there was a lot I didn't realize. Beenhakker had made repeated attempts to get Hasse Borg to name a price for me. Hasse refused. He didn't want to get locked into a figure.

"The kid's not for sale," he said, and that was definitely smart. It was a high-stakes game.

Beenhakker informed him, "If I don't get a price, I won't come to La Manga."

"That's your problem. Just forget about it in that case," Hasse Borg replied, or at least that's what he claims, and Beenhakker relented.

He flew to Spain, and the first thing he would see was our match against Moss. I have no recollection of him on the sideline afterward. I only saw John Steen Olsen and the coach, Co Adriaanse, over by the opposition's goal. Apparently, Beenhakker had climbed up onto a shed beyond the goal line to get a better view, and, of course, he must have been prepared to be disappointed. It wouldn't have been the first time he had traveled a long way to see a talent that didn't live up to expectations, and it wasn't an important match either. There was no reason for anyone to make much of an effort, and maybe it would all just turn out to be a wild-goose chase. No one knew. The Ajax guys were chatting among themselves, and I felt a little nervous. I couldn't keep still.

Early on in the first half, I got a pass from the right. I was just outside the penalty area, and we were in our pale blue uniforms. The clock read 15:37, if you go by the flickering video recording that's up on YouTube. It was warm, but there was a good breeze blowing in from the coast, and it didn't look like a critical situation. The play was cautious. Then I saw a gap—a chance. It was one of those images that just pop into my head, one of those flashbulb moments that whiz into your thoughts, which I've never been able to explain properly. Soccer isn't something you plan in advance. Soccer just happens, and as soon as I got the ball I chipped it over a defender, one of those little lobs that you instantly feel is perfect, and then I just went for it. I accelerated past two defenders and reached the ball a few meters inside the penalty area, ideally positioned for a backheel.

I backheeled it over another defender, ran up and shot with my left foot on the volley, and for a moment you're left wondering, you have time to think even though everything happens in under a tenth of a second: Will it go in? Will it miss? Nope, it just sailed in. That was one of the most beautiful goals I'd scored, and I ran out across the pitch, screaming, with my arms stretched wide. The journalists who were there were convinced I was shouting, "Zlatan, Zlatan!" Come on, why would I be shouting my own name? I was yelling, "Show time, show time!"

That was a "show time" goal, and I can just imagine what Beenhakker was thinking. I bet he was bowled over. He'd probably never seen anything like it. Later on, I found out that it also made him worried. He'd found what he was looking for: a big player who was dangerous around the goal and technical, who'd just scored an epic goal as if to order. He was smart enough to realize that, with this performance, my value had rocketed, and if any other big clubs had spies around the pitch, there would be a crazy bidding war, so Leo Beenhakker resolved to act immediately. He jumped down from the roof of the shed and went to find Hasse Borg.

"I want to meet that guy right now," he said—because, you know, in the soccer world it's never just about the player; it's about the person as well. It's no good if someone's a brilliant player if he's got the wrong attitude. You're buying the whole package.

"I don't know if that's possible," said Hasse Borg.

"What do you mean, not possible?"

"We might not have time. We've got loads of activities and things like that."

Beenhakker was fuming, because of course he knew what was going on.

There were no activities. Hasse Borg must have been creaming himself. The guy had just been handed every trump card in the deck, and now he wanted to seem difficult and play out every one of his tricks.

"Eh? What are you talking about? He's a young kid. You're at your training camp. Of course there's time."

"Maybe just a little while, then," said Hasse Borg, or something along those lines, and so they agreed that we would meet at the Ajax group's hotel, which was some distance away.

We drove there. In the car, Hasse Borg stressed how important it was for me to convey a good, positive attitude. But I was relaxed. Ajax might have wanted to acquire me and, sure, that was definitely big, and some other time I probably would have been nervous.

I wasn't used to big shots from abroad in those days, much less big business deals. After a goal like that, though, you're king of the world. It was easy to turn on the charm. Hasse Borg and I went to their hotel and shook hands with everyone, said, "How do you do?," and chatted about this and that, and I smiled and said I was really committed to soccer, and I knew it was hard work, all that kind of thing. It was a little theater performance where everybody was displaying their goodwill. There were definitely serious and suspicious undertones. Everybody was checking me out, thinking, Who is he, really? The main thing I remember is Leo Beenhakker. He leaned forward and said, "If you fuck with me I'll fuck you two times back," and—well, that made an impression on me.

Beenhakker was speaking my language, and he had a glint in his eye. Clearly, he and his guys had done their homework. They probably knew everything about me, even that episode in Industrigatan. Not that it crossed my mind then. His words could be interpreted as a warning, though, and I recall that we went back to our hotel very shortly afterward, and I remember I was barely able to sit still.

There's one game on the pitch.

There's another on the transfer market, and I like them both, and I know quite a few tricks. I know when to keep my mouth shut and when to do battle. I've learned the hard way. In the beginning, I knew nothing. I was just a kid who wanted to play soccer, and after that meeting in La Manga I didn't hear a single word about Ajax, not for a while.

I went home, and in those days I was driving around in a convertible Merc—not the one I'd ordered, but a loaner I was given while I was waiting for the actual one—and I don't think I was heading anywhere in particular. I was just cruising around, feeling like a pretty cool dude, and there was a miniature soccer ball in the backseat in case I felt like practicing some moves. In other words, it was a completely ordinary day in Malmö.

There were still a few weeks to go until the Allsvenskan season opener, and I was going to play with the under-twenty-one national squad in Borås, but otherwise things were quiet. I just went to training sessions and stuff, and hung out with my pals and played videogames. Then the phone rang. It was Hasse Borg. Nothing strange about that. We phoned each other often. But this time he sounded different.

"Are you busy?" he asked, and I couldn't exactly say that I was.

"Are you ready? Are you good to go?"

"Sure. What's up?"

"They're here now."

"Who are?"

"Ajax. Come to the St. Jörgen Hotel. We're waiting for you," he said, and sure, naturally, I drove there.

I parked outside the hotel, and of course my heart was pounding. I realized things were happening now, and I had told Hasse Borg that I wanted to be sold for a record sum. I wanted to go down in history. There was a Swedish player who had been signed by Arsenal for £3 million ($4.5 million), which was a lot in those days, and a Norwegian by the name of John Carew, who Valencia had paid £5 million ($7.5 million) for. That was a record in Scandinavia, and I was hoping to beat it. My God, though, I was nineteen years old.

It wasn't easy to be tough when the chips were really down—and, remember, we wore warmups in the projects. Sure, I'd tried out different looks when I was at Borgarskolan. But now I was back in Nike gear again and had a little cap on, and it was all wrong. When I walked into the St. Jörgen, I was greeted by John Steen Olsen, and of course, I realized that everything was top secret. Ajax is a corporation listed on the stock exchange, and this would be insider information if anything got out. Just then I caught sight of Cecilia Persson, and stopped short. What was Cecilia doing there? I wasn't expecting to bump into people from Rosengård at the St. Jörgen Hotel. It was a different world. It was a long way from the projects. But there she was.

She and I had grown up on the same block; she was the daughter of my mom's best friend. Suddenly, I remembered that she worked in the hotel as a cleaner. She was a cleaner just like Mom, and now she was eyeing me suspiciously, probably thinking, What's Zlatan doing here with these guys? I shushed her, going, "Don't say anything!" I went up the elevator and entered a conference room, and there was a load of suits standing there: Beenhakker, his finance guy, and then Hasse Borg, of course, and I realized immediately that there was something not right about the atmosphere in there.

Hasse was really nervous and on edge, he was full of adrenaline, but of course he was playing it cool: "Hi there, kid. You understand we can't say a word about this yet. But do you want to go to Ajax? They want you." Even though I'd had my suspicions, it blew me away.

"Definitely!" I replied. "Ajax is a great training ground." Then everybody nodded, and there was lots of smiling and stuff.

Even so, there was still something weird in there, and I shook people's hands and was told that I would now negotiate my personal contract. For some reason, Beenhakker and his guys left at that point, leaving me on my own with Hasse Borg. What the hell was going on with Hasse? He had a huge wad of *snus* tucked inside his lip, and he showed me a stack of papers.

"Have a look at this. This is what I've drawn up for you," he said, and I looked down at the papers. It said 160,000 kronor (around $19,000) a month, which was definitely a lot of money—it was like, Wow, am I gonna get that? I had no clue whether it was a good rate on the market, and I said so.

"Is that good?"

"Damn right it's good," said Hasse. "It's four times what you're earning now," and I thought, Okay, I'm sure he's right, I guess it is a lot of money, and I could sense how tense he was.

"Go for it," I said.

"Great, Zlatan! Congratulations!" Then he went out, saying he was going to negotiate a little, and when he came back in, he was beaming with pride. He looked as if he'd just closed the greatest deal in the world.

"They'll stump up for your new Mercedes as well—they'll pay for it," he added. I thought that was awesome too, and replied, "Wow, cool."

I still knew nothing else about the deal, didn't even consider that the part about the car was just small potatoes to them—because, really, do you think I was prepared for those negotiations?

Was I, hell! I didn't know a thing about what soccer players earned or what gets deducted in tax in the Netherlands, and I really didn't have anyone who was speaking for me or representing my interests. I was nineteen years old and came from Rosengård. I knew nothing about the world. I had about as much of a clue as Cecilia out there, and, as you know, I thought Hasse Borg was my friend, sort of like my second dad. I didn't realize that he had only one thing on his mind: earning money for the club, and in fact it was only much later that I even grasped what that pumped-up vibe in the room was all about. Of course, the men in suits were still in the middle of their negotiations.

They hadn't decided on a price for me yet, and the whole reason they had called me in was because it's obviously easier to agree to a transfer if you sign the player and set his salary first, because then you know what sort of money you're talking about, and if you're so slick that you make sure the guy gets paid less than anybody else on the whole team, then it's easier to get a fat sum for him. So, in short, it was a strategic game, and I was sacrificed. I had no idea then. I just strolled out into the foyer and even gave a little shout of joy or some-thing, and I think I was really good at keeping my mouth shut. The only person I told was my dad, and he was smart enough to have his doubts about the whole thing. He just didn't trust people. As for me, I just let it happen, and the following day I went up to Borås to play with the under-twenty-one national team against Macedonia. It was a qualifying match for the UEFA European Championship, and my debut with the Swedish youth squad, and it should have been a major thing. But my mind was obviously on other things, and I remember I met with Hasse Borg and Leo Beenhakker again and signed the con-tract. They had finished their negotiations by then.

We still had to keep it secret until two o'clock that afternoon, when the news would be announced in the Netherlands, and I found out that a whole load of agents from abroad had come to town to check me out. But they'd come too late. I was set for Ajax. I was walking on air, and I asked Hasse Borg, "How much was I sold for?" and the answer—I'll never forget it.

He had to repeat it. I just couldn't comprehend it: maybe he gave the figure in guilders first, and I wasn't familiar with that currency. Then I realized how much it was, and I just completely lost it.

All right, I had been hoping for a record sum. I'd wanted to go for more than John Carew, but it was something else to see it written down in black and white. It was mind-boggling. Eighty-five fucking million kronor (around $10 million)! Above all, no Swede, no Scandinavian—not even Henke Larsson, not even John Carew—had been sold for anywhere near that much, and of course I realized it would get reported all over. I wasn't unfamiliar with publicity.

Even so, when I bought the papers the following day—it was completely insane. It was a Zlatan orgy in the press. It was the guy with the golden shorts. It was Zlatan the Incredible. It was Zlatan this and Zlatan that, and I read and savored it, and I remembered when me and Chippen and Kennedy Bakircioglü from the national youth squad went out for something to eat in Borås. We were sitting there in a café having a soft drink and a pastry, when suddenly some girls around our age came up, and one of them said, sort of shy, "Are you the eighty-five-million-kronor guy?" I mean, what can you say to something like that?

"Yep," I said, "that's me." My cell was ringing constantly.

People were sucking up to me and congratulating me and generally being envious—all except one, that is: Mom. She was absolutely beside herself. "My God, Zlatan, what's happened?" she wailed. "Have you been abducted? Have you gone and died?" She'd seen me on TV and hadn't really caught what they were saying, and of course what normally happens if you're from Rosengård and end up in the media, is that it's bad news.

"It's all right, Mom. I've just been sold to Ajax," I told her, and then she got angry instead. "Why didn't you say anything? Why do we have to find out about these things from the TV?"

She calmed down—I find it really touching when I think about it—and the next day John Steen Olsen and I headed down to the Netherlands, and I was wearing that pink sweater and the brown leather jacket, which were the coolest clothes I owned, and I gave a press conference in Amsterdam. There was a massive commotion, with photographers and journalists sitting and lying all over the place, and I was beaming. I looked down. I was happy and uncertain. I was big and small at the same time, and I tasted champagne for the first time in my life and made a face, sort of like, What kind of shit is this? Beenhakker gave me the number-nine shirt, which had been worn by van Basten.

It was almost too much, and in the midst of all this some guys were making a documentary about me and Malmö FF entitled *Blådårar* ("Blue Maniacs"), and they came along to Amsterdam and filmed me with the club's sponsor in a Mitsubishi car showroom, and I'm walking around in my brown leather jacket and checking out all the cars.

"It's weird to just come in here and pick one. I guess you get used to it," I say, and then grin.

It was that first, amazing feeling that anything was possible. It was a fairy tale, it really was, spring was in the air and I went out to the Ajax complex and stood there in the empty stands, thinking, with a lollipop in my mouth, and all the while the journalists were getting more and more out of control. They ran the story about the ghetto kid who got the chance to live his dream, and the next day they wrote about how Zlatan had gotten a taste for life as a pro and a life of luxury, and this was when the Allsvenskan season was about to start. Hasse Borg had made a deal that I would stay at Malmö FF for another six months, so I went straight back to the training complex from Amsterdam. It was a little chilly that day, I remember.

I'd just gotten a haircut and I was happy and hadn't seen my teammates in a while. Now they were all just sitting there in the locker room with newspapers on their laps, reading about me and my "life of luxury." There's a scene in the film. I stride in, laughing, take off my jacket, and give a little shout of joy, a wild sort of "yee-ha," and they look up. I almost feel sorry for them.

They all look miserable. Of course, they're all green with envy, and worst of all is Hasse Mattisson, the one who fought with me at Gunnilse. He looks totally destroyed, but still, he's a good guy. He's the team captain, and he means well. He makes an attempt: "I've gotta say, congratulations. That's fantastic! Might as well seize the chance," he says, but he's fooling no one—least of all the camera.

The camera pans from his sad eyes to me, and I'm sitting there on the bench beaming, happy as a little kid, and maybe, I dunno, I might have been a little manic during those days. Stuff had to be happening all the time. I wanted action, more action—keep the drama and the show going. That's why I did a whole load of stupid stuff. I got blond streaks in my hair, and I got engaged—not that it was such a dumb thing to get engaged to Mia. She was a nice girl, she was studying web design and she was blond and pretty, and she was going places. We'd met in Cyprus the previous summer, where she was working in some bar, and we exchanged phone numbers and started hanging out together in Sweden and having fun together. The engagement was kind of a whirlwind thing, and because I wasn't experienced in dealing with the media yet, I told Rune Smith from the *Kvällsposten* tabloid about it. That's the one where he asked, "What did she get for an engagement present?"

"Whaddaya mean, present? She got Zlatan."

She got Zlatan!

It was the kind of remark that just popped out, that sounded cocky, totally in line with my media image, and one that still gets dredged up all the time. The only thing was, a few weeks later, Mia got nothing. I broke off the engagement because a friend had convinced me that you have to get married within a year, and I was just generally doing a lot of impulsive things. I was on fast-forward. There was too much happening around me. Our Allsvenskan season opener was approaching, and, as you can imagine, that was where I was supposed to show I was worth those 85 million kronor. The previous day, Anders Svensson and Kim Källström had scored two goals in their Allsvenskan season openers, and people were saying I wouldn't be able to cope with my new star status. Maybe I was just an overhyped teenager. As often happened in those years, they were saying that I'd just been built up by the media, and I felt I had to perform. It was a lot to deal with, and I remember that Malmö Stadium was reaching the boiling point. It was April 9, 2001.

I had my blue Merc convertible and was as proud of it as anything. When Rune Smith interviewed me before the match, though, I didn't want to be photographed with it. I didn't want to seem too cocky. It felt like it would just come back and bite me in the ass, and I was hearing some concerns: the pressure would get too big and stuff, and that wasn't all that easy to deal with. I was nineteen, and everything had happened so fast. Still, I got a buzz from it. Things were on another level now. Yet that feeling of wanting to get back at everybody who hadn't believed in me and circulated petitions and everything else was something I'd had for a long time. I'd been driven by revenge and rage ever since I started playing, and now there were tons of expectations and concerns hanging in the air. We were going to be playing AIK. That was no easy opener.

The last time we'd played them we were humiliated and got relegated to the second division. Now, ahead of this season, many people saw AIK as one of the favorites to win the Allsvenskan League, and, really, what were we? We'd just come out of the Superettan without even leading the league. Even so, people thought the pressure was on us, and they were saying it was mainly due to me, the 85-million-kronor kid. The stands were packed at Malmö Stadium, nearly twenty thousand people were there, and as I ran out through the long tunnel with the blue floor toward the pitch, I could hear the roar outside. This was big, I realized, this was our return to the Allsvenskan, and yet it was almost incomprehensible.

There was a sea of banners and placards in there, and as we lined up they were shouting something I couldn't hear at first. It was "We love Malmö," and my name as well. It was like a giant chorus, and the banners said things like "Good luck, Zlatan!," and I just stood there on the pitch and soaked up everything with my hand to my ear as if to say, Give me more, give me more. To be honest, all the doubters were right about one thing at least. The stage was set for a flop. It was too much.

The starting whistle went off at a quarter to nine, and the roar got even louder. In those days, the main thing wasn't scoring goals. It was the show, the artistry, everything I'd been practicing over and over again, and early on I forged a tunnel toward an AIK defender and managed a few dribbles. Then I faded out of the action, and AIK took command of the match with one chance after another, and for a long time it didn't look good for us. Maybe I wanted too much. That was something I was aware of even then. If you want too much, it's easy to get stuck.

I tried to ease up, and in the thirtieth minute I got the ball outside the penalty area off Peter Sörensen. It didn't feel like a promising chance at first. Then I feinted. I backheeled the ball and advanced, and shot a broadside into the goal and, my God, it hit me like a punch—here comes the explosion, now it's happening, and I went down on my knees in a goal celebration as the entire stadium roared, "Zlatan, Zlatan, Super-Zlatan!" and all kinds of stuff. After that it was as if I was being carried aloft.

I did one fancy move after another, and in the ninth minute of the second half I got another nice ball from Sörensen. I was on the right side and rushed down toward the goal. A shot wasn't open, not at all, and everybody was thinking, He'll make an assist, he'll pass it. But I had a shot anyway. From that impossible angle, I got the ball in and the crowd went absolutely nuts. I walked across the pitch really slowly with my arms stretched wide—and that face I made! That's power. That's, Here I am, you bastards who just complained and tried to get me to give up soccer.

It was revenge, it was pride, and I imagine everybody who'd thought the 85 million kronor was too high a price was eating their words now, and I'll never forget the journalists afterward. The atmosphere was electric.

One of them said, "If I say the names Anders Svensson and Kim Källström, what do you have to say?"

"I say Zlatan, Zlatan," and people laughed, and I stepped out into the spring evening, and there was my Mercedes convertible, and it was amazing.

It took me a long time to reach my car. There were kids everywhere who wanted my autograph, so I spent ages doing that—nobody should be left out, that was part of my philosophy. I had to give something back, and only afterward did I climb into my new car and blast out of there while the fans screamed and waved their autograph books, and that would have been plenty. It wasn't over yet. That was just the beginning, and the next day the newspapers came out, and what do you think? Did they write anything?

They wrote reams.

Back when we crashed out of the Allsvenskan, apparently I'd said, "I want people to forget me. Nobody should know I exist. Then when we're back, I'll strike down on the pitch like a bolt of lightning," and the papers dug up that quote.

I became the bolt of lightning that struck. I was suddenly the most amazing thing, and people even started talking about Zlatan Fever in Sweden. I was everywhere, in every branch of the media, and people were saying it wasn't just young kids and teenagers reading. It was little old ladies at the post office, it was old men at the liquor store, and I heard jokes like "All right, how are things? How you doing?" "I think I've caught Zlatan Fever." I was walking on air. It was absolutely incredible. Some guys even recorded a song that swept the nation. It was played everywhere. People had it as their ringtone: "Oh hiya, Zlatan and me, we're from the same town," they sang. I mean, how do you deal with something like that? They're singing about you. Sure, there was another side to it all as well, and I saw that in our third match in the Allsvenskan. It was April 21. It was in Stockholm, where we were away to Djurgården.

Djurgården was the team that had been relegated to the Superettan along with us and that also made it back up at the same time—Djurgården won the league and we finished second, and, to be fair, they had really trounced us in the Superettan, first by 2–0 and then 4–0, so in that sense they definitely had the psychological advantage. Still, we'd beaten both AIK and Elfsborg 2–0 in our first matches, and, above all, Malmö FF had me. Everybody was going, "Zlatan, Zlatan!"—I was hotter than volcanic lava, and people were saying that Lars Lagerbäck, the coach of the Swedish national team, was sitting in the stands to observe me.

Of course, even more people were worked up now: What the hell's so special about that guy? One of the tabloids got hold of Djurgården's defensive lineup. They were three burly dudes, I remember, standing with their arms folded in the center spread underneath the headline "We're the ones planning to put a stop to Zlatan the overhyped diva," and I guess I was expecting a really nasty atmosphere on the pitch. There were reputations at stake, so of course there was going to be a lot of trash-talking, but a shiver still went over me when I came on at Stockholm Stadium.

The Djurgården fans were seething with hatred, or, if it wasn't hatred, at least it was the worst mind games I've ever experienced: "We hate Zlatan, we hate Zlatan!" It was thundering all around me. The entire arena was baiting me, and I heard a bunch of other chants, loads of nasty shit about me and my mom.

I'd never experienced anything like it, and, okay, I could understand it in a way. The fans couldn't run down and play ball themselves, so what could they do? They targeted the best player from the opposing side, tried to break me. I suppose it's only natural. That's how it is in soccer. But this crossed the line, and I was furious. I'd show them, and in a way I played more against the spectators than against the actual team. Just as in the match against AIK, though, it took a while before I got into the game.

I was tightly marked. I had those leeches from the newspaper on me, and Djurgården dominated for the first twenty minutes. We'd just brought in a guy from Nigeria. Peter Ijeh was his name, and he had a reputation as a brilliant goal-scorer. He would lead the league in goal-scoring the following year. But at this point he was still in my shadow. Well, who wasn't? In the twenty-first minute he got a pass from Daniel Majstorović, our center back, who would later become a good friend of mine.

Peter Ijeh made it 1–0, and then in the sixty-eighth minute he made a nice through pass to Joseph Elanga, the other African recruit we'd made that year, and Elanga managed to break free of a defender and shoot 2–0. The spectators booed hysterically, they yelled, and of course I was useless, I was no good. I hadn't scored any goals, just like those defenders had said I wouldn't, and sure, up to that point I hadn't been particularly good.

I'd done a few tricks and a backheel down by the corner flag, but otherwise it was more Ijeh's and Majstorović's match than mine, and there was no magic in the air when, two minutes later, I got the ball around the midfield. Things soon changed, because suddenly I drew a player, it just happened, and then another one, and I thought, Wow, this is easy, I'm in control, and I went on.

It was like a dance, and even though I wasn't conscious of it I dribbled past every one of the defenders from that newspaper article and toed the ball into the net with my left foot, and I'm telling you, that feeling was not just joy. It was revenge. This is for all of you, I thought, this is for your chants and your hate, and I assumed my war with the spectators would continue after the final whistle went.

I mean, we had humiliated Djurgården—the final score was 4–0.

Do you know what happened next? I was surrounded by Djurgården fans, and nobody wanted to fight or hate anymore.

They wanted my autograph. They were crazy about me, and when I look back on that time, there's a lot of stuff just like that, about how I managed to turn everything around with a goal or a fancy move. You know, there was no movie I loved more than *Gladiator* in those days. There's a scene in it that everybody knows—right?—where the emperor comes down into the arena and tells the gladiator to take his mask off, and the gladiator does it and says, "My name is Maximus Decimus Meridius . . . And I will have my vengeance, in this life or the next."

That was how I felt, or wanted to feel. I wanted to stand up to the whole world and show everybody who'd doubted me who I really was, and I couldn't imagine anyone who'd be able to stop me.

7

It was High Chaparral, as I like to say. It was a three-ring circus, and I said all kinds of stupid stuff, like how the Swedish national squad would have won the Euro 2000 championship if they'd had me. It might have been cocky and cool then, I dunno, but it didn't seem so funny when I really was called up.

That was in April as well. I'd just scored that goal against Djurgården, and the papers were totally crazy. They had me in the headlines constantly, and I guess people who read them wouldn't exactly think I was the most humble guy in the world, and that made me a little worried. Would the big guys, like Patrik Andersson and Stefan Schwarz, think I was a mouthy little shit?

It was one thing to be a star at Malmö FF. But come on, the national squad was something else! There were guys there who'd won the World Cup bronze, and, believe it or not, I was well aware of the attitude in Sweden that it's not a good idea to stick out and stuff, especially when you're the new kid on the block. God knows I'd come in for a lot of crap on the youth team, and I wanted to be liked.

I wanted to be part of the gang, but it didn't get off to a good start. We headed off to a training camp in Switzerland, and all the journalists were just buzzing around me the whole time. It was almost embarrassing. Come on, I wanted to say, Henke Larsson is standing over there, go over and talk to him instead, and yet I couldn't let it go. At a press conference in Geneva I was asked whether I thought I was similar to any other great player in the world.

"No," I replied. "There's only one Zlatan"—and how humble was that on a scale of one to ten? I realized immediately I had to make amends. I tried to keep a low profile after that, and, to be honest, I didn't need to make much of an effort. I felt shy around all the big names, and apart from Marcus Allbäck, who I shared a room with, I didn't talk to many of them. I stood around on the sidelines.

"He's a loner. He goes his own way," the papers wrote, and sure, that sounded exciting. Made me sound like Zlatan the intriguing artiste.

In fact, I was just awkward, and I didn't want to get anyone else worked up, especially not Henrik Larsson, who I know as "Henke"— he was like a god to me. He was playing for Celtic then, and it was that year—2001—that he was awarded the Golden Boot as the top goal-scorer in all the European leagues. Henke was awesome, and when I heard he and I would be in the starting lineup against Switzerland, it felt great.

That was another one of those surreal things, and several newspapers ran long stories about me before the match. They wanted to run a big feature about me now, ahead of my international debut, and there was some director of studies from Sorgenfri in those articles— Sorgenfri was the school where they gave me a remedial teacher, and she said I was the most unruly pupil she'd had in thirty-three years of teaching, or something like that: I was the hooligan at Sorgenfri School. A one-man show. It was a bunch of blah blah blah, but there was other stuff as well, loads of expectations that I would be a massive success on the national side. People really wanted to see me as both a hooligan and a star, and I was feeling the pressure.

Still, there was no great success. I was substituted at halftime, and I wasn't called up for the big World Cup qualifiers that year against Slovakia and Moldova. Lagerbäck and Söderberg relied on Larsson and Allbäck up front instead, and that should have given me a little more anonymity. I was hardly even a regular member of the squad.

Nothing worked out the way it should have for me. I remember the first time I played with the national squad in Stockholm. We were up against Azerbaijan at Råsunda Stadium, and I was still sort of a fish out of water. Stockholm was a different world for me. It was like New York. I was lost and awkward, and there were loads of hot chicks in the city. I was just gawping at everything.

I was starting as a reserve, and there was a capacity or near-capacity crowd at Råsunda. There were 33,000 people there, and all the big guys seemed confident and used to the whole thing, and I sank down on the bench and felt like a little boy.

Then, fifteen minutes into the match, something happened. The crowd started shouting. They were bellowing my name, and I can't describe it, I got so pumped up, I got goose bumps. All the big names were out there on the pitch. There was Henke Larsson, there was Olof Mellberg, there was Stefan Schwarz and Patrik Andersson. But the crowd wasn't shouting their names. They were shouting my name, and I wasn't even playing. It was almost too much, and I didn't get it. What had I done, exactly?

A few matches in the Allsvenskan League, that's all. And yet I was more popular than guys who'd played in big championship games and won the World Cup bronze. It was completely nuts, and everybody on the team was looking at me. Whether they were happy or pissed, I haven't got a clue. All I know is that they didn't get it either. This was something completely new. This hadn't happened before, and after a while the crowd went back to yelling the usual chant, "Come on Sweden, come on!" and I bent over to do up my laces, just for something to do or because I was nervous. It was like an electric shock.

The spectators thought I was warming up, and they boomed, "Zlatan, Zlatan!" again, completely wild now, and of course I took my hands away from my shoes. I mean, I was sitting on the bench, and to take over the show in that way would have completely overstepped the mark, so I tried to make myself invisible.

Secretly, though, I was loving it. I felt a massive rush. The adrenaline was pumping, and when Lars Lagerbäck really did tell me to warm up, I rushed onto the pitch, absolutely delighted, no lie. I was soaring around, there was "Zlatan, Zlatan!" coming from the stands, and we were ahead 2–0. I lobbed the ball with my heel, a beautiful little move from the projects, and I got the ball back and fired it at the goal, and all of Råsunda and the evening exploded, and even Stockholm felt like my town.

The only thing was, it was like I brought Rosengård along with me. One time that year, I was in Stockholm with the national squad. We went out to Undici, Tomas Brolin's nightclub, and we were just sitting there. Then one of my pals from the projects started talking:

"Zlatan, Zlatan, can I have your hotel key?"

"What's up?"

"Just give it to me!"

"Okay, okay."

He got it, and I thought nothing more of it. When I got in that night, my pal was there and he had shut the closet and was acting all secretive and jumpy.

"What have you got in there?" I asked.

"Nothing special. And don't touch it," he replied.

"What?"

"We can make some cash from them, Zlatan!"

You know what it was? It was insane. It was a whole load of Canada Goose down coats he'd stolen from Undici. So I didn't always keep the most respectable company, if truth be told, and life at Malmö FF started to have its ups and downs. It was a funny thing to stay with a club when I'd already been sold to another one, and I wasn't the most well-balanced guy. Sometimes, I would just go off.

I'd explode. I'd always done that, but now there was this whole situation surrounding me, and that "bad boy" stuff was starting to bite. When we were playing away against Häcken, I'd gotten a warning in the previous match for shouting at the referee, and there was a certain amount of uneasiness in the air. Was that madman Zlatan going to do something again?

Häcken was coached by Torbjörn Nilsson, the former star player, and they had Kim Källström, who I knew from the national under-twenty-one squad. There were some nasty tackles early on, and a little way into the match I took Kim Källström down from behind. I elbowed another guy and was sent off, and then the real outburst came. On the way to the locker room I kicked over a loudspeaker and a microphone, and, well, the sound technician who'd set up that stuff didn't exactly appreciate it. He called me an idiot, and I turned around and went up to him, saying, Who the hell are you calling an idiot?

Then our equipment manager split us up, and there was a big to-do and newspaper headlines and about seven million pieces of advice from all quarters, saying things like I had to change my behavior, and all that. Otherwise, things could go badly at Ajax . . . Bullshit. Bull-shit! The *Expressen* tabloid even interviewed a psychologist who said I ought to seek help, and of course my immediate reaction was, Who the fuck is he? What does he know?

I didn't need any psychologist. I just needed peace and quiet. True, it was no fun being stuck on the bench and watching IFK Göte-borg humiliate us 6–0. Our flow from the season opener had van-ished and our manager, Micke Andersson, came under a fair amount of criticism as well. I really didn't have anything against him, and we didn't have much contact either. If I had a problem, I'd go to Hasse Borg. But there was one thing that was starting to annoy me. I thought Micke had too much respect for the older players on the team. He was frightened, pure and simple, and he couldn't have been too happy with me since I'd been sent off again against Örebro. There were some tensions, and we played a practice match. It was summer. Micke Andersson acted as the referee, and there was some confron-tation with Jonnie Fedel, the goalie, who was one of the oldest on the team, and, of course, Micke called it in Jonnie's favor. I saw red and went up to Micke.

"You're scared of the older guys. You're even fucking afraid of ghosts," I bellowed. There was a bunch of balls lying on the pitch. I started kicking them, boom, boom, boom!

They went flying like missiles and landed on the cars outside, setting off the alarms, and whistles and horns started and everything just came to a standstill, and I stood there with a fierce housing proj-ects attitude, while my teammates glared at me. Micke Andersson tried to calm me down, and I screamed at him, "What are you, my mother?"

I was furious and headed off to the locker room, where I emptied my locker, ripped down my name, and declared that I would never come back. I'd had enough. Goodbye, Malmö FF; so long, you idiots, and I drove off in my Toyota Celica and didn't turn up to any more practices, just played on my PlayStation and hung out with my friends instead. It was sort of like I was cutting school, and of course Hasse Borg called, sounding absolutely hysterical.

"Where are you? Where are you? You've got to come back!" And, of course, I was reasonable. Four days later, I turned up and was polite and charming again, and to tell the truth, I didn't think my outburst was really such a big thing. That stuff happens in soccer, it's part of it; there's a lot of adrenaline in the sport. Besides, I didn't have long left with the team, I was on my way to the Netherlands, and I didn't actually believe there would be any penalty or ridiculous consequences. I was thinking more about how they would see me off. Only a few months before, Malmö FF had been in crisis. They had a 10 million kronor (about $1.2 million) hole in their finances and really couldn't afford to purchase any top players.

Now they were the richest club in Sweden, I'd given them a massive amount of capital, and even Bengt Madsen, the chairman of Malmö FF, had said in the papers, "A player like Zlatan is born only once in every fifty years!" So, no, it wasn't so strange to think that they were planning a big send-off, or at least a "Thanks for the 85 million," especially when they'd said farewell to Niclas Kindvall in front of thirty thousand spectators in the match against Helsingborg the previous week. Sure, I noticed that they were all a little scared of me. I was the only one who could sabotage the deal with Ajax by doing something even crazier, and my last match in the Allsvenskan was approaching.

It was on June 26, away at Halmstad, and I was gearing up for a good farewell performance. It was no big thing for me, don't get me wrong. I was finished with Malmö. In my mind, I was already in

Amsterdam. Even so, a period of my life was coming to an end, and I remember looking at the list of names on the wall of who would be going along to Halmstad. Then I looked again.

My name wasn't there. I wouldn't even be sitting on the bench. I was going to stay at home, and, of course, I realized that was my punishment. That was Micke's way of showing who was in charge, and, okay, I accepted it, what else could I do? I didn't even get angry when he told the press that I was "under pressure and out of balance," and "needed some rest," basically saying he was dropping me because he was such a kindhearted guy; in fact, I was naïve enough to believe that the club's management was still planning something, maybe some event with the supporters.

Soon afterward I was summoned to Hasse Borg's office, and, as you know, I don't like that sort of thing. I think I'm going to get a talking-to or something. There was so much going on then that I just went without expecting anything, and there in the office stood Hasse and Bengt Madsen, looking generally uptight, and I wondered, What's this all about, is this a funeral?

"Zlatan, our time together is drawing to a close."

"You don't mean—"

"We'd like to say—"

"So you're going to see me off in here?" I said, looking around. We were in Hasse's stupid, boring office, just the three of us in there. "So you're not going to do it in front of the fans?"

"Well," said Bengt Madsen, "people say it's bad luck to do it before a match."

I just looked at him. *It's bad luck?*

"You said goodbye to Niclas Kindvall in front of thirty thousand people, and that went all right."

"Yes, but—"

"Whaddaya mean, *but*?"

"We'd like to give you this gift."

"What the hell is this?"

It was a ball, an ornament made out of crystal.

"This is a memento."

"So this is how you're thanking me for the eighty-five million kronor?" What were they thinking? That I would take it along to Amsterdam and weep when I looked at it?

"We'd like to express our gratitude."

"I don't want it. You can keep it."

"You can't just—"

Yes, I could. I put the crystal thing on the table. Then I got out of there. That was my farewell from the club—no more, no less—and sure, I wasn't happy about it. Nevertheless, I shook it off. I mean, I was on my way out of there, and really, what was Malmö FF anyway? My real life was about to start now, and the more I thought about it, the bigger it got.

I wouldn't just go to Ajax. I was the club's most expensive player, and while Ajax might not be Real Madrid or Manchester United, it was definitely a big club. Only five years earlier, Ajax had played in the Champions League final. Six years ago, they'd won the whole tournament, and Ajax had had players like Cruyff, Rijkaard, Kluivert, Bergkamp, and van Basten—especially van Basten, he'd been absolutely brilliant, and I was going to be wearing his number. It was crazy, really. I was going to score goals and make a difference, and sure, that was awesome, but it was also beginning to dawn on me that it meant incredible pressure.

Nobody spends 85 million kronor without expecting something in return, and it had been three years since Ajax had won their league. For a club like Ajax, this was a minor scandal. Ajax is the finest team in the Netherlands, and their supporters expect the team to win big. You had to deliver the goods, not go around all cocky and do things your own way from the get-go, definitely not start off by going, "I'm Zlatan, who the hell are you?" I would fit in and learn the culture. The only thing is, stuff continued to happen around me.

On the way home from Göteborg, in a little place called Bottnaryd near Jönköping, I got stopped by the police. I'd been going 110 km an hour in a 70 zone—not exactly flooring it when you consider what I would do later on. I did lose my license for a while, though, and the press didn't just print massive headlines about this nonevent. They made sure they dredged up the business from Industrigatan as well.

They compiled entire lists of all the scandals I'd been involved in and all the times I'd been sent off, and of course it all made its way to the Netherlands. Even though the club's management was already aware of most of it, now the journalists in Amsterdam got in on it as well. No matter how much I wanted to be a good guy, I was labeled a bad boy even before I started. There was me and one other new guy, an Egyptian called Mido who'd been a success with KAA Ghent in Belgium. We both had reputations as being out of control, and to cap it all, I was hearing more and more about the coach I'd met in Spain, Co Adriaanse.

He was supposed to be like a goddamn Gestapo officer and know everything about his players, and there were some crazy stories about the punishments he dished out, including one about a goalkeeper who happened to answer his cell phone during practice: he had to spend a whole day on the club's switchboard, even though he couldn't speak a word of Dutch. It was like, "Hello, hello, don't understand," all day long; and then there was one about three guys on the youth squad who'd been out partying. They had to lie on the pitch while the others walked on top of them in their cleats. There were quite a few of those stories, not that they worried me.

There's always a load of talk about the coaches, and in fact I've always liked guys with discipline. I get on well with coaches who keep their distance from their players and don't get too close. That's how I'd grown up. Nobody went, Poor little Zlatan, of course you'll get to play. I didn't have a dad who came to practice sessions and sucked up to everyone and insisted that people should be nice to me, no way. I've had to look out for myself, and I'd much rather get chewed out and be on bad terms with a coach and get to play because I'm good, rather than get along with him and be allowed to play because he likes me.

I don't want to be mollycoddled. That just messes me up. I want to play soccer, nothing else. Sure, I was still nervous as I packed my bags and headed off. Ajax and Amsterdam were something completely new. I didn't know a thing about the city, and I remember the flight and landing and the woman from the club who came to meet me.

Her name was Priscilla Janssen. She was a gofer at Ajax, and I really made an effort to be nice, and I greeted the guy she had with her. He was around my age and seemed shy, but he spoke really good English.

He said he was from Brazil. He'd played for Cruzeiro, a famous team—I knew that because Ronaldo had played there. Just like me, he was new at Ajax, and he had a long name I didn't really catch. Apparently I could call him Maxwell, and we exchanged phone numbers and then Priscilla drove me in her Saab convertible out to the little terraced house the club had arranged for me in Diemen, a small town far away from the city. There I sat with a fancy brand-name bed and a 60-inch TV and nothing else, playing on my PlayStation and wondering what was going to happen.

8

It was no big deal to be on my own. If there was one thing I'd learned growing up, it was to look after myself, and I was still feeling like the coolest guy in Europe.

I'd turned pro and been sold for crazy amounts of money. Still, my terraced house was bare inside. It felt very remote, and I didn't even have any furniture or anything else that made it feel like a home, and to be honest, the fridge started to get bare pretty soon too. Not that I was gripped by panic and relived my childhood or anything. It was okay. I'd had an empty fridge in my apartment in Lorensborg as well. I could cope with anything. Then again, in Malmö I'd never had to go hungry—not least because I would stuff myself at Kulan, the restaurant at Malmö FF, and I'd often sneak out a little something extra hidden in my warmups, a yogurt or something to keep me going in the evenings, but also because I'd had Mom over in Cronmans Väg and my friends.

In Malmö, I usually didn't need to cook or worry about empty fridges. Now, in Diemen, I was back to square one. It was ridiculous. I was supposed to be a professional guy. I didn't even have a box of cornflakes, and I hardly had any cash, and I sat there in my terraced house on my fancy bed and called pretty much everyone I knew: my friends, Dad and Mom, my sister and my little brother. I even rang Mia, even though we'd broken up. I was like, Can you come here? I was lonely, restless, and hungry, and finally I got ahold of Hasse Borg.

I thought he could cut a deal with Ajax, maybe he'd lend me a little money and make sure Ajax reimbursed him later. I knew Mido had done something similar with his previous club. It didn't work. "I can't do that," Hasse Borg said. "You'll have to look after yourself." That made me lose it.

He'd sold me. Couldn't he help me in a situation like this?

"Why not?"

"I can't do that."

"And where's my ten percent?"

I got no answer and got angry—all right, I admit I had only myself to blame. I hadn't realized it takes a month before you get your wages, and then I'd had a problem with my car. It was my Merc convertible. It had Swedish plates. I couldn't drive it in the Netherlands. I'd only just gotten it, and the whole idea had been to cruise around Amsterdam in it, but now I'd had to sell it and order another Mercedes—an SL55—and that hadn't exactly helped my finances.

So there I sat in Diemen, broke and hungry, and got an earful from my dad about how I was an idiot who'd bought a car like that when I didn't have any money, and of course that was true. That didn't help. I still didn't have any cornflakes at home, and I still hated empty fridges.

That's when I happened to think of the Brazilian guy from the airport. There were a few of us new players that season. There was

me, there was Mido, and then there was him, Maxwell. I'd hung out
a bit with both of them, not only because we were all new. I felt most
comfortable among the black guys and the South Americans. It was
more fun, I thought: more relaxed and there wasn't so much jealousy.
The Dutch guys wanted nothing more than to get out of there and end
up in Italy or England, so they were constantly eyeing one another—
wondering who had the best prospects—whereas the Africans and
the Brazilians were mostly glad to be there. It was like, Wow, we get
to play for Ajax? I felt more at home with them, and I liked their
sense of humor and their attitude. Maxwell was certainly nothing
like the other Brazilians I'd meet later. He was no party animal, not a
guy who needed to go nuts on a regular basis—not at all. He was
really sensitive, close to his family, and was constantly phoning
home. He was a nice guy through and through, and if I have anything
bad to say about him, it's that he's too nice.

"Maxwell, I'm in a crisis here," I said over the phone. "I haven't
even got any cornflakes at home. Can I come and stay at your place?"

"Sure," he said. "Come right over."

Maxwell lived in Ouderkerk, a small town with a population of
only seven or eight thousand, and I moved in with him and slept on a
mattress on the floor for three weeks until I got my first paycheck,
and it wasn't a bad time. We cooked together and chatted about our
training sessions, the other players, and our old lives in Brazil and
Sweden. He'd tell me about his family and his two brothers, who he
was very close to—I remember that in particular, because one of
those brothers died in a car crash not long after. That was terribly sad.
I really liked Maxwell.

I got myself straightened out a bit while I was at his place, and
things started to loosen up a little. I got back that feeling that this was
something really great, and I got off to a good start in the preseason.
I scored goals against the amateur teams we played, and I did a load

of tricks, just like I thought I would. Ajax was known for playing fun, technical soccer, and the newspapers wrote stuff like Well, well, well, looks like he's worth those 85 million kronor, and sure, I noticed that Co Adriaanse, the manager, was tough on me. I thought that was just his style. I'd heard so much about him.

After every match he'd give us grades out of ten, and one time when I'd scored a bunch of goals, he said, "You made five goals, but you made two bad passes as well. That's a five." I thought, Okay, I get it, the standards here are tough. I kept at it, and in fact, I didn't think anything could stop me now. For one thing, I remember meeting a guy who had no idea who I was.

"So, are you any good?" he asked.

"I'm not even gonna touch that one!"

"Do the opposing side's fans boo and jeer at you?"

"Hell yeah, they do."

"Okay. You're pretty wicked then," he replied, and I've never forgotten that. Anybody who's any good is on the receiving end of boos and trash talk. That's how it works.

The end of July saw the launch of the Amsterdam Tournament. The Amsterdam Tournament is a classic top-level preseason tournament in the Netherlands, and that year, Milan, Valencia, and Liverpool would be taking part, which of course was fantastic.

This was my chance to introduce myself to Europe, and I immediately noticed, Good grief, this was nothing like the Allsvenskan League! In Malmö, I used to have all the time in the world with the ball. Now they were all over me in a flash. Everything just went so much faster.

We were up against Milan in the first match. Milan was going through a rough patch at the time, but the club had dominated European soccer in the nineties, and I tried hard not to care about the fact that they had defenders like Maldini. I really put some effort into it, and got a few free kicks and some applause, and I made some nice moves. It was tough, though, and we lost 1–0.

In the second match we played Liverpool. Liverpool had won the Cup treble that year, and they had possibly the strongest defensive pair in the Premier League with Sami Hyypiä, a Finn, and Stéphane Henchoz from Switzerland. Henchoz hadn't just been on top of his game that year. He had done something that was the talk of the soccer world. In the FA Cup final, he'd blocked a shot on the goal line with his hand, and that nasty bit of work that the referee never saw had helped Liverpool to win.

Both he and Hyypiä were on me like leeches. A little way into the match, I fought my way to the ball down by the corner flag and went into the penalty area, and there stood Henchoz. He was blocking me on the goal side and, of course, I had several choices. I was in a tight spot, but I could send in a cross or play it back or try to advance toward goal.

I tried doing a feint with one foot, a cool thing Ronaldo and Romário did a lot, which was one of the moves I'd watched on the computer when I was a junior and had practiced for hours and hours until I could do it in my sleep and didn't even need to think in order to pull it out of the bag. It just came naturally. This particular one was called the Snake, because if you do it well it's like a snake slithering alongside your feet. It's not all that easy. You need to have your outer side behind the ball and quickly nudge it to the right and then suddenly angle it with the tip of your shoe to the left, and get past— boom, boom! quick as a flash, having total control, with the ball glued to your foot, like a hockey player cradling the puck.

I'd used that move many times at Malmö and in the Superettan League, but never against a world-class defender like Henchoz. It was just that I'd already felt it against Milan, and the whole atmosphere got me going. It was more fun to dribble toward a guy like him, and now things got even more intense. Swish, swish, it went, and Stéphane Henchoz flew toward the right. He couldn't keep up at all and I whizzed past, and the entire Milan squad sitting along the sideline stood up and screamed. The entire Amsterdam Arena screamed.

This was definitely show time, and afterward, when I was surrounded by journalists, I came out with that line, and I promise you, I never plan what I'm going to say. It just happens, and it happened a lot in those days before I got more cautious around the media. "First I went left," I said, "and he did too. Then I went right, and he did too. Then I headed left, and he went out to buy a hot dog," and that got repeated all over the place; it became a famous quote. Somebody even made a commercial with it, and people were saying that Milan was interested in me. I was called the new van Basten and all sorts of stuff, and I felt like, Wow! I'm awesome. I'm the Brazilian from Rosengård, and truly, that should have been the start of a fantastic season.

Still, there were tough times ahead, and in hindsight the warning signs had been there from the start—partly because of me: I didn't have my shit together. I went home too often and started losing weight and looking spindly, but it was also the coach, Co Adriaanse. He criticized me publicly, not so seriously at first. It got worse later on, after he was sacked. Then he said I was wrong in the head. Now, early on, it was just the usual stuff, that I played too much for myself, and I started to realize that even my moves against Henchoz weren't necessarily appreciated at Ajax unless they led to something concrete.

Instead, they could be seen as an attempt to stand out and show off to the spectators rather than playing for the team. At Ajax, they played with three men up front instead of two, the way I was used to. I was in the center. Not flitting out toward the edges and doing loads of individual stuff. I was supposed to be more of a target player, one who got up in there and took passes and, above all, scored goals. I started to wonder if that stuff about Dutch soccer being fun and technical was true anymore. It was as if they'd decided to become more like the rest of Europe, but it wasn't easy to interpret the signals.

There was a lot that was new, and I didn't understand the language or the culture, and the coach didn't talk to me. He didn't talk to anybody. He was completely stone-faced. It felt wrong just to look him in the eye, and I lost my flow. I stopped scoring goals, and then my excellent preseason didn't really benefit me anymore—quite the opposite, in fact. All the headlines and comparisons with van Basten were just turned against me, and I started to be seen as a disappointment, a bad purchase. I was replaced in the front line by Nikos Machlas, a Greek who I'd hung out with quite a lot, and in those situations when I get dropped and lose my form, my head starts buzzing, like: What am I doing wrong? How am I going to break out of this?

That's the kind of person I am.

I'm really not one to go around all satisfied, thinking, Wow! I'm Zlatan! Not at all. It's like there's a film constantly playing in my head and I ask myself over and over, Should I have done this or that differently? I watch other people: What can I learn from them? What am I missing? I go over my mistakes all the time—along with the good stuff. What can I improve? I always, always take something with me from matches and training sessions and, of course, that's tough sometimes. I'm never really satisfied, not even when I have reason to be, but it helps me improve. It's just that at Ajax I got bogged down in those thoughts, and I didn't have anybody to talk to, not really.

I talked to the walls at home. I thought people were idiots, and naturally I'd phone home and moan and groan. There was a cloud hanging over me. Still, I really shouldn't put the blame on anybody else. Everything just felt sluggish, and I wasn't doing well at all. It was as if life in the Netherlands just didn't agree with me, and I went up to Beenhakker and asked him, "What's the coach saying about me? Is he happy, or what's going on?" And Beenhakker, he's a different sort of guy to Co Adriaanse: he doesn't just want to have obedient foot soldiers.

"It's all right. It's going fine. We're being patient with you," he replied.

I was homesick, and I didn't feel appreciated, not by the coach, not by the press, and certainly not by the fans. Those Ajax supporters are not to be treated lightly. They're used to winning—they're like, What the hell, you only won 3–0?

When we only managed a draw against Roda they threw rocks, sections of pipe, and glass bottles at us, and I had to stay in the arena and seek shelter. There was a constant stream of shit, and instead of all that "Zlatan, Zlatan!" I'd heard early on, even at Ajax, I was now getting boos and jeers, and not from the opposing fans. That would have been completely normal, but no, this was from our own fans, and it was tough. It was like: What the hell is this?

Still, you just have to put up with it in this sport, and in a way I could understand them. I was the club's most expensive acquisition. I really shouldn't be a reserve. I was supposed to be the new van Basten and score one goal after another, and I made every effort I could. I made too much of an effort.

A soccer season is long, and you can't put everything on show in a single match. But that's what I tried to do. As soon as I arrived I wanted to do my whole repertoire all at once, and that's why I got stuck, I think. I wanted too much, and that's why it wasn't enough, and I guess I hadn't learned to handle the pressure yet, in spite of everything. Those 85 million kronor were starting to weigh me down like a damn backpack, and I spent a lot of time sitting around in my terraced house in Diemen.

I have no idea what the press thought of me in those days. I'm sure many of them imagined that me and Mido were out on the town, partying. In fact, I stayed home and played videogames, day and night, and if we had a Monday off, I'd fly home on Sunday evening and come back on the 6 a.m. flight Tuesday morning and head straight to practice. There were no nightclubs, none of that stuff, but even so, I wasn't being professional.

I was totally irresponsible, to be honest—I didn't sleep or eat properly and got mixed up in all sorts of stupid stuff in Malmö. I went around with cherry bombs and stuff—illegal fireworks that we'd toss into people's gardens. We did all kinds of crazy stuff to get our adrenaline going. There'd be smoke and clumps of grass and crap flying all over the place. There was loads of racing around in cars, because that's how I function. If nothing's going on with soccer, I've got to get my kicks somewhere else. I need action, I need speed, and I wasn't looking after myself.

I continued shedding weight, and as a center forward at Ajax I was supposed to be sturdy and able to drive myself forward. I was down to 165 pounds, or even less. I got really thin, and I was probably worn out. I hadn't had a break. I'd done two preseasons in the space of six months, and as for food, well, what do you think? I ate junk. I could only make toast and boil pasta, and that whole flood of favorable newspaper coverage had dried up. There was no "Another triumph for Zlatan." It was "Zlatan booed." "He's off balance." He's this, that, and the other—and people were talking about my elbows.

There was a hell of a lot of talk about my elbows.

It started in a match against Groningen, where I elbowed a defender in the back of the neck. The referee didn't see anything, but the defender dropped to the ground and was taken off on a stretcher, and people claimed he got a concussion. When the guy came back in after a while he was still groggy, but, worst of all, the Netherlands Soccer Association took it upon themselves to study the TV footage and decided to give me a five-match suspension.

That was definitely not what I needed. It was bullshit, and things didn't exactly get off to a good start when I returned after my suspension. I elbowed another guy in the back of the neck, and, of course, he was taken off on a stretcher as well. It was as if I'd gotten a stupid new habit, and even though I avoided a suspension that time I didn't get to play much afterward, and it was hard, and the fans weren't exactly delighted, so I phoned Hasse Borg. It was idiotic, but that's the sort of thing you do when you're in a desperate situation.

"Shit, Hasse, can't you buy me back?"

"Buy you back? Are you serious?"

"Get me out of here. I can't take it."

"Come on, Zlatan, there's no money for that, you must realize that. You've got to be patient."

I was tired of being patient. I wanted to play more, and I was so homesick it was unreal. I felt totally lost, and I started phoning Mia again, not that I knew whether it was her or something else I was missing. I was lonely and I wanted my old life back. What did I get? I got another kick in the teeth.

It started when I discovered that I was being paid less than everybody else on the team. I'd suspected as much for a while, and finally it became clear. I was the most expensive transfer, but I got paid the least. I'd been purchased to be the new van Basten. And still I earned peanuts, and, I mean, what was that down to? It wasn't hard to figure out.

Remember what Hasse Borg said: "Agents are crooks" and all that? Like a bolt from the blue, I understood: he'd screwed me over. He'd pretended to be on my side, but in reality he was working only for Malmö FF. The more I thought about it, the more enraged I got. Right from the beginning, Hasse Borg had made sure nobody came between us, nobody who could represent my interests. That's why I'd had to stand there like a fool at the St. Jörgen Hotel in my warmups and let the guys in suits with their finance diplomas shaft me. It felt like a punch in the gut. Let's get this straight: money has never been the main thing for me. To be tricked and exploited, though, to be seen as some stupid falafel boy you can cheat and make money out of— that made me furious, and I wasted no time. I rang Hasse Borg.

"What the hell is this? I've got the worst contract on the entire club."

"What do you mean?" He was playing dumb.

"And where's my ten percent?"

"We invested it in an insurance policy in England."

In an insurance policy? What the hell was that? It meant nothing to me, and I said, Okay, it could be anything, an insurance policy, a briefcaseful of banknotes, a bucket in the wilderness, it didn't make a difference: "I want my money now."

"That's not possible," he said.

It was tied up, it was invested in something I didn't have a clue about, and I decided to get to the bottom of it. I got myself an agent, because this much I'd realized: agents aren't crooks. Without an agent, you haven't got a chance. Without help, you'll just stand there and get screwed by the guys in suits again. Through a friend, I got ahold of a guy called Anders Carlsson who worked at IMG in Stockholm.

He was all right, wasn't exactly going to set the world on fire. He was the sort of guy who'd never spit out his chewing gum in the street or cross over the line but who still wants to seem a little tough, though it doesn't really suit him. Still, Anders helped me out a lot in the beginning. He got the insurance documents, and that's when I got my next shock. It didn't say 10 percent of the transfer fee. It said 8 percent, so I asked: "What's this?" I found out they'd paid something called advance tax on my wages, and I thought, What kind of shit is that? Advance taxes on somebody's wages? I'd never heard of it, and I said, "This isn't right. This is a new trick." And what do you think happened? Anders Carlsson got on the case, and that was all it took for me to get that 2 percent back. Suddenly, there was no more advance tax on my wages, and then it was all over, I was finished with Hasse Borg. It was a lesson I'll never forget. It scarred me, and don't think for a second that I'm not fully on top of everything when it comes to my money and contracts these days.

When Mino rang me up recently, he asked, "What'd you get from Bonnier for your book?"

"I don't really know."

"Bullshit! You know exactly how much," and of course he was right.

I'm in complete control. I refuse to be cheated and taken advantage of again, and I always try to be one step ahead in negotiations. What are they thinking? What do they want, and what are their secret tactics? And then I remember. Things get etched in, and sure, Helena often says I shouldn't dwell on things so much, saying, "I'm tired of hating Hasse Borg."

No, I won't forgive him. No chance. You don't do something like that to a young guy from the projects who doesn't know anything about that stuff. You don't pretend to be like a second dad to him while you're looking for every possible loophole to screw him. I'd been the guy on the youth squad they didn't believe in, I was the one they least expected to get called up onto the first team. But then . . . when I was sold for big money, their attitudes changed. They wanted to milk every drop out of me. One minute I barely existed, and the next I was there to be exploited. I won't forget that, and I often wonder: Would Hasse Borg have done the same thing if I'd been a nice kid with a lawyer for a father?

I don't think so, and even back then at Ajax I made my feelings known. I basically said that he'd better watch out. I guess he didn't really get it, and later, in his book, he wrote that he was my mentor, he was the man who'd taken care of me. The thing is, I think he got the idea later on. We bumped into each other in an elevator a few years ago. This was in Hungary.

I was there with the Swedish national team. I got into the elevator, and it stopped on the fourth floor, and then out of nowhere he got in. He was in town on some junket. He was busy tying his tie and then he caught sight of me. Hasse is always going, "All right there, how's it going?"—that sort of thing—and he said something along those lines and put out his hand.

I didn't move a muscle, nothing at all. All he got was an ice-cold, black stare, and he got really nervous, that's for sure. He just stood there, psyched out, and I didn't say a word. I stared him down, and then in the lobby I strode out and left him behind. That was our only encounter since all that business, so, no, I won't forget. Hasse Borg is someone with two sides to him, and I was really hurting from all that at Ajax. I'd been cheated and insulted, I was being paid less than everybody else, and the club's own fans were booing me. There was one thing after another. There were my elbows. There was crap everywhere, the lists of my mistakes, the thing with the police in Industrigatan for the ninety-eighth time, and people saying I was off balance. People missed the old Zlatan. There was talk about me day in, day out, and my thoughts kept going around and around in my head.

I was looking for solutions every hour, every minute, because I wasn't going to give up, no way. I didn't have it easy growing up; people forget that. I'm not a talent who just waltzed out into Europe.

I've fought against the odds. I've had parents and managers against me right from the start, and a lot of what I've learned I've picked up in spite of what others have said. Zlatan just dribbles, they've complained. He's this, he's that, he's wrong. I just live my life: I listened, I didn't listen; and now at Ajax I was really trying to figure out the culture and learn how they thought and played.

I thought about what I needed to do to improve. I trained hard and tried to learn from the others. At the same time, I didn't give up my style. Nobody was going to get rid of what made my game my own— not that I was pigheaded or a troublemaker, I just kept fighting, and when I'm working on the pitch, I can seem aggressive. That's just a part of my character. I demand as much from others as I demand from myself. Clearly, Co Adriaanse was annoyed with me. I was difficult, he said later, I was full of myself, I went my own way, blah blah blah; and of course he's free to come out with whatever he wants to say, I'm not going to get into it with him. I accept the situation. The manager is the boss. I can only say that I really made an effort to fit in.

Things didn't improve. Nothing happened, other than we heard Co Adriaanse was going to get axed, and that was good news, after all. We'd been thrashed by Henrik Larsson and Celtic in the Champions League qualifier and by FC Copenhagen in the UEFA Cup, but I don't think it was the scores that brought him down. We were doing well in the league.

He had to go because he couldn't communicate with us players. None of us had any contact with him. We were living in a vacuum. It's true that I like tough guys, and Co Adriaanse was really hard. But he crossed the line, there was nothing funny about his dictatorial style—no sense of humor, nothing—and of course we were all curious: who was going to replace him?

There was talk of Rijkaard for a while, and that did sound good, not because a good player necessarily makes a good coach, but still, Rijkaard had been legendary with van Basten and Gullit in Milan. It ended up being Ronald Koeman. I knew him as well; he'd been a brilliant free kicker at Barcelona. He brought Ruud Krol with him, who's another great player, and right away I noticed they understood me more, and I started to hope that things would take a turn for the better.

They got worse. I was benched five matches in a row, and Koeman sent me home from one practice session. "You're not into it," he yelled. "You're not giving it your all. You can go home." Sure, I got out of there; my mind was on other things. It was no big thing, but, of course, there were big headlines. Even Lars Lagerbäck was in the papers saying he was worried about me, and there was talk that I might lose my spot on the national squad, and that was no fun—not at all.

The World Cup was coming up in Japan that summer, and that was something I'd been looking forward to for a long time. I was also worried that my shirt, number nine at Ajax, would be taken away from me, not that I really cared. I don't give a damn what it says on my back. But it would be a sign that they didn't believe in me anymore. At Ajax, people talked about numbers constantly.

Number ten should be like this. Number eleven like that, and there was none better than nine, van Basten's old number. It was a special honor to wear that one, and if you didn't make the grade, you lost it. That was how it worked, and now people kept saying that I wasn't bringing enough to the team, and, unfortunately, there was some truth in that.

I'd only scored five goals in the league. That made six in total, and for the most part I'd sat on the bench and got more and more boos from our own fans. While I warmed up and got ready to go in, they'd roar, "Nikos, Nikos! Machlas, Machlas!" It didn't matter how bad he was, they didn't want me in there. They wanted to keep him, and I thought, Shit, I haven't even started playing, but they're already against me. If I made a bad pass there'd be a massive racket up there, boos or the same crap again: "Nikos, Nikos! Machlas, Machlas!" As if it wasn't bad enough that I wasn't playing well, I had that stuff to tackle as well, and sure, it looked as if we were going to win the league title.

I couldn't bring myself to be happy about it, though. I hadn't been a serious part of it, and I couldn't close my eyes to that any longer. There were too many of us in my position on the club. Somebody would have to leave, and it looked like it was going to be me, I could feel it in my gut, and people were saying that I was just the number-three center forward, after Machlas and Mido.

Even Leo Beenhakker, my friend, was quoted in the Dutch media saying, "Zlatan is often the player who launches our attacks. But he doesn't follow through on goal," and then he added, "If we sell him, we'll certainly make sure it's to a good club."

It was hanging in the air, and there were more and more of those statements. Koeman himself said, "In purely qualitative terms, Zlatan is our best striker, but it takes other qualities as well to succeed in the number-nine shirt at Ajax. I doubt whether he can achieve them," and then came the wartime headlines: "Decision Tonight," said one; "Zlatan on the Transfer List!" another. It was impossible to tell what was true and what wasn't, but the fact was that I'd been purchased for a huge sum of money and turned out to be a disappointment, and believe me, I felt it. It was as if I was about to be revealed as the overhyped diva after all.

I hadn't lived up to expectations. This was my first major setback. But I refused to give up. I'd show them. That thought kept going around in my head, day and night, and, really, I had no other choice, whether I was going to be sold or not. I had to show I was good whatever happened. The only thing was, How was I supposed to do that when I didn't get to play? It was a catch-22. It was hopeless, and I sat there on the bench, fuming: Are they stupid, or what? It was like being back on Malmö FF's youth squad.

That spring, we qualified for the final in the Holland Cup. We were going to face Utrecht at De Kuip in Rotterdam, the same stadium where the UEFA Cup final had been played two years earlier, and the crowd was electric. It was May 12, 2002. There were fireworks and stuff and brawls in the stands. Ajax is Utrecht's archrival. No other team is more important to beat, and their fans were burning with hatred and hungry for revenge after our league victory. You could almost smell it, and for us it was a chance to take home the double and show that we really were back after a few lean years. Obviously, I'd hardly get a chance to be a part of it.

I spent the entire first half and a good chunk of the second sitting on the bench and saw Utrecht make it 2–1 with a penalty and, believe me, we felt it. The wind went out of our sails completely, the Utrecht supporters were going nuts, and, not far away from me, Koeman sat moping in his suit and his red tie. He seemed to have completely given up. Put me in there, I thought, and in the seventy-eighth minute I actually got to play. Something had to happen and, of course, I was impatient. I was up for it and wanted everything all at once, as usual, that year, and we kept up the pressure, but the minutes ticked away and things seemed hopeless. We didn't get it in, and I remember I had one shot that I really thought would go in, but it hit the crossbar.

It was no use, and then it was full time and a few minutes of stoppage time, but it was still hopeless. There would be no Cup celebration, and the Utrecht fans were cheering. Their red banners were waving around the stadium, and you could hear their songs and chants and you could see their flares, and there were thirty, then twenty seconds left. That's when a long pass came into the penalty area past several Utrecht defenders and reached Wamberto, one of the Brazilians on our team, and he was probably offside, but the linesman didn't see it, and Wamberto put his foot on the ball and scored, and it was crazy. We were saved in the final seconds of stoppage time, and the Utrecht fans clutched their heads in desperation. It wasn't over yet.

We went into extra time, and in those days many Cup matches were decided by a golden goal—like sudden death in ice hockey—and that's what would happen now. The team that scored a goal would immediately win the match, and just five minutes into extra time a pass came, this time from the left, and I jumped up and headed it, and got the ball back soon after.

I took it down on my chest. I was boxed in really tight, but I turned and kicked it with my left foot—not a brilliant shot, by any means. The ball bounced on the grass. My God, it was well placed, and went into the net. I tore off my shirt and rushed out to the left, completely delirious with joy and as thin as a rake. You could see my rib cage. It had been a tough year. There had been a load of crap in the press and my game had been frozen for long periods. But now I was back. I'd done it. I'd shown them all, and the entire stadium went insane. It was absolutely pulsating with joy and disappointment, and the main thing I remember is Koeman, who ran over to me and shouted into my ear, "Thank you very much. Thank you very much!"

That was a happiness I can't even describe, and I just ran around there with the whole team and felt everything let loose.

9

I was a typical bloody Yugo, she thought, with a gold watch and a flash car, and I played my music too loud. I was definitely not her type. I didn't know any of that, though.

I thought I was pretty awesome, and I was sitting there in my Merc SL outside the Forex currency exchange at Malmö Central railway station while Keki, my little brother, was exchanging some money inside. The season was over in the Netherlands, and this might have been either before or after the World Cup in Japan—I don't remember, but it doesn't matter—anyway, there I was and this girl burst out of a taxi. She was angry about something.

Who the hell is that? I wondered.

I'd never seen her before, and in those days I still felt pretty much at home in Malmö. I'd been going back there whenever I got a chance, and I thought I knew everything there was to know. But this girl . . . where had she been hiding? She wasn't just pretty. She had a wicked attitude, as if to say, Don't try anything with me. And she was a bit older, which was exciting. I asked around: Who is she? Who is that girl? I found out through an acquaintance that her name was Helena. Okay, Helena, I thought. Helena. I couldn't get her out of my head.

Even so, nothing more came of it. There was so much going on around me, and I was restless; nothing really stuck. Then one day I went to Stockholm again with the national squad, and I mean, that city—where do all the good-looking girls come from? It's crazy: they're everywhere. Me and some friends went to the Café Opera, and of course it caused a bit of a stir, and as usual I sized up the situation with that look I'd grown up with: Any problems coming up? Is there somebody going to give us shit? There's always something.

Things were better then. This was before everybody took my picture with their cell phones (and a lot of them don't even ask. They just snap a picture right in my face, and sometimes I jump all over them). This time, I was just having a look around and suddenly I caught sight of her—I thought, Wow, it's the girl from Forex. I went over and started chatting to her—"All right, are you from Malmö as well?"—and she started going on about how she worked at such and such a place, and I didn't have a clue. That career stuff was totally beyond me in those days, and I was probably pretty arrogant. That's how I rolled back then.

I didn't want to let anybody get too close. I've since regretted it. I should have been nicer, and I was happy when I saw her in Malmö again. I started seeing her around all the time. She had a black Mercedes SLK which was often parked by Lilla Torg square, and I would often cruise by there. In those days, I no longer had my Merc SL; I'd changed it for a red Ferrari 360.

Everybody in town knew that was my car. There was a lot of "Check it out, there goes Zlatan," and it's true, if I wanted to keep a low profile, that car wasn't a bright idea. But the guys who'd sold me the Mercedes had promised me: you'll be the only one in the country with that one. That was just sales talk. It was bullshit. I saw another one just like it that summer and thought, They can go to hell. I don't want this car anymore, and then I phoned some people who sold Ferraris and asked, Have you got any in stock? Sure, they said, and so I went there and picked one out and traded in my SL as part payment. It was a stupid thing to do—I lost money on the deal, and my finances weren't in great shape in those days. But I didn't care.

I took pride in my cars—it was a matter of principle—so that's why I cruised around in a Ferrari and felt, well, cool. Sometimes I'd see her in her black Merc, the girl called Helena, and I'd think, Gotta do something about that, I can't just look, so I got her number off an acquaintance and spent some time thinking it over. Should I call her?

I sent her a text, something like "All right, how's it going? Think you've seen me around," and then I finished with "The guy in the red one"—the guy in the red Ferrari, that is—and got a reply.

"The girl in the black one," she wrote, and I thought, This could be the start of something, who knows?

I phoned her and we met up, nothing special at first, just lunch a few times, and I went along out to her house in the country, and I checked out her interior design stuff, the wallpaper and traditional ceramic-tiled wood stoves and all that, and honestly, I was impressed. It was something completely new to me. I'd never met a single girl who lived like that, and I don't think I still really grasped what it was she did. She had something to do with marketing for Swedish Match, a tobacco company, but I understood she was pretty high up in her line of work, and I liked that.

She wasn't at all like the younger girls I'd met. There was none of the hysteria, not at all—she was cool. She liked cars. She'd left home when she was seventeen and worked her way up, and I wasn't exactly a superstar to her. Or as she put it, "Come on, Zlatan, you weren't exactly Elvis who'd beamed in." I was just a crazy guy to her who wore hideous clothes and was totally immature, and sometimes she'd tease me a bit.

"Evil super-bitch deluxe," I'd reply, or *Evilsuperbitchdeluxe* as all one word, in a single breath, because she'd go around in wicked stiletto heels and tight jeans and fur coats and stuff. She was like Tony Montana in *Scarface,* only a girl, whereas I was slobbing around in warmups again. The whole thing between us was so wrong it somehow felt right, and we had a good time together. "Zlatan, you're an absolute idiot. You're so much fun," she said, and I really hoped she meant it. I enjoyed being with her.

She came from a respectable traditional family in a small town called Lindesberg—the kind of family where they say, "Darling, could you please pass me the milk," whereas in my family we'd generally threaten to kill one another over the dinner table, like I said; and there were many times when she didn't even understand what I was saying. I didn't understand anything about her world, and she knew nothing about mine. I was eleven years younger and lived in the Netherlands and was a nut job with hinky friends. It wasn't an ideal situation.

That summer, some friends and I went down to crash a party she'd organized for loads of celebs and big shots in the resort town of Båstad during the annual tennis tournament there. The people at the door didn't want to let us in—at any rate, they weren't going to let my pals in—and it turned into a big song-and-dance. As I say, there was always something.

Like the time I played in an international match in Riga and flew into Stockholm in the evening, and I took a taxi with Olof Mellberg and Lars Lagerbäck to the Scandic Park Hotel. Our game hadn't been much to write home about. We'd only managed to draw 0–0 against

Latvia in the World Cup qualifier. I always have a hard time getting to sleep after matches, especially when I've played badly. My mistakes whirl around in my head, so some pals and I decided to go and check out a club, Spy Bar, in the city center. It was late, and I was walking up a flight of stairs.

I hadn't been standing there very long before a girl came up and was coming on really strong, and, of course, I had some buddies nearby. If you see me out and about, you can be sure I'll have some homeboys around somewhere. Not just because of all the to-do around me. It's something about my personality. I easily end up with the bad guys. We gravitate toward each other, and it doesn't bother me a bit. They're as nice as all the rest. Sure, things can get out of hand, and this girl, she came up close and said something silly, she just wanted to get a reaction, and suddenly her brother turned up and grabbed me, and, well, he shouldn't have done that.

You don't mess with my friends. One of them took the brother and another grabbed her, and I realized, Nope, I don't want to be a part of this. I wanted out, but you see, that was the first time I'd been to Spy Bar and it was late and packed with people and I couldn't find the way out.

I ended up in the men's room instead. Over where I had been standing there was already a big commotion, and I started to get stressed out. I'd just played in an international match.

This will make the headlines, I thought, there'll be a scandal. Then a new security guy turned up, and it was no more Mr. Nice Guy.

"The owner wants you to leave the premises."

"Tell that swine there's nothing I'd rather do," I hissed, and so he and a few others followed me out, and I got out of there.

It was half past three in the morning—I know that because I was caught on one of the security cameras—and what do you think happened? Did they bother with any confidentiality stuff? Not quite. It ended up in the *Aftonbladet* tabloid and in all the headlines, and you have no idea—it was as if I'd murdered seven people. The papers were screaming all kinds of stuff and they claimed I'd been reported for sexual assault. Sexual assault? Can you imagine? That's just sick, and, as usual, anyone who'd happened to touch me that night went to the papers and milked it for all it was worth.

I headed back to Amsterdam. We had matches coming up, including a Champions League game against Lyon, and I refused to speak to the press. Mido went out and spoke on my behalf. We troublemakers had to help each other out. Really, I'd had about enough now, and it didn't surprise me at all when it emerged that it was the *Aftonbladet* that had made sure the girl reported me to the police, and I issued a public statement, saying I was going to stick it to that paper. I was going to sue them. What do you think happened? I didn't get a damn thing, only an apology, and so I started to be more on my guard. I started to change.

There had been too much bad stuff in the papers, and sure, I'd never wanted just the usual dull fluff in the media: Zlatan trains, Zlatan is good, Zlatan looks after himself. Not at all. This had crossed the line, though, and I wanted to get noticed for my soccer again. It had been a long time since anyone had written anything positive about that.

Even the World Cup had been a disappointment. I'd had such high hopes, and for a while it had seemed as if I wouldn't get to go at all. Lagerbäck and Söderberg did select me in the end, and I liked both of them—especially Söderberg, of course, the whole team's teddy bear. At one training session I picked him up and hugged him out of sheer joy. I cracked two of his ribs. He could hardly walk, but he was nice. I shared a room with Andreas Isaksson. Andreas was the third goalie then, a good guy, I guess. But his habits! He went to bed at nine o'clock and I'd be lying there festering, and of course my cell would ring. I'd be like, "Yeah, great, finally somebody to talk to." But Andreas just grumbled and I'd hang up. I didn't want to disturb him. I'm a nice guy, really. The following evening my phone rang around the same time and he was asleep again, or pretending to be asleep.

"What the fuck, Zlatan," he hissed, and then I snapped—I mean, what is this? Asleep at nine o'clock? "If you open your mouth again I'm going to throw your bed out the window." That was a good line— not just because we were on the twentieth floor, but also because it got results.

The following day, I had my own room, which was great, but otherwise I wasn't doing so well personally. We were in the group of death, as it was called, with England, Argentina, and Nigeria, and there was such an amazing atmosphere, such great stadiums and perfect pitches, and I wanted to get in there and play more than ever. I was seen as too inexperienced. I was put on the bench. Even so, I was voted Man of the Match in a telephone vote. Totally crazy! I was seen as the best one on the pitch, and I hadn't even taken my warmups off. That was the old Zlatan Fever again, and in fact I only played five minutes against Argentina and a little while against Senegal in the final of the group phase, where I did get a few chances. No, I thought Lars and Tommy were still sticking with the same eleven too much and not giving us younger players a chance. That was how things were, and I got out of there and headed back to Amsterdam.

I had a strategy. I wasn't going to worry as much about what other people said, just go for it. That was my objective, but it didn't help much, not at first. Things started pretty much as they had ended—on the bench. Competition for places up front was still fierce, and I had my critics, including Johan Cruyff, who was always talking trash about me, and who was up there already back then with his views about my technique.

Other things happened too: Mido, my friend, declared publicly that he wanted to be transferred. Not a particularly good tactic. He wasn't exactly a diplomat; he was like me, only worse. Later on, when he'd been on the bench against Eindhoven, he came into the locker room and called us all miserable cunts. That sparked off a massive blowup and insults were flying, and I responded by saying that if anybody was a cunt it was him, and then he picked up a pair of scissors that were lying there on the bench and flung them at me. The scissors whizzed past my head, straight into the concrete wall and made a crack in it. Of course I went over and gave him a smack, a slap. But ten minutes later we left with our arms around each other, and much later I found out that our team manager had kept those scissors as a souvenir, something to show his kids, telling them, Zlatan nearly got these in his face.

At any rate, things were kind of up and down with Mido, and now he'd screwed up again. Koeman had fined him and shut him out, and now there was another guy. His name was Rafael van der Vaart, a Dutchman, a real arrogant sort, like a lot of the white guys on the team, even if he wasn't exactly upper-class. He'd grown up in a trailer and lived like a Gypsy, as he put it, and he'd played soccer in the street with beer bottles for goalposts, and he claimed that had sharpened his technique. At the age of ten he'd been signed to the Ajax youth academy and trained hard—and, sure, he was good. Only the previous year he'd been voted European Talent of the Year, or something. He tried to be a tough guy and he wanted to get noticed and be a leader, and there was a rivalry between us right from the start.

Now he had injured his knee, and with both him and Mido out of action I got to start at home to Lyon. This was my debut in the Champions League—I'd only played in a qualifier before—and, of course, that was great. The Champions League was a longtime dream of mine, and the pressure in the stadium was intense. I'd brought over a bunch of friends and got them tickets far down on the byline near the goal, and I remember I got a ball early on from Jari Litmanen, the Finn. I liked him.

Litmanen had played for Barcelona and Liverpool and had just joined us, and he was a catalyst for me. A lot of guys at Ajax played mainly for themselves. They wanted nothing more than to get sold to a bigger club, and it often felt like we were competing more against one another than against the other clubs. Litmanen really was a team player. He was the real deal, I thought, and now when I got the ball off him I went down the sideline and was fronted by two defenders, one right in front of me and another to my right. I'd been in similar situations many times, and had gone over them again and again.

It was kind of similar to that time with Henchoz in the Liverpool match, but there were two guys now, and I dribbled it to the left, a two-footer, and the defenders were both on me. It was looking like a dead end, but then I sensed a gap between them, a little corridor, and before I even had a chance to think about it I was through and got in front of the goal, saw another opening and shot, a low shot that struck the post and went in, and I went absolutely nuts.

It wasn't just a goal, it was a beauty as well. I raced over to my buddies on the sideline and cheered with them, and the whole team followed me, completely wild, and not long after that I scored another goal. It was incredible. That was two goals in my Champions League debut, and people started saying that Roma was after me, and Tottenham as well.

I was on a roll, and, normally, if things are going smoothly in soccer, I haven't got a problem in the world. Things weren't going well in my personal life, though. I just wasn't settling in down there. I was in a sort of vacuum. I was going back to Sweden far too often and doing stupid stuff, and I was still in touch with Helena, mainly via texting, without really knowing where that was leading. Was it just a crazy thing, or was it something more?

In October, we played a UEFA Cup qualifier against Hungary at Råsunda Stadium. It felt good to be back. I hadn't forgotten the chants from the year before, but things didn't start off well, and some of the Stockholm papers wrote things like I was an overhyped player who just elbowed his way through. This was an important match. If we lost, our European Championship dreams would go up in smoke, and both I and the national squad had something to prove. Hungary scored 1–0 after just four minutes, and it didn't seem to make any difference how many chances we had. We just couldn't equalize; it felt hopeless. Then, in the seventy-fourth minute, a high cross came over from Mattias Jonson, and I went up to head it. The goalie flung himself against me and tried to punch the ball away, and I don't know if he actually made contact with it. He definitely bashed into me, and everything went black. I went down.

I was out for five, ten seconds, and when I came to, the players were standing in a circle around me and I didn't know what was going on. What's this? What's going on? Everyone in the stands was screaming, and the guys looked both happy and concerned.

"It was a goal," said Kim Källström.

"Really? Who scored it?"

"You did. You headed it in."

I felt groggy and nauseous, and a stretcher came out and I got onto it. The team doctor was there, and I was carried off, but then I heard the chanting again: "Zlatan, Zlatan!" The whole stadium was shouting, and I waved to the spectators. I was really on a high, and the whole team came alive. Okay, so the score stayed at 1–1, and we ought to have won. For one thing, Kim Källström had a blatant penalty in the final minutes, which the referee chose not to see. I remembered that, feeling so awful and yet so good, and soon afterward I got sick in another way, with a terrible fever that affected only 250 people in all of Sweden—and something unexpected happened that changed a lot of things.

It was December 23, 2002. I was at Mom's place. I might not have had a great start to the season, but I was pretty happy, in spite of everything. I'd scored five goals in the Champions League, more than in the Dutch League, in fact, and I remember Koeman had told me, "You know, Zlatan, we're in a league as well," but somehow that's how I functioned. A stronger opposition got me going, and anyway, now I was at home in Rosengård.

We were off until the beginning of January, when we would go to a training camp and play matches in Cairo, and I really needed some rest. It was crowded at Mom's, and people were shouting and making noise and arguing with one another. There was no peace and quiet anywhere. There was me, Mom, Keki, and Sanela, and we usually had a Christmas like everybody else, a simple Christmas dinner at four o'clock and then opening presents afterward, and sure, it could have been really nice. Now, though, I just couldn't be bothered. I had a headache and my whole body ached. I needed to get away and get some peace and quiet, or at least talk to somebody other than my family. The only thing was, who could I call?

Everybody was with their own families, I mean, Christmas is sacred. Maybe Helena? I gave it a try. Not that I expected anything much. She worked all the time, and presumably she was at her parents' place in Lindesberg. But she answered. She was at her place out in the country. She said she didn't like Christmas.

"I feel so rotten," I said.

"Poor thing!"

"I can't deal with this circus here at home."

"So come over here," she said. "I'll take care of you." To be honest, that was kind of surprising.

We'd mainly just had coffee together and texted each other before then. I still hadn't spent the night at her place, but of course, that sounded perfect, so I headed out. I just said, "Sorry, Mom, gotta go."

"So now you're not going to spend Christmas with us either?"

"Sorry," I said. Out in the country, Helena put me to bed. It was silent and peaceful outside, which was exactly what I needed. It was really nice, and it didn't feel at all strange to be with her instead of with my family. It was both natural and exciting. Even so, I didn't get any healthier.

I was wiped out, and the next day was Christmas Eve. I'd promised Dad I'd drop by. My dad doesn't celebrate Christmas. He sits on his own, as usual, and does his own thing. He and I had become very close since that day there on pitch no. 1 in Malmö. All that stuff from my childhood when he didn't really care was gone, and he'd been down several times to watch my matches, and partly in honor of him I'd had my Ajax shirt changed so it said Ibrahimović instead of Zlatan. But now he was drunk as a skunk again, and I couldn't deal with it, not for a second, so I went straight back to Helena's place.

"Back already?"

"I'm back."

That was basically all I managed to say. I got so ill, with a temperature of about 106. I'm not joking. Never felt so lousy in my life. This was a superflu bug. I was completely out for three days, and Helena had to shower me and wipe my forehead and change the sheets because they were soaked through with sweat, and I was delirious and whimpering—and there was something about that. I dunno. Up until that time I'd basically been that strutting Yugo around her. The guy who played at being a mafioso in extravagant cars and who was a lot of fun—at least I hoped I was—but maybe wasn't exactly the guy for her.

Now I was completely broken, an absolute wreck, and she liked that in a way, she says. I became human. My whole exterior cracked, and afterward when I got a little better, she went out and rented some DVDs, and that was the first time I'd seen any Swedish cop shows like the *Beck* series, and it was a bit of a revelation to me. It was like, Wow! I didn't know Sweden could do this sort of stuff! I became an instant fan, and we sat there together and watched one movie after another and had a really nice time—not that we got it on right away, not at all.

She was in and out during that time. She left for work and came back and looked after me, and sure, we didn't always understand each other. We still didn't know what we wanted, and we were still totally different and completely wrong, and all the rest. It started there, I think. It felt good to hang out with her, and when I was back in the Netherlands I missed her, like, Where is she? "Can't you come down here?" I asked, and she did. She visited me in Diemen. That was nice. But you can't say she was impressed by my terraced house. By then I'd started to like it out there, and I made sure the fridge was full.

But she claims she had to scrub my floors, that the place was in a terrible state, and that I had about three plates and none of them matched, and the walls were all a mess of purple, yellow, and apricot, and the green carpets didn't go with anything and the whole place was a disaster. Besides, my clothes were pathetic, and I just lay in bed with my videogames, and there were cables and trash everywhere, and nothing was tidy. "Evil super-bitch," I said.

Evilsuperbitchdeluxe, all in one breath.

———

I missed her when she left, and I started phoning and texting more often, and I think I settled down a bit. Man, this was a classy girl. She taught me stuff, like what fish knives look like, and how to drink wine. In those days, I thought you should gulp down vintage wines like a glass of milk. But oh no, you were supposed to sit there and sip it. I was starting to get it. It didn't come easily to me. I was still going back up to Malmö all the time, and not just for cuddles.

One day, me and some friends went out to Helena's place and did some handbrake turns on her gravel paths, and she was upset and yelled that they'd been all raked and nice and everything was wrecked now, and, of course, I felt guilty. I had to do something about it, I thought. I sent my little brother. He went out there and was handed a rake, but I mean, we haven't got a clue about rakes and stuff in my family. My bro didn't exactly do a brilliant job, and she told me again that I was a complete idiot, but, fortunately, we had a good laugh about it.

Another time I'd given her a Sony Vaio laptop. Then we had a bit of a falling-out and I didn't want her to have that computer anymore. So I gave Keki a new assignment. Go and get it back, I told him. Keki usually does as he's told, or at least some of the time. So he went out there, but what do you think happened? Helena said we could eat shit, she wasn't going to give anything back, and soon after that we became friends again. Still, things were a mess. There was the matter of the firecrackers, for one thing. We bought them off a guy who made them illegally at home—they were tight little bundles of power, and in those days we had a friend who owned a hot dog stall in Malmö. Nothing bad about him, quite the contrary. But we agreed that we'd set off a little explosion at his place, just for a laugh, and in order to do that, we needed a vehicle that wasn't linked to us, and since Helena had plenty of contacts, I asked her, "Can you get us a jeep?"

Of course. She got us a Lexus. She must have believed we were going to do something pretty nice, in spite of everything.

But we headed over to the hot dog place and tossed a firecracker into the mailbox on the front, and the mailbox went up in the air. It just rumbled and then exploded into seven million pieces, and that same night, when we were still out and about, we called Keki.

"Wanna have a little fun?"

He probably didn't, but we drove over to his girl's place, where they were in bed asleep, and tossed two firecrackers into her garden. There was a massive bang there too, and a ton of smoke and crap and clumps of grass flew up in the air. Of course the girl sat bolt upright: "What the hell was that?" Keki just played dumb: "My God, what can it be? How strange! How annoying." Of course he knew, and—well, you realize it was just kid pranks, the sort of thing I've always needed and, in fact, the sort of thing that still happens. It's true, my time with Ajax was my most out-of-control phase. That was before Mino Raiola and Fabio Capello got me to shape up.

I remember when I bought my elder brother some furniture from IKEA. I let him pick out whatever he wanted. I'd already started helping my family out quite a bit. I bought my mom a terraced house in Svågertorp and eventually bought my dad a car, even though he was so proud and didn't want to accept anything. But this time at IKEA I had a friend along with me, and we had all our stuff on those carts. One of the carts rolled forward a little too far. It happened to go past the checkout, and my friend noticed immediately—he was a smart guy—and I gave it another push:

"Keep going, go, go!"

So we ended up getting a load of the stuff for free, and of course we enjoyed that. Don't think it was about the money, though. It was the buzz. It was the adrenaline. It was like when we were kids in the department store. But, sure, of course, sometimes things turned out badly. Like that time with the Lexus. It was spotted in some suspicious location and it was reported all over, and that was embarrassing for Helena. It was like, "You know that car you rented, it was seen in connection with some explosion." She got into hot water because of me. Sorry, Helena. And then there was a Porsche Cayenne.

She'd straightened it out for us in the same way. But we happened to drive it into a ditch and had a minor crash on the way back from Båstad. She was furious, and I can understand that. Then, to cap it all, she was burgled. Helena had worked hard—not just in her marketing job, she'd also taken on extra work in a bar in order to buy her house in the country, and lots of nice stuff, furniture, a motorbike, and stereo equipment. She'd worked hard to be able to afford that stuff, so it must have hurt when somebody broke in one day and ripped off her Bang & Olufsen gear and a load of other things. I understand that.

Helena thought I knew who'd done it. She still does. But I haven't got a clue. That's the truth. Of course, news spread quickly in my old circles. We hear about all the nasty stuff that goes on. One night when I was parked outside Mom's place, some guy swiped the tires from my Merc CL. I heard about it at five in the morning, and by then word had gotten out and there were police photographers out there and journalists, and I stayed indoors. I started to put out feelers, and it didn't take long before I knew who'd stolen them. A week later, I got the tires back. I never did find out who broke into Helena's place, though, and, to tell the truth, sometimes I just don't know how she managed to be so patient with me. She'd been saddled with a little maniac. But she managed, she was strong, and I think she got to see some results too.

Before, I'd been fairly lonely and didn't really have anybody to act as a sounding board for everyday things or stuff that was bothering me. Now, though, I had some structure and something to look forward to. Helena started coming down to the Netherlands more often, and we became a little like a family, especially when she got that fat little pug called Hoffa that we fed pizza and mozzarella in Italy.

But a lot of things happened before then. This was when my career took off, and I got my revenge.

10

There had been a lot of Marco van Basten in my life. I'd inherited his shirt number and I was supposed to resemble him on the pitch and all that, and sure, it was flattering. I was starting to get tired of it, though. I didn't want to be a new van Basten. I was Zlatan, nothing else. I wanted to scream, No, don't bring that guy up again, I've heard enough about him. Sure, it was as cool as anything when he turned up in person—it was like, Wow! Is he talking to me?

Van Basten is a legend, one of the best strikers ever, maybe not in the same class as Ronaldo, but still, he'd scored over two hundred goals and completely dominated at Milan. That was just over ten years since he'd been voted Best Player in the World by FIFA, and now he'd just completed a coaching course run by the Soccer Association and was going to be an assistant coach for the Ajax youth squad, his first step on that path. That's why he was there with us at our training sessions.

I was like a little boy around him, at least at first. Then I got used to it. We spoke nearly every day, and we had some good times together. He would get me fired up before every match. We'd chat and make bets and joke around.

"Well, how many goals are you gonna score this time? I say one."

"One? You're kidding. I'll get at least two."

"Bullshit. Wanna make a bet?"

"How much are you willing to lose?"

We kept it up, and he gave me lots of advice, and he was really a cool guy. He did things his own way and didn't give a damn what the bosses thought. He was totally independent. I'd come in for criticism because I didn't work enough at the back, or even because I just stood around on the pitch while the opposing side was attacking, and I'd done some thinking about it and wondered what to do about it. I asked van Basten.

"Don't listen to the coaches," he said.

"So, what then?"

"Don't waste your energy defending. You've got to use your strength in attacking. You'll serve your team best by attacking and scoring goals, not by wearing yourself out defending." That became another one of the things I picked up: you've got to save your energy for scoring goals.

We headed to a training camp in Portugal and, by that time Beenhakker had resigned as director and was replaced by Louis van Gaal. Van Gaal was a pompous ass. He was a little like Co Adriaanse. He wanted to be a dictator, without a hint of a gleam in his eye. As a player, he'd never stood out, but he was revered in the Netherlands because, as a manager, he'd won the Champions League with Ajax and received some medal from the government.

Van Gaal liked to talk about playing systems. He was one of those in the club who referred to the players as numbers. There was a lot of Five goes here and Six goes there, and I was glad when I could avoid him. In Portugal, I couldn't escape. I had to go in for a meeting with van Gaal and Koeman and listen to how they viewed my contribution in the first half of the season. It was like a performance review with grades, the kind of thing they loved at Ajax. I went into an office there and sat down in front of van Gaal and Ronald Koeman. Koeman smiled. Van Gaal looked sullen.

"Zlatan," said Koeman, "you've played brilliantly, but you're only getting an eight. You haven't worked hard enough at the back."

"Okay, fine," I said, wanting to leave.

I liked Koeman, but couldn't cope with van Gaal, and I thought, Great, an eight will do me. Can I have a break now?

"Do you know how to play in defense?"

Van Gaal was sticking his oar in, and I could see that Koeman was getting annoyed too.

"I hope so," I replied.

Then van Gaal started to explain, and, believe me, I'd heard it all before. It was the same old stuff about how Nine—that is, me—defends to the right, while Ten goes to the left, and vice versa, and he drew a bunch of arrows and finished with a really harsh "Do you understand? Do you get all this?," and I took it as an attack.

"You can wake up any of the players at three in the morning," I said, "and ask them how to defend and they'll rattle it off in their sleep: Nine goes here and Ten goes there. We know that stuff, and we know you're the one who came up with it. But I've trained with van Basten, and he thinks otherwise."

"Excuse me?"

"Van Basten says Number Nine should save his strength for attacking and scoring goals, and, to tell the truth, now I don't know who I should listen to, van Basten—who's a legend—or van Gaal?" I said, putting special emphasis on the name van Gaal, as if he were some completely insignificant figure. And what do you reckon? Was he happy?

He was fuming. *Who should I listen to, a legend or van Gaal?*
"I've gotta go now," I said, and got out of there.

———

There was more talk about how Roma was after me, and the manager at Roma was Fabio Capello: real tough, people said, he had no problem benching or chewing out any star at all. It was Capello who'd coached van Basten in Milan in the glory days and made him better than ever, so of course I talked it over with van Basten: "What do you think? Wouldn't Roma be great? Would I be able to cut it?"

"Stay with Ajax," he said. "You need to improve as a striker before you go to Italy."

"How come?"

"It's a lot tougher there. Here you might get five, six chances to score a goal in a match, but in Italy it might be only one or two, so you've got to be able to take advantage of them," he explained, and sure, in a way, I agreed.

Things hadn't really loosened up for me yet. I wasn't scoring enough goals, and I had loads to learn. I needed to become more effective in the goal area. Still, Italy had been my dream from the very beginning and I thought my playing style would fit in there. So I went to speak to my agent, Anders Carlsson.

"What's happening? What have you got in the works?"

Of course, Anders meant well. He went off to make some inquiries and turned up again. What had he come up with?

"Southampton is interested," he said.

"What the fuck! Southampton! Is that my level?" Southampton!

———

Around this time, I'd bought a Porsche Turbo. It was amazing—and completely lethal. It felt like a go-kart. I drove it like a maniac. Me and a friend had taken it out to Småland in southeastern Sweden, near Växjö, and I'd stepped on the gas. I got it up to 250 km an hour. That was nothing unusual in those days. The only thing was, when I slowed down, we heard police sirens.

The cops were after us, and I thought, Okay, pull yourself together, what to do? I can stop and say, Sorry, here's my license. Come on, what about the headlines? Did I want them? Would a controversy about Zlatan, the maniac on the roads, help me in my career? Hardly! I looked behind us. We were on a highway with oncoming traffic, and the police were about four cars behind us. They wouldn't get anywhere, they were boxed in, and I had Dutch plates. They couldn't trace me, and I thought, They haven't got a chance, and when we turned onto a bigger road I put it in second and accelerated. I floored it and got up to 300 km an hour, and I could still hear the sirens going—*wee, wee*—but getting fainter and fainter. The police car vanished in the distance, and when we couldn't see it in the rearview mirror anymore we zipped into an underpass and waited—it was like in a film—and we managed to get away.

There were a number of those episodes with that car, and I remember I drove Anders Carlsson, my agent, in it. He needed to go to his hotel and then on to the airport, and we came to a bend in the road and there was a red light. I couldn't be bothered with that, not in that car. I gunned it—*vroom!*—and he said, "I think that was a red light."

"Oh, was it?" I replied. "I must have missed it," and then I gave it some more—left, right, into the city center.

I was really putting my foot down and could see that he was really sweating. When we reached the hotel he opened the door and got out of there without a word. The next day, he phoned me, absolutely beside himself.

"That was the worst goddamn thing I've ever been through."

"Whaddaya mean?" I said. I pretended not to know what he was talking about.

"That ride."

———

Anders Carlsson wasn't the right guy for me. That was becoming increasingly obvious. I needed a different agent, one who wasn't such a stickler for rules, and traffic lights. By chance, Anders had just left IMG and set up on his own, so he had given me a new contract to sign. Because I hadn't done it yet, I was a free man. The only thing was, what was I going to do with my freedom? I didn't have a clue, and in those days I didn't have many people I could talk soccer with.

I had Maxwell, of course, and a few others on the squad, but not really. There was so much competition everywhere and I didn't know who I could trust, especially when it came to agents and transfers. Every single player on the team wanted to move up to the big clubs, and it felt as if I needed somebody from the outside. I thought of Thijs.

Thijs Slegers was a journalist. He had interviewed me for *Voetbal International,* and I'd liked him right away. We'd talked on the phone a bit after that interview. He became something of a sounding board, and even back then he had a good idea of what was what. He knew what I was like and what kind of people I liked.

I dialed his number and explained the situation: "I need to find a new agent. Who would be best for me?"

Thijs is cool. He said, "Let me think about it." And sure, I let him think about it, I didn't want to rush into anything.

"Listen," he said later. "There are two agents I can think of. One is the firm that works for Beckham. They're supposed to be terrific, and then there's another guy. But, well—"

"Well, what?"

"He's a mafioso."

"Mafioso sounds good," I said.

"I suspected you would say that."

"Terrific. Set up a meeting!"

The guy wasn't actually a mafioso. He just looked and acted like one. His name was Mino Raiola, and I'd heard of him before. He was Maxwell's agent, and he'd tried to get in touch with me via Maxwell a few months earlier—because that's the way he works: Mino always goes via intermediaries. He always says, "If you approach them yourself, you don't have the upper hand. You're standing there with your cap in your hand."

It hadn't worked too well with me, though—I'd just acted cocky, and I told Maxwell, "If he's got something specific to bring to the table, he can show up; otherwise, I'm not interested," but Mino just sent this message: "Tell this Zlatan to go fuck himself." Although that had pissed me off at the time, I was getting excited now that I found out a little about him. I had grown up with that attitude: Go fuck yourself, and stuff. I feel comfortable with that housing project talk, and I suspected that Mino and I had similar backgrounds. Neither of us had been handed anything on a plate. Mino was born in southern Italy, in the province of Salerno. When he was just a year old, his family moved to the Netherlands and opened a pizzeria in the city of Haarlem. Mino had to clean and wash dishes and help out as a waiter when he was a boy. He worked his way up. He started looking after the books and that sort of thing.

He started making something of himself even as a teenager. He was involved in thousands of things: he studied law, made deals, and learned languages. He also loved soccer and wanted to become an agent early on. In the Netherlands, there used to be a really crazy system where players had to be sold according to a price that was based on their age and a bunch of statistical crap, and he went against all that. He challenged the entire Netherlands Soccer Association, and he didn't start off dealing with small fry. Back in 1993, he sold Dennis Bergkamp to Inter, and in 2001, he got Pavel Nedvěd to Juventus for 41 million euros.

Even so, Mino wasn't all that big, not yet, but he was considered to be on his way up, and he was completely fearless and prepared to pull any number of tricks, and that sounded good. I didn't want to have another nice boy. I wanted to be transferred and get a good contract, and so I decided to make an impression on this Mino. When Thijs set up a meeting for us at the Okura Hotel in Amsterdam, I wore my cool brown leather jacket from Gucci. I had no intention of being the idiot in the warmups who gets screwed over again. I put on my gold watch and drove there in my Porsche, and I parked right outside just to be safe.

It was like, Here I come, and I went into the Okura, and, well, that hotel! It's right alongside the Amstel Canal and is amazingly elegant and luxurious, and I thought, This is it, I've got to play it cool now, and I went into the sushi restaurant in the hotel. We'd booked a table there, and I didn't really know what sort of person to expect, probably some sort of pinstriped fella with an even bigger gold watch. But who the hell turned up? A guy in jeans and a Nike T-shirt—and that belly, like one of the guys in *The Sopranos*.

Was he supposed to be an agent, that weirdo? And then when we ordered, what do you think they brought us? A few pieces of sushi with avocado and prawns? We got a massive spread, enough to feed five people, and he started stuffing himself. Then he started talking, and he was really sharp and to the point. There was no sugarcoated crap, and I knew immediately that this was going to work, it was sounding great, and I said to myself, I want to work with this guy. We think alike. I was all set to shake hands on a deal.

Do you know what he did next, that cocky bastard? He took out four pages he'd printed off the Internet. They had a bunch of names and numbers on them, like Christian Vieri: 27 matches, 24 goals; Filippo Inzaghi: 25 matches, 20 goals; David Trézéguet, 24 matches, 20 goals; and, finally, Zlatan Ibrahimović: 25 matches, 5 goals.

"You think I'm going to be able to sell you with statistics like these?" he said, and I thought, What is this, some kind of attack?

I retaliated. "If I'd scored twenty goals, even my mother could have sold me," and silenced him. He wanted to laugh, I know that now. But he carried on with his game. He didn't want to lose the upper hand.

"You are right. But you—"

Now what? I thought. It felt like there was another attack coming.

"You think you're pretty great, huh?"

"What are you talking about?"

"You think I'm going to be impressed by your watch, your jacket, your Porsche. But I'm not. Not at all. I just think it's ridiculous."

"All right."

"Do you want to become the best in the world? Or the one who earns the most and can traipse around in this kind of gear?"

"Best in the world!"

"Good. Because if you become the best in the world, you'll get the other stuff too. But if you're just after the money, you won't end up with anything, you get that?"

"I get it."

"Think about it, and let me know," he said, and we concluded the meeting. I left and felt, Okay, I'll think about it. I can play it a little cool too and let him wait. But I'd hardly got into my car before I started feeling antsy. I phoned him up.

"Listen, I don't like waiting, I want to start working with you right away."

He was silent.

"All right," he said. "But if you're going to work with me, you have to do what I tell you."

"Sure, absolutely."

"You're going to sell your cars. You're going to sell your watches and start training three times as hard. Because your stats are crap."

Your stats are crap! I should have told him to go to hell. Sell my cars? What did they have to do with him? He was going too far, no doubt about it. Still, he was right, wasn't he? I gave him my Porsche Turbo. Not just to be a good boy; for its own sake. It was just as well I got rid of that car. I was going to kill myself in it. Things didn't stop there, though.

I started driving around in the club's lame little Fiat Stilo, and I put away my gold watch. I put on an ugly Nike watch instead, and went around in warmups again. Things were going to be tough now, and I trained for all I was worth. I pushed myself to the limit, and it struck me that all that stuff was true. I had been too pleased with myself, thinking I was all that great. But it was the wrong attitude.

It was true that I hadn't scored enough goals and I'd been too lazy. I hadn't been motivated enough. I was realizing that even more, and began to give everything I had in practice and matches. But it's true, it isn't easy to change overnight. You start off at full tilt, then you can't be bothered. Fortunately, I didn't have a chance to slack off. Mino was on me like a leech.

"You like it when people tell you you're the best, don't you?"

"Yeah, maybe."

"But that's not true. You're not the best. You're shit. You're nothing. You've got to work harder."

"You're the one who's shit. All you do is nag. You should train yourself."

"Go fuck yourself."

"Fuck you."

Things often got aggressive between us, or rather, it *seemed* aggressive. That's how we were brought up, and of course I got it, that whole attitude, "You're nothing," and all that, was just his way of getting me to change my attitude, and I really think he succeeded. I started saying those things to myself.

"You're nothing, Zlatan. You're shit. You're not even half as good as you think you are! You've got to work harder."

It got me going, and it got me more of a winner's mind-set. There was no more talk of getting sent home by the coach. I put everything into every situation and I wanted to win every little match or competition, even in practice, and sure, I had some pain then in my left groin, but I didn't care. I just kept going. I had no intention of giving in. Didn't even care that it was getting worse and worse. I gritted my teeth. Several other players on the squad were injured then. I didn't want to give the manager any more problems, and I often played on painkillers. Tried to just ignore it. But Mino could see it—he realized. He wanted me to work hard, not break myself.

"This can't go on, fella," he said. "You can't play injured." I finally started taking it seriously and went to see a specialist, and it was decided that I would have an operation.

At the Rotterdam University Hospital they inserted a reinforcement in my left groin, and afterward I had to rebuild my strength in the club's training pool. That was no fun. Mino told the physio that I'd had it too easy.

"This guy has just been goofing off, having fun. Now he's got to be made to fight and tire himself out! Really give it to him." I had to wear a damned heart monitor and some kind of life vest that held me up, and then I would run in the water until I reached my absolute maximum level, and afterward I was ready to puke my guts out. I collapsed by the edge of the pool. I just had to rest. I couldn't move. I was totally exhausted, and one time I needed to pee. It just got worse and worse. There was no way I'd make it to the toilet. There was a hole by the side of the pool so I pissed into that hole. What else could I do? I was completely finished.

We had a disciplinary rule at Ajax: we weren't allowed to go and eat until they said, "Dismissed," and I would often make a break for it as soon as I heard the first syllable. I was always ravenously hungry. Now I couldn't even raise my head. No matter how much they shouted, I just lay there like a wreck by the side of the pool.

———

I kept that up for two weeks, and the strange thing is, it wasn't just hard work. There was something pleasant in that pain. I enjoyed the opportunity to exert myself to the point of exhaustion, and I started to understand what hard work means. I entered a new phase and felt stronger than I had for a long time. When I returned after my physiotherapy, I gave everything I had on the pitch, and now I started to dominate.

I gained self-confidence, and posters started appearing—"Zlatan, the son of God," that sort of thing. People shouted my name. I became better than ever, and of course it was terrific, but it was also the same as always: when somebody shines, there are others who get jealous. There was already some tension on the squad, particularly among the younger players, who also wanted to get noticed and get sold to the big clubs.

I imagine that Rafael van der Vaart was one who wasn't entirely pleased about these developments. Rafael was probably one of the most popular players in the country then. He was certainly the favorite among those fans who didn't really like foreigners on the pitch, and Ronald Koeman made him team captain, even though Rafael was no more than twenty-one years old. I'm sure it was a massive ego boost for him, and he was also the main quarry for the tabloid press. He'd gotten together with some celeb chick, and maybe it wasn't so easy for him to deal with my successes on the pitch in those circumstances. I bet Rafael saw himself as the big star and didn't want to have a rival. I dunno. He was also desperate for a transfer, just like all the rest of us. He'd do anything to get ahead, I think. Then again, it's true, I didn't know him, and I didn't care, either.

This was early summer 2004, and the tensions between us didn't really explode until August. In May and June, things were still pretty cool. We'd secured the league title again, and Maxwell, my friend, was voted Best Player of the Series, and I was happy for him. If there's anyone I don't begrudge anything, it's him. I remember we drove to Haarlem to eat at the pizzeria where Mino had grown up, and I talked to Mino's sister there. There was one thing she said she was wondering about. It was about their father. "Dad's started driving around in a Porsche Turbo," she said. "It's a bit odd, really. It's not exactly the sort of car he's had in the past. Is it anything to do with you?"

"Your dad—"

I missed that Porsche, but I hoped it was in safer hands now, and that summer I really wanted to stay away from crazy stuff and just focus on soccer. The European Championship tournament was coming up in Portugal. This was my first big international tournament where I was an established member of the Swedish national squad, and I remember Henrik Larsson phoned. "Henke," as I call him, was a role model for me. He was finishing up his time at Celtic then. He would be sold to Barcelona after that summer and, right after our loss to Senegal in the World Cup, he'd declared, "I'm not going to play for the national team any longer. I want to focus on my family." Of course, you had to buy it, especially from a guy like him.

But he was missed. We were going to be playing in the same group as Italy and needed all the strong players we could get ahold of, and I guess most people had lost hope in him then. But now he was saying he regretted his decision and wanted back in, and that made me perk up.

Now it would be me and him up front. That would make us stronger. I could sense each day how the pressure on us was increasing, and there was more and more talk about how this could be my big international breakthrough, and I realized everybody was going to be watching me, including scouts and coaches from abroad. In the days before we left for the tournament, the fans and the journalists were swarming around me, and in situations like that it was nice to have Henke there. He'd been involved in some high-level uproar himself, but the commotion surrounding me was absolutely insane then. I'll never forget how I asked him later on, "Henke, what should I do? If anybody should know, it's you. How should I deal with all this?"

"Sorry, Zlatan. You're on your own now. There's no player in Sweden who's ever experienced this kind of circus before!"

There was a Norwegian who turned up one time with a damn orange. People had been going on about oranges ever since John Carew, who was with Valencia, had criticized my playing and I responded, "What John Carew does with a soccer ball, I can do with an orange." Now this Norwegian journalist was there and wanted me to show what I could do with a piece of fruit.

But, I mean, come on, why should I make that guy famous as well? Why should I perform his little trick?

"You can take your orange, peel it, and eat it up. It'll give you some good vitamins," I said, and of course, that became a thing in the media as well—get a load of him, all cocky and arrogant—and there was more and more being said about how my relationship with the media was so tense.

Really, though, was that so strange?

11

Nobody knew about Helena and me, not even her mom. We'd made a huge effort to keep it a secret. The tiniest thing about me made headlines, and we didn't want journalists to go digging around in our relationship before we even knew where it was going.

We did everything we could to throw them off our trail, and early on we benefited from our differences. Nobody could believe I was with someone like her, a career woman eleven years older than me. If we were spotted in the same place, like a hotel or something, the dime still didn't drop, and that was lucky. That helped us. All that sneaking around had its price, though.

Helena lost some friends and felt isolated and alone, and I got more furious than ever with the media. The previous year, I'd flown to Gothenburg to play in an international match against San Marino. Things had started to loosen up at Ajax by then, and I was in a good mood and was talking fairly freely, like in the old days, including with a journalist from the tabloid. I really hadn't forgotten what that paper did with the episode at Spy Bar. Even so, I didn't want to hold a grudge, so I was chatting away, even talking about starting a family in the future—nothing unusual, not at all. It was just idle chat—stuff like It'd be nice to have kids sometime in the future. But do you know what that journalist did?

He wrote up his article in the form of a personal ad: "Who wants to win the Champions League with me? Sporty guy, aged twenty-one, 6-foot-4, 185 pounds with dark hair and eyes, seeks woman of suitable age for a serious relationship," he wrote, and what do you think? Was I happy? I was outraged. I mean, what sort of respect did that show? A personal ad! I wanted to deck the bastard, so it wasn't a very happy occasion when I encountered him the very next day in the dark tunnel in the stadium leading out to the pitch.

If I understood correctly, the paper had already heard I was furious. I think it was somebody from the national team who'd tipped them off, and now he wanted to apologize and get back to business as usual. There was already a load of money to be made off my name in those days. Believe me, I wasn't having any of it, and I guess I should be happy I restrained myself fairly well. I managed to restrict it to hissing, "What kind of clown are you? And what the fuck are you trying to say? That I've got problems with girls or something?"

"I'm sorry, I just wanted to—" He was spluttering. He couldn't utter a coherent sentence.

"I'm never gonna speak to you again," I yelled, and walked off, and honestly, I thought I'd frightened him, or at least got them at the paper to behave with more respect in the future. But it got worse. We won the international match 5–0 and I scored two goals. So what do you think *Aftonbladet* ran as a headline the next day, "Go Sweden"? "Next Stop: The European Championships"? Not quite! They went with "Shame on You, Zlatan!," although it wasn't exactly as if I'd pulled my pants down or thrashed the referee.

I'd taken a penalty—which went in. The score stood at 4–0, and I'd been fouled inside the penalty area. Okay, sure, Lars Lagerbäck had his list of penalty kickers and Kim Källström was at the top of that list, but he'd just scored a goal and I thought, This is my thing, I'm really in form, I'm up for it, and when Kim came up I moved the ball to the other side of my body, as if to say, Don't take my toy away, and he put out his hand—like, Give it here! I slapped his hand, gave him five instead, placed the ball on the penalty spot and kicked it, no more than that—it wasn't the best thing I've ever done and I did apologize afterward, but come on, it wasn't the Balkan War. It wasn't a housing project riot. It was a goal in a soccer match. Even so, the paper got six pages out of it, and I didn't get it. What the hell, coming out with personal ads and "Shame on You, Zlatan!" when we won 5–0?

"If anybody should be ashamed, it's *Aftonbladet,*" I said at a press conference the following day.

———

After that, I boycotted that paper, and when the European Championship tournament got under way in Portugal, there was no cause for a thaw in relations. I continued the war, but I was running a risk. If I didn't talk to them, they had nothing to lose, and the last thing I wanted was for the relationship between Helena and me to get out. That would be a disaster for our final preparations, so we had to be careful. What could I do? I missed her.

"Can't you come down here?" I asked. She couldn't. She had too much to do. But then, some of her bosses had bought tickets to the championships and couldn't go. They asked, "Does anybody else want to go instead?" and she thought, It's a sign, I'll go—and she came along for a few days. As usual, we snuck around, and not even anybody on the national squad took any notice of her. The only one who seemed to suspect something was going on with her was Bert Karlsson, a Swedish media figure and businessman who bumped into her at the airport and wondered what a girl like her was doing among all the soccer fans in their replica shirts and silly hats. We still managed to keep it under wraps, and I could focus on soccer.

We were a great bunch on the national team. We were all good guys—well, there was one prima donna among us. The prima donna was all like, "At Arsenal, you know, this is how we do it. That's how you ought to do it. Because they know about that stuff at Arsenal, and I play for them." Pretty much like that.

That made me furious. "My back is killing me," he said. Oh dear, oh dear. "I can't go in the regular bus. I need my own bus. I need this, I need that." I mean, who the hell did he think he was, coming along and lording it over us? Lars Lagerbäck talked things over with me about him.

"Please, Zlatan, try to handle this professionally. We can't have any conflicts on the squad."

"Listen," I said. "If he respects me, I'll respect him. Full stop," and there was a fair amount of fuss about that.

Otherwise, though, my God, the atmosphere was incredible. When we came on for our first match against Bulgaria in Lisbon it was as if the whole stadium was in yellow, and everybody was singing Markoolio's Euro 2004 song, it was all so awesome and we totally annihilated Bulgaria.

It was 5–0, and people's expectations for us were ratcheted up. Still, it was as if the championships hadn't really gotten under way yet. The big match everybody was waiting for was the one against Italy on July 18 in Porto, and it was no secret that the Italians were out for revenge. They'd only managed a draw in their first match against Denmark, and of course none of them had forgotten their defeat to France in the previous European Championship finals in

Rotterdam. Italy was dead set on winning and they had an incredible team with Nesta, Cannavaro, and Zambrotta at the back, Buffon in goal, and Christian Vieri out in front, and sure, Totti, the big star, was out, having spat on an opponent in the match against Denmark, but still, I admit I was nervous meeting these guys.

This was my most important match up to that point, my dad was sitting in the stands and it was a major occasion. Right from the start, I sensed that the Italians respected me. They seemed to be thinking, What's that guy gonna come up with next?, and I battled with their defense. We weren't playing around. The Italians put on a fierce offensive and, just before halftime, Cassano, a young guy who'd taken Totti's place, made it 1–0 from a cross from Panucci, and nobody can say they didn't deserve it. The Italians pressed us hard. Gradually, we worked our way into the match and had some chances in the second half. Still, the match belonged to the Italians, and getting a draw against them is no easy thing. Italy is often said to have a crazy defense. Then, with just five minutes remaining, we got a corner from the left.

Kim Källström hit it, and things started to get messy in the penalty area. Marcus Allbäck was on the ball, then Olof Mellberg as well, and there was general chaos. The ball was still up in the air and I rushed toward it, and at that moment I saw Buffon running up and Christian Vieri standing on the goal line, so I leapt up and gave it a kick. It was a bit like kung fu. In the photos, my heel is level with my shoulder, and the ball flew in a perfect arc over Christian Vieri, who tried to head it, and there wasn't much room to spare between his head and the crossbar. But it went in, right in the top corner, and that was against Italy.

It was the European Championship. It was a backheel with just five minutes left, and I ran out, totally crazy, and the whole team came after me, just as crazy, all of them except one, who was running in the other direction. Still, who cares? I threw myself onto the pitch, and everybody piled on top of me, and Henrik Larsson yelled, "Enjoy it!" Just like that. As if he immediately grasped the magnitude of it, and okay, the match ended in a draw. But it felt like we'd won, and we made it into the quarterfinal against the Netherlands, and of course that one was tense as well.

The Dutch fans in their orange outfits and hats were booing and jeering at me, as if I were playing on the wrong team, and the match was incredibly close, with loads of chances. It was still 0–0 at full time, and we went into extra time. We had shots that hit the crossbar and the goalposts. We should have scored several times over. We ended up having to go into a penalty shootout, and it seemed as if the entire stadium was praying to God.

There were nerves on all sides and, as usual, many couldn't even bear to look. Others booed and tried to psych us out. The pressure was incredible. Things got off to a good start, though. Kim Källström landed his penalty, and so did Henke Larsson. It was 2–2, and I was up next. I was wearing a black hairband. I had long hair, and gave a little smile, I dunno why. But I felt pretty cool, in spite of everything— I was nervous, but, even so, there was no sense of panic—nothing like that, not at all—and Edwin van der Sar was in goal. It really should have gone in.

Nowadays, when I take a penalty, I know precisely where it's going to go, and it's in the net. That day, though, I had such a strange feeling, and that feeling hit me just as I approached the ball. It was as if I was just going to shoot, and I did. I just shot, as if it would be a surprise where the ball ended up, and I completely missed. I was totally off target. It was a disaster, and we were out of the tournament— Olof Mellberg missed too—and believe me, that's not a happy memory. It was shit. We had a good team. We should have gone much further. Still, those matches set off an entire course of events.

August is an uncertain time. The transfer window closes on the thirty-first, and there are rumors of transactions buzzing all over the place. People talk about the "silly season." It's still the preseason, and the papers haven't got much else to write about. Is he going to this team? Or that one? How much are the clubs willing to spend? Things get blown out of proportion, a lot of players get stressed out, and it was particularly evident with us at Ajax.

All the young guys at the club wanted to get sold, and people were casting nervous glances at one another. Has he got something in the works? What about him? And why isn't my agent calling? There was a lot of tension and jealousy, and I was waiting and hoping myself, but I still tried to concentrate on soccer. I remember we played a match against Utrecht, and the last thing I thought would happen was that I'd get substituted. But that's exactly what happened. Koeman waved me over, and I got so furious I even kicked an advertising sign by the side of the pitch, thinking, What the hell are you doing, putting me on the bench?

Even in those days I was in the habit of phoning Mino after matches. It was nice to be able to talk everything over with him and have a little moan about things in general, but this time I really let loose.

"What kind of idiot takes me out of the game? How can he be so stupid?," and even though Mino and I were rough with each other, I was expecting some support in this situation—along the lines of, Yeah, I agree with you, Koeman must have suffered a brain hemorrhage, poor you.

What Mino said was "Of course he took you off. You were the worst one on the pitch. You were shit."

"What the hell are you saying?"

"You were useless. He should've put you on the bench sooner."

"Listen," I said.

"What?"

"You can go to hell. Both you and the coach."

I hung up, showered, and drove home to Diemen, and my mood did not improve. When I got home, I saw someone standing at the door. It was Mino. He had some nerve, that idiot, I thought, and I hadn't even gotten out of my car before we were yelling at each other again.

"How many times do I need to tell you?" he roared. "You were shit, and you can't fucking kick over advertising signs. You need to grow up."

"Go to hell."

"Go fuck yourself!"

"Fuck you! I want out of here!" I screamed.

"In that case, you can move to Turin."

"What are you talking about?"

"I might have Juventus lined up."

"You what?"

"You heard me," and I had. It's just that I didn't get it, not in the midst of that blowup.

"Have you lined up Juventus for me?"

"Maybe."

"Are you the most amazing thing ever, you bloody idiot?"

"Nothing is certain yet, but I'm working on it," he said, and I thought, Juventus!

That was a little different from Southampton.

———

Juventus were possibly the best club in Europe back then. They had stars like Thuram, Trézéguet, Del Piero, Buffon, and Nedvěd, and while the club had lost the Champions League final to AC Milan the previous year, on paper at least there was no team that was anywhere near them. The players were superstars, all of them, and the club had just signed Fabio Capello, the manager from Roma who'd been after me for several years, and I really started to hope. Come on, Mino, I thought, bring this one home!

Juventus was run by Luciano Moggi in those days. Moggi was a tough guy, a power broker who'd worked his way up from nothing to become one of the bigwigs of Italian soccer. He was the king of the transfer market.

That guy had transformed Juventus. The club won their league year after year under his leadership. Luciano Moggi wasn't exactly known for being whiter than white. He'd been involved in a bunch of scandals with bribes, doping, and criminal trials and shit, and there were rumors that he belonged to the Camorra in Naples. Of course, that was bullshit. The guy really did look like a mafioso, though. He liked cigars and flash suits and, as a negotiator, he didn't stop at anything. He was a master at making deals, and he was an opponent to be reckoned with. But Mino knew him.

They were old enemies, you could say, who'd become friends. Mino had arranged a meeting with Moggi back when he was trying to get his business off the ground. It didn't get off to a good start. Moggi's office was like a damned waiting room. There were about twenty people outside, and everyone was impatient. But nothing happened. Time just ticked away and, finally, Mino blew a fuse. He stormed out, absolutely furious: What the hell, blowing off a meeting like that? Most people would probably just have accepted the situation. Moggi was a big shot. Mino has no respect for that kind of thing. If people are rude to him, it doesn't matter who they are. So he went looking for Moggi later that day at Urbani, the restaurant in Turin frequented by the club's staff and team members.

"You treated me badly," he hissed.

"Who the hell are you?" Moggi asked.

"You'll find out when you buy a player off me," Mino roared, and he hated the guy for a long time after that.

He'd even introduce himself to other soccer bosses, "I'm Mino. I'm against Moggi," and because Moggi was a man who made enemies easily, that was often a good line to use. The only problem was, sooner or later Mino was going to have to do business with Moggi, and, in 2001, Juventus wanted Pavel Nedvĕd, one of Mino's big players. Nothing was finalized, nothing at all. Mino had Real Madrid in the works as well, and he and Nedvĕd were only supposed to meet Moggi in Turin to discuss things. Then Moggi raised the stakes and called around to journalists, photographers, and supporters. He put together an entire welcoming committee before negotiations had even started, and neither Nedvĕd nor Mino could wriggle out of it.

Not that it bothered Mino, really. He wanted Nedvĕd at Juventus, and that coup gave him the opportunity to bargain for a better contract, but, for the first time, he was impressed by Moggi. The guy may have been a bastard that time, but he knew his game, and the two of them declared peace and became friends—"I'm Mino. I'm with Moggi," sort of. Not that they exactly cozied up together. Still, there was a certain respect there, and clearly a number of other clubs had dissed me. Moggi was the only one who'd been seriously interested. But it wasn't going to be easy.

Moggi didn't have a lot of time for us. We'd be able to meet him in secret for half an hour in Monte Carlo. That was when the Formula 1 Monaco Grand Prix was on, and I guess Moggi was in town on business. The Fiat Group owns both Ferrari and Juventus, and we were going to meet him in a VIP room at the airport. Traffic was terrible, and we couldn't get there by car. We had to run, and Mino isn't exactly in tip-top physical condition. He's overweight. He was huffing and puffing. He was all sweaty, and he wasn't exactly dressed for a business meeting.

He was wearing Hawaiian shorts. He had on a Nike shirt and running shoes with no socks and was drenched in sweat. We came barging into the VIP room there at the airport, and the air was thick with smoke. Luciano Moggi was puffing on a fat cigar. He's a bit older and bald, and you realize instantly that this guy has power. He's used to people doing what he says. Now, though, he just stared at Mino's clothes.

"What the hell are you wearing?"

"Are you here to check out what I look like?" Mino hissed back, and that was where things started.

———   ———

Around that time, we had an international match against the Netherlands in Stockholm. It was just an exhibition match, but none of us had forgotten our loss in the Euro 2004 tournament and, naturally, we wanted to prove we could beat the Netherlands. The entire squad was out for revenge—it was offensive, quite aggressive soccer, and early on in the match I got a ball outside the penalty area. I immediately had four Dutchmen on me. One of them was Rafael van der Vaart, and all of them were going for me. It was a tough situation, and I powered my way through and got the ball to Mattias Jonson, who was standing unmarked.

He made it 1–0, and afterward van der Vaart was lying in pain on the pitch. He was stretchered off with a torn ligament in his ankle, nothing serious. But he might miss a match or two, and he went and claimed in the papers that I'd injured him on purpose. I winced. What kind of shit was that? There wasn't even a free kick awarded, so how could he say that stuff about doing it on purpose? And that guy was supposed to be my team captain!

I phoned him up and said, "Listen up, I'm sorry, it's a shame about your injury, I apologize, but it wasn't intentional, you got that?"

And I said the same thing to the journalists. I said it a hundred times. Still, van der Vaart carried on, and I couldn't understand it. Why the hell was he going around trashing his teammate? It didn't make any sense. Or did it?

I started to wonder—because, don't forget, this was August and the transfer window was open. Maybe he wanted to fight his way out of the club? Or fight me out as well, for that matter? It wouldn't exactly be the first time somebody tried that kind of trick, and the guy had the media on his side down there.

I mean, he was the Dutchman. He was the darling of the gossip pages, and I was a bad boy and all that—the foreigner. "Are you serious?" I asked him when I saw him at practice. He clearly was.

"Okay, okay," I said. "I'll say it one last time. It wasn't intentional. D'you hear me?"

"I hear you."

He still didn't back down even a millimeter, and the atmosphere on the club got more and more heated. The whole team divided into two camps. The Dutch were on Rafael's side, and the foreigners were on mine. Finally, Koeman called us in to a meeting, and by that time I was completely obsessed with this thing. What the hell, accusing me of something like that? I was absolutely seething, and we all sat in a circle there at the meeting in our lunchroom on the third floor, and I could immediately sense it in the air. This was serious. The management insisted that we should patch things up. We were key players, and we had to get past this. But there weren't any openings right away. Rafael came out harder than ever.

"Zlatan did it on purpose," he said, and I saw red. What the hell? Why wasn't he giving this up?

"I didn't injure you on purpose, and you know that, and if you accuse me again I'll break both your legs, and that time it will be on purpose," I said, and, of course, everybody on van der Vaart's side immediately started going, "You see, you see, he's aggressive. He's nuts," and Koeman tried to calm things down.

"Now, we don't need to go that far, we can sort this out." Honestly, though, that didn't feel very likely, and we were summoned in to see Louis van Gaal, the director. He and I had argued in the past, and it was no fun having to go into van Gaal's office together with van der Vaart. I didn't exactly feel surrounded by friends, and van Gaal immediately launched into his power play.

"I am the director here," he said. Yeah, thanks for that information.

"And I'm telling you," he continued, "to bury the hatchet. When Rafael is injury-free, you will play together."

"No way," I replied. "As long as he's on the pitch, I'm not playing."

"What are you saying?" countered van Gaal. "He's my captain, and you will play with him. You'll do it for the club."

"Your captain?" I asked. "What kind of crap is that? Rafael has been going to the papers and claiming I injured him on purpose. What kind of captain is that? One who attacks his own teammates? I'm not playing with him—no chance. Never, ever. You can say whatever you want."

Then I left. The stakes were high. Of course, I had a boost from knowing that I had Juventus in the works. Nothing was signed yet, but I was really hoping, and I talked about it with Mino: What's happening? What are they saying? Our fortunes kept changing, and at the end of August we were going to play NAC Breda in the league. The papers were still writing about our conflict, and the journalists were on van der Vaart's side more than ever. He was their favorite. I was the thug who'd injured him.

"Get ready to get jeered off," Mino said. "The spectators are going to hate you."

"Good," I said.

"Good?"

"That kind of stuff gets me fired up, you know that. I'll show them."

I was up for it. I really was. The situation was complicated, and I told Koeman about Juventus. I wanted to prepare him, and discussions like that are always delicate. I liked Koeman. He and Beenhakker were the first ones who'd understood my potential at Ajax, and I had no doubt he'd understand me now. Who wouldn't want to go to Juventus? Koeman was hardly going to let me go willingly, and I knew he'd recently been quoted in the media saying that certain people seemed to think they were bigger than the club, and it was obvious he meant me. I had to choose my words carefully, and right from the start I decided to use a few expressions van Gaal had used with me.

"I really don't want this to turn into an argument as well," I said to Koeman. "But Juventus wants me, and I hope you can sort it out. An opportunity like this only comes along once in a lifetime," and sure, just as I thought, Koeman understood—he'd been a pro himself.

"I don't want you to leave us," he said. "I want to keep you here. I'll fight for it!"

"Do you know what van Gaal said?"

"What?"

"He said he doesn't need me for the league, that you'll do well anyway. He needs me for the Champions League."

"What the hell? He said that?"

Koeman went mad. He was furious with van Gaal. He felt that statement meant his hands were tied and limited his chances to fight for me. That was exactly what I wanted, and I remember I went out onto the pitch and thought that now it was do or die. It was a crucial match for me. The Juventus crew would be observing me closely. But it was crazy. It felt like the Dutch were spitting at me. They jeered and yelled, and partway up in the stands sat everyone's golden boy, Rafael van der Vaart, receiving applause. It was just ridiculous. I was seen as a bastard. He was the innocent victim. Soon, though, all that would change.

We were playing against Breda and, with twenty minutes remaining, we were ahead 3–0. As a replacement for Rafael van der Vaart we'd brought in a young guy from the Ajax youth academy called Wesley Sneijder, and that kid was good. He was an intelligent player. He scored 4–1. He broke through, and just five minutes after his goal I got the ball some twenty meters outside the penalty area. I had a defender on my back and I nudged and forced my way around him and broke loose, and then I dribbled past another guy. That was the beginning. That was the intro.

I made as if to shoot and got nearer the penalty area and feinted again. I was trying to find a shooting position. But I kept getting new defenders on me. They were swarming around me, and maybe I should have passed, but I didn't see any chances. Instead, I went forward with a burst of speed and some nimble slalom dribbling, spun round the goalkeeper as well, and used my left foot to slot the ball into the empty net. That was an instant classic.

It was christened my Maradona goal, because it was somewhat reminiscent of Maradona's goal against England in the 1986 World Cup quarterfinal. It was a dribble past the entire team, and the whole stadium exploded. Everybody went nuts. Even Koeman was leaping about like a madman, regardless of how much I wanted to leave him. It was as if all the hatred against me was transformed into love and triumph.

Everybody was cheering and screaming, they were all on their feet, jumping up and down—all except one, that is. The cameras panned across the roaring stadium to Rafael van der Vaart. He was sitting there, stock-still. He was expressionless, didn't move a muscle, even though his own team had scored a goal. He just sat there, as if my performance was about the worst thing that had ever happened to him—and maybe it was. Because, don't forget, before the kickoff, they'd all been booing me.

Now they were only screaming one name, and it was mine. Nobody cared about van der Vaart, and the goal was replayed on TV throughout that evening and the following day. It was later voted Best Goal of the Year by Eurosport viewers. But I was focusing on something completely different. Time was running short. The transfer window would not be open for many more days, and Moggi was kicking up a fuss. Or faking it—it was always hard to tell. Suddenly, Moggi announced that Trézéguet and I couldn't play together, and David Trézéguet was the big goal-scorer at Juventus.

"What kind of idiocy is that?" said Mino.

"Their playing styles don't fit together. It won't work," he replied, and that didn't sound good—not at all.

———

When Moggi got something into his head, it wasn't easy to get him to change his mind. Then Mino saw a way out. He realized that Capello, the manager, had a different view. Capello had wanted me for a long time, and sure, absolutely, Moggi was the director. But Fabio Capello was not one to be taken lightly either. That guy can put any star in his place with a single glance. Capello is one tough guy, and so Mino invited them both out to dinner, and he started off with a fierce opener.

"Is it true that Trézéguet and Zlatan can't play together?"

"What kind of nonsense is that? What's that got to do with our dinner?" Capello responded.

"Moggi said their playing styles don't work together, isn't that right, Luciano?"

Moggi nodded.

"So my question to Fabio is this: Is that right?" Mino continued.

"I don't give a damn whether it's right or not, and neither should you. What happens on the pitch is my problem. Just get Zlatan here, and I'll take care of the rest," Capello replied, and, really, what could Moggi do?

He couldn't give the coach instructions on what to do on the pitch. He was forced to give in, and of course Mino relished that. He got exactly what he wanted. Still, nothing was finalized, and the Dutch soccer gala was being held in Amsterdam.

Mino and I were there to celebrate Maxwell, who was receiving the award for Best Player in the league, and we were both happy for him. There wasn't a lot to celebrate, though. Mino was really worked up. He went back and forth, talking to the directors of Juventus and Ajax, and there were new problems and question marks arising all the time, whether they were real problems or just things invented to improve people's bargaining positions. The situation seemed deadlocked, the transfer window was closing the following evening, and I was completely beside myself.

I was sitting at home in Diemen playing on my Xbox—*Evolution,* I think, or *Call of Duty,* both awesome games. That almost helped me to forget everything. But Mino kept calling me every few minutes. He was annoyed. My bag was packed and Juventus had a private plane waiting for me at the airport. So, definitely, the club wanted me. They couldn't agree on a fee, though. There was one thing and another, and the management at Ajax didn't seem to think the offer was serious. The Italians didn't even have a lawyer there in Amsterdam, and I tried to pressure Ajax myself. "As I see it, I'm not playing with you anymore. I'm finished with you!" I told van Gaal and his guys.

Nothing helped. Nothing happened, and time was passing, and I was totally wrapped up with my Xbox—you should see me when I'm like that. I'm totally focused. My fingers dance over the controls. It's like a fever. All my frustration came out in the game. I was just clicking away while Mino was fighting to clinch the deal. He was tearing his hair out. Why couldn't Moggi even send a lawyer to Amsterdam? What kind of blasé style was that?

It could have been part of the game, of course. Difficult to tell. Nothing felt certain, and Mino decided to make a move. He phoned his own lawyer. "Get on a flight to Amsterdam," he told him, "and pretend you represent Juventus," and sure enough, the lawyer flew in and played his little charade, and that helped: the negotiations picked up. They didn't come to an agreement, though, and, finally, Mino lost it. He phoned again.

"Fuck it," he said. "Bring your lawyer and get on a plane here. We'll hammer it out here." I put down my game controller and headed out—I barely locked the door, in fact.

I just went straight to the stadium, where the club's management was sitting with Mino's lawyer, and there was no mistaking that everybody got really stressed when I walked in.

The lawyer whirled around and said only one thing: "There's just one document missing, one single document. Then everything will be set."

"We haven't got time. We've got to go, Mino says we're not gonna bother," I replied, and we drove to the airport and Juventus's private plane.

––––––––

I'd already called my dad at this point: "Hey, this is urgent, I'm in the middle of putting together a deal with Juventus. Do you want to be here for it?"

You bet he did, and I was happy about that. If this came together, it would be my boyhood dream come true, and it would be great to have Dad there—me and him, after we'd been through so much together. I know he immediately headed to the Copenhagen airport and flew to Milan, where Mino's guy picked him up and drove him to the club's offices. That's the office where all the transactions in the transfer market are registered.

He got there before me and, when I turned up with the lawyer, I was knocked for a loop—like, Is that you? It wasn't the Dad I was used to, definitely not the one who used to sit at home in his workman's dungarees listening to Yugo music on headphones. This was a guy in a nice suit, a man who could pass for an Italian bigwig, and I felt proud—and really shocked, to be honest. I'd never seen him in a suit before.

"Dad."

"Zlatan."

That was really nice, and there were journalists and photographers standing around outside. The rumor had gotten around. It was big news in Italy. Still, nothing was finalized. The clock was ticking. There wasn't much time left to play around, and Moggi carried on making a fuss and bluffing, and, unfortunately, it was producing results. My price had gone down, from Mino's original demand of 35 million euros to 25, 20, and finally 16 million euros, and sure, of course, that was still a lot. It was twice as much as Ajax had once paid. But it shouldn't have been a big thing to Juventus. The club had sold Zidane to Real Madrid for 86 million euros. They could damn well afford it. The Ajax men didn't need to be worried. But they were nervous, or at least claimed to be. Juventus didn't even manage to scare up a bank guarantee. Sure, there may well have been a genuine explanation for that.

Despite all their successes, Juventus had made a loss of 20 million euros the previous year, but that was nothing unusual for big clubs—quite the opposite. No matter how much they took in, their costs always seemed to be getting bigger. No, that business about not having a bank guarantee, I wonder if that wasn't another trick, another negotiating bluff. Juventus was one of the biggest clubs in the world, and ought to be able to come up with the money. Without a bank guarantee, though, Ajax refused to sign anything, and more time passed. It was hopeless, and, sure enough, Moggi sat there in his chair puffing on his fat cigar, and people thought he had things under control, as if he was saying, This will sort itself out, I know what I'm doing. Meanwhile, Mino was standing a little way away with his headset on, screaming at the Ajax management.

"If you don't sign, you won't get any of the sixteen million. You won't get Zlatan. You won't get anything. You understand? Not a damn thing! And do you think Juventus is going to try and get out of paying? Juventus! You guys are nuts. But sure, do what you like, just pass all this up. Go ahead!"

Those were tough words. Mino knows his stuff. Still, nothing happened, not a thing, and the atmosphere kept getting tenser. I guess Mino needed to find an outlet for his energy. Or maybe he was just screwing around. There were loads of soccer things in there, and Mino picked up a ball and started doing tricks with it. It was wild. What was he playing at? I didn't get it. That ball flew around and bounced and hit Moggi in the head and on the shoulder, and everybody was wondering, What's this all about? Is he playing one-up in this situation? In the middle of a goddamn negotiating crisis? It wasn't exactly the time for games.

"Stop that! You're hitting people on the head."

"No, no, come on now," he countered. "We'll play for it. Try and get it, come on, Luciano, get up and show us your skills. Here comes a corner, Zlatan. Get in there. Head it, you dumb bastard."

He kept that up, and, to be frank, I have no idea what the legal staff and all the others in there were thinking. One thing's for sure: Mino gained a new supporter that day—my dad. Dad was just laughing. He was thinking, What kind of guy is this? How cool can he be? To do tricks in front of a big shot like Moggi. That was Dad's style. It was like singing and dancing in the wrong setting. It was doing his thing no matter what, and, ever since that day, Dad hasn't just collected cuttings about me. He also pastes in everything about Mino as well. Mino is my dad's favorite eccentric, because he noticed something: Mino wasn't just a nut job, he also landed the deal. Ajax didn't want to miss out on both me and the money, and their management signed at the last moment. It was past ten o'clock then—at least I think so—and the club's office really should have closed at seven. But we brought it home, and it took a while to sink in. Me, a pro in Italy? Crazy.

Afterward, we drove to Turin. On the highway, Mino rang ahead to Urbani, Juventus's regular restaurant, and asked them to stay open late, and of course it wasn't hard to persuade the staff. We were welcomed like kings just before midnight, and we sat down and ate and went over the whole deal. Honestly, I was especially happy Dad was there to see everything.

"Proud of you, Zlatan," he said.

———

Me and Fabio Cannavaro went to Juventus at the same time, and we held a joint press conference at the Stadio delle Alpi in Turin. Cannavaro is a guy who jokes and laughs all the time. I liked him immediately. He went on to be voted World Player of the Year a few years later, and he helped me out a lot in those early days. But then, after the press conference, Dad and I flew straight to Amsterdam, where we said goodbye to Mino before continuing to Gothenburg, where I was going to be playing in an international match.

That was a frantic period, and I never returned to my terraced house in Diemen. I left it behind, simple as that, and for quite a while I lived at the Hotel le Meridien on the Via Nizza in Turin. I lived there until I moved into Filippo Inzaghi's apartment on the Piazza Castello.

So it was Mino who went to Diemen to pick up my old stuff. When he entered the house, he heard some noises from upstairs, and froze. Was it a burglar? There were clearly voices coming from up there, and Mino crept upstairs, ready for a fight.

But he didn't meet any burglars. It was my Xbox, which was still on and had been humming along for three weeks, ever since I'd dashed off to take Juventus's private plane to Milan.

12

"Ibra, come in here."

Fabio Capello, possibly the most successful European manager of the past ten years, was calling me, and I thought, What have I done now? My whole childhood fear of meetings returned, and Capello could make anyone nervous. Wayne Rooney once said that when Capello walks past you in the corridor, it feels sort of like you're dead. That's the truth. He would usually just pick up his coffee and pass you by without so much as a glance. It was almost creepy. Sometimes he'd mutter a brief "Ciao." Otherwise, he'd just disappear on his way, and it felt as if you weren't even there at all.

I said that the stars in Italy don't jump just because the coach says so. That doesn't apply with Capello. Every single player toes the line when he shows up. People behave around Capello, and I know of a journalist who asked him about it.

"How do you get that sort of respect from everyone?"

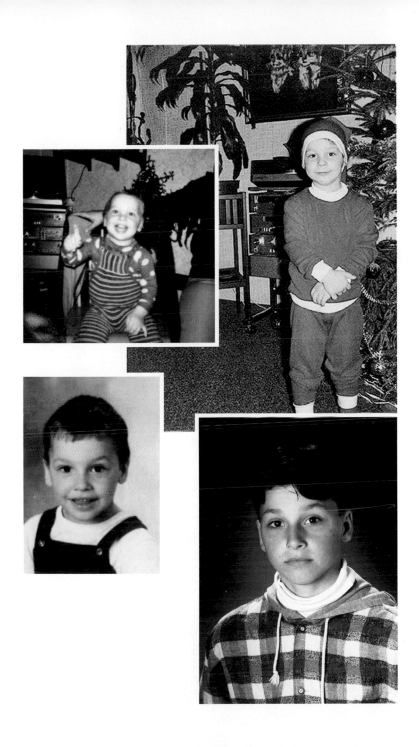

With Sanela on
Dad's Opel.

ROSENGÅRD
"MAN KAN TA EN KILLE FRÅN ROSENGÅRD
MEN MAN KAN INTE TA ROSENGÅRD FRÅN EN KILLE"
CITAT ZLATAN

You can take a guy
out of Rosengård
but you can never
take Rosengård out
of the guy.

ABOVE: Dad with
Vincent, Maxi, and me.
Dad's apartment.

RIGHT:
MBI's boys' team.

LEFT: Malmö FF's boys' team.

BELOW: With Lionel Messi in Barcelona.

ABOVE: With Gennaro Gattuso in Milan.

RIGHT: Celebrating with Maxwell in Ajax.

With Thierry Henry
in Barcelona.
© Reuters/
Gustau Nacarino

With Patrick
Vieira.

Capocannoniere
in Serie A.

LEFT: With Luciano Moggi and Maxi.

BELOW: José Mourinho suddenly turns up behind Pep Guardiola and me during the Champions League semifinal.
© *Bildbyrån*

"Welcome Maximilian"— the Ultras celebrate Maxi's birth.

With Helena and Maxi.

At home in Malmö.

Returning to Milan with Mino Raiola, Vincent, and Maxi.

© Bildbyrån

"You don't get respect. You take it," Capello replied, and that's something that's stuck with me.

When Capello gets angry, hardly anyone dares to look him in the eye, and if he gives you an opportunity and you don't take it, you might as well be selling hot dogs outside the stadium, basically. You don't go to Capello with your problems. Capello isn't your pal. He doesn't chat with the players, not like that. He's the *sergente di ferro,* the iron sergeant, and it's not a good sign when he calls for you. Then again, you never know. He breaks people down and builds them up. I remember one session where we'd just started on some positional training.

Capello gave a blast on his whistle and yelled, "Get inside. Off the pitch," and nobody knew what was going on.

"What have we done? What's this about?"

"You've been slacking off. You've been shit!"

There was no more training that day, and it was confusing, but, of course, he had something in mind. He wanted us to come back the next day all fired up like warriors. I liked that style, because, like I said, I didn't grow up with lots of cuddles. I like guys with power and attitude, and Capello believed in me.

"You have nothing to prove, I know who you are and what you can do," he said on one of my first days there, and that made me feel secure.

I could relax a little. The pressure had been terrible. A lot of newspapers had questioned the transfer, and they wrote that I didn't score enough goals. A lot of them thought I'd just be sitting on the bench: How can Zlatan make it on a team like that?

"Is Zlatan ready for Italy?" they wrote.

"Is Italy ready for Zlatan?" Mino countered, and that was exactly right.

You had to respond with cocky retorts like that. You had to be tough back to them, and sometimes I wonder whether I would've made it without Mino. I don't think so. If I'd landed at Juventus the way I arrived at Ajax, the press would have eaten me alive. In Italy, they're soccer mad, and where Swedes write about a match the day before and the day after, in Italy they keep it up all week long. It just keeps going, and you're being judged constantly. They look you up and down and, until you get used to it, it's tough.

Now I had Mino. He was my protective wall, and I was on the phone to him constantly. I mean, Ajax, what was that? A nursery school in comparison. If I was going to score a goal in a practice, I didn't just have to get past Cannavaro and Thuram, there was Buffon in goal as well, and nobody treated me with kid gloves just because I was new—quite the opposite.

Capello had an assistant called Italo Galbiati. Galbiati is an older fellow—I called him the Oldie. He was a good guy. He and Capello are a little like good cop, bad cop. Capello says the harsh, tough stuff, while Galbiati takes care of the rest, and after the very first practice Capello sent him over to me.

"Italo, let him have it!"

All the others on the team had gone in to shower, and I was completely exhausted. I would have gladly called it a day as well. But a goalie from the youth team came over from the sideline, and I flashed what was going on. Italo was going to feed me balls—bam, bam! They came at me from all angles. There were crosses, passes, he chucked the ball, he gave me wall passes, and I shot at goal, one shot after another, and I was never allowed to leave the box—the penalty area. That was my area, he said. That's where I was supposed to be and shoot, shoot, and there was no chance of taking a break or taking it easy. The pace was relentless.

"Go after them, harder, more determined, don't hesitate," Italo yelled, and the whole thing became a routine, a habit.

Sometimes Del Piero and Trézéguet came down as well, but most of the time it was just me. It was me and Italo, and there would be fifty, sixty, a hundred shots at goal. Now and then, Capello would turn up, and he's just the way he is.

"I'm gonna knock Ajax out of your body," he said.

"Okay, sure."

"I don't need that Dutch style. One, two, one, two, play the wall, play nice and technical. Dribble through the whole team. I can get by without that. I need goals. You understand? I need to get that Italian mind-set into you. You've got to get that killer instinct."

That was a process that had already started in me. I'd had my discussions with van Basten, and with Mino, but I still didn't see myself as a real goal-getter, even though my position was out there in front. I felt more like the guy who had to know everything, and there were still a lot of feints and tricks from Mom's yard in my head. Under Capello, I was transformed. His toughness was infectious, and I became less of an artiste and more of a bruiser who wanted to win at any price.

Not that I hadn't wanted to win before. I was born with a winner's mind-set. Even so, don't forget: soccer had been my way to get noticed. It was with all my moves on the pitch that I'd become something more than just another kid from Rosengård. It was all the Wow!'s and Check that out!'s that got me going. I grew with the applause I got for my moves, and for a long time I'd probably have called you an idiot if you thought an ugly goal was worth just as much as a nice one.

Now, though, I was starting to realize that nobody's going to thank you for your artistry and your backheels if your team loses.

Nobody even cares if you've scored a dream goal if you don't win, and, gradually, I got to be tougher and even more of a warrior on the pitch. Of course, I didn't stop that Listen/Don't listen business either. No matter how strong and tough Capello was, I held on to my own stuff. I remember my Italian lessons. It wasn't always easy with the language. On the pitch, it was no problem. Soccer has its own language. Outside, I was completely lost sometimes, and the club sent a tutor for me. I was supposed to meet her twice a week and learn grammar. Grammar? Was I back at school here? I didn't need that. I told her, "Keep the money and don't say anything to anybody—not your boss, nobody. Stay at home. Just pretend you've been here, and really, don't take it personally," and, sure enough, she did as I said.

She took off and pretended. I just said, "Thanks, see ya," but don't think that means I ignored the Italian.

I really did want to learn, and I picked it up in other ways, in the locker room and at the hotel, and I found it easy to grasp. I learned fast, and I was dumb and cocky enough to yak away even when my grammar was wrong. Even in front of journalists, I'd start off in Italian before switching to English, and I think they appreciated that. They thought, Here's a guy who might not be able to do it, but he's trying; and that's the way I did it with most things—I listened/I didn't listen.

Still, I was soon transformed both in my head and my body. I remember my first match with Juventus. It was September 12, 2004, and we were playing against Brescia, and I started on the bench. The Agnelli family, who owns the team, were up in the VIP section, and they were obviously checking me out—thinking, Is he worth the money? After halftime, I came on for Pavel Nedvěd, who's one of Mino's guys as well and who'd been honored as the European Player of the Year the previous year. He's probably the biggest training addict I've ever met. Nedvěd would go cycling on his own for an hour before our training sessions. Afterward, he'd go running for another hour. He wasn't an easy guy to replace, and sure, it's no disaster if things go badly in your first match. But it doesn't help either, and I remember I was running along the left baseline and got two defenders on me. The situation felt deadlocked. Then I made a burst, broke through, and heard the supporters shouting from the stands, "Ibrahimović, Ibrahimović!" That was awesome, and it wouldn't be the last time.

People started calling me "Ibra" then—it was Moggi who thought of it—and even "Flamingo" for a while. I was still really skinny. I was six foot five but weighed only 185 pounds, and Capello didn't think that was enough.

"Have you ever done any weight training?" he asked.

"Never," I said.

I'd never even picked up a barbell, and he regarded that as a minor scandal. He got the physio to drive me hard in the gym, and for the first time in my life I started to care about what I was stuffing into my face—all right, maybe there was still too much pasta, and that would become apparent later on. Everything was more thorough at Juventus, and I put on weight and became a heavier, more powerful player. At Ajax, the guys were sort of left to fend for themselves. Strange, really, with all those young talents. In Italy, we ate both before and after our training sessions, and before our matches we stayed at a hotel and had three meals a day together. So it was no wonder I got bigger.

I got up to 216 pounds at my heaviest, and that felt like too much. I got a little clumsy, and had to ease up on the weight training and do more running instead. But, overall, I changed into a tougher, faster, and better player, and I learned to be absolutely ruthless against the big stars. It's not worth it to step out of the way. Capello made me understand that. You've got to stand your ground. You can't let the stars hem you in—the opposite, in fact. They've got to get you going, and I moved my positions forward. I grew. I got respect—or, rather, I took it.

Step by step, I became who I am today, the one who comes out of a loss so seething with rage that nobody dares come near, and sure, that can seem negative. I frighten a lot of younger players. I yell and make noise. I have outbursts of rage.

I've retained that attitude since Juventus and, just like Capello, I stopped caring about who people were. They could be called Zambrotta or Nedvěd, but if they didn't give their all at practice, they'd hear about it. Capello didn't just knock Ajax out of me. He made me into a guy who comes to a club and expects to win the league, no matter what, and that's helped me a lot, no doubt about it. It transformed me as a soccer player.

It didn't make me any calmer, though. We had a defender on the team, a French guy called Jonathan Zebina. He'd played for Roma with Capello and had won the Scudetto with them in 2001. Now he was with us. I don't think he was doing very well there. He had personal problems, and he played aggressively in practice. One day, he tackled me really violently.

I went up to him, right in his face: "If you wanna play dirty, say so beforehand, and I'll play dirty too!"

Then he headbutted me—bang! just like that—and things happened fast after that. I didn't have time to think. It was sheer reflex. I hit out at him, and it happened right away. He hadn't even finished headbutting me. I must have hit him hard. He dropped down on the grass, and I have no idea what I expected to happen. Maybe a furious Capello running up, shouting. But Capello just stood there a little way off, totally ice-cold, as if the thing had nothing to do with him. Of course, everybody was talking, saying things like What happened? What was that about? The whole place was buzzing, and I remember Cannavaro—Cannavaro and I always helped each other out.

"Ibra," he said, "what have you done?" For a moment, I thought he was upset.

But then he winked, as if to say, that damned Zebina deserved it. Cannavaro didn't like the guy either, not the way he'd been behaving recently, but Lilian Thuram, a Frenchman, took a completely different view.

"Ibra," he began, "you're young and stupid. You don't do stuff like that. You're crazy." He didn't have a chance to continue. A roar echoed over the pitch, and there was only one person who could shout like that.

"Thuuuraaam," Capello screamed. "Shut your mouth and get out of there." Of course, Thuram made himself scarce, he was like a little kid, and I left as well. I had to cool down.

Two hours later, I saw a guy in the massage room who was pressing some ice against his face. It was Zebina. I must have hit him hard. He was still in pain. He would have a black eye for a long time, and Moggi slapped a fine on both of us. But Capello never did a thing. He didn't even summon us to a meeting. He said only one thing:

"That was good for the team!"

That was it. That's what he was like. He was tough. He wanted adrenaline. You could get into fights, and be as tightly wound as an animal. There was one thing you were definitely not allowed to do: question his authority or act recklessly. Then he'd get all over you. I remember when we were playing in a Champions League quarterfinal against Liverpool. We lost 2–0, and before the match Capello had explained our tactics and determined who would be marking who in Liverpool's corners. But Lilian Thuram decided he was going to mark another guy. He went for a different Liverpool player, and at that point they scored. In the locker room afterward, Capello did his usual round, back and forth, while the rest of us sat there on the benches in a circle around him, wondering what was going to happen.

"Who told you to mark a different player?" he asked Thuram.

"Nobody, I thought it was better that way," Thuram replied.

Capello breathed in and out a couple of times.

"Who told you to mark a different player?" he repeated.

"I thought it was better that way."

It was the same explanation again, and Capello asked the question a third time and got the same answer once more. Then the outburst came—it had been lying in wait inside him, like a bomb.

"Did I tell you to mark a different player? Is it me who makes the decisions here or somebody else? It's me, you hear? It's me who tells you what to do. You got that?"

Then he gave the massage table a kick and it spun toward us with a hell of a speed. In situations like that, nobody dares to look up. Everybody just sat there around him, staring at the floor: Trézéguet, Cannavaro, Buffon—each and every one. Nobody moved a muscle, and nobody would do something like what Thuram had done ever again. Nobody wanted to meet those same furious eyes. There was a lot of that. It was tough. Expectations were running high. Still, I continued to play well.

Capello had taken out Alessandro Del Piero to make room for me, and no one had benched Del Piero in ten years. Putting Del Piero on the bench was like benching the club icon, and it outraged the fans. They booed Capello and screamed at Del Piero—*"Il pinturicchio, il fenomeno vero,"* referring to his nicknames, which meant "The little painter, the real phenomenon."

Alessandro Del Piero had won the league seven times with Juventus and had been a key player every year. He'd brought home the Champions League trophy with the club, and he was loved by the family that owned the team. He was the big star. No, no ordinary coach would put Del Piero on the bench. But Capello was no ordinary coach. He never cared about history or status. He just went out with his team, and I was grateful for that. It also put pressure on me, though. I had to play especially well when Del Piero was on the bench, and, as it turned out, I was hearing his name less and less from the stands. I heard "Ibra, Ibra!," and in December the fans voted me Player of the Month, and that was big.

I was about to make a serious breakthrough in Italy, and yet—and of course I knew this—it takes so little in soccer. One minute you're a hero, the next you're shit. The special training with Galbiati had produced results, no doubt about that. Through being fed balls in front of the goal I'd become more effective and tougher in the box. I'd absorbed a whole range of new situations into my bloodstream, and I didn't need to think so much—it just happened: bam, bam!

Don't forget, though: being dangerous in front of the goal is a feeling, an instinct. You either have it or you don't. You can conquer it, sure, but you can just as well lose it again when your confidence disappears, and I'd never seen myself as just a goal-scorer. I was the player who wanted to make a difference at every level. I was the one who wanted to be able to do everything and, sometime in January, I lost my flow.

I failed to score a goal in five appearances. In three months, I only scored one goal—I don't know why. It just happened that way, and Capello started going after me. As much as he'd built me up before, now he was putting me down. "You haven't done a damn thing. You were worthless out there," he said, but still, he let me play.

He still had Del Piero on the bench, and I assumed he was shouting to motivate me—at least, I hoped so. Surely Capello wanted the players to believe in themselves, but they couldn't be sure and cocky either. He hates overconfidence, so that's why he does that. He builds players up and knocks them down, and I had no idea where I stood now.

"Ibra, come in here!"

————

My fear at being summoned will never leave me, and I started to wonder: Have I stolen a bike again? Headbutted the wrong guy? On the way to the locker room, where he stood waiting, I tried to come up with some smart excuses. It's hard when you don't know what it's about, you can only hope for the best, and when I went in, Capello was wearing only a towel.

He'd taken a shower. His glasses had fogged up, and the locker room was in just as much of a state as usual. Luciano Moggi loved nice things. But the locker rooms were supposed to be gross. That was part of his philosophy. "It's more important to win than to have a nice-looking place," he often said, and, okay, I suppose I can go along with that. But if there were four of us showering at the same time, the water would rise up past our ankles, and everybody knew it was no use complaining. Moggi would just see it as a confirmation of his theory:

"You see, you see, it doesn't have to be pretty in order to win"—so that's why the place looked the way it did, and Capello came up to me half-naked in that filthy room, and I wondered again: What is this? What have I done to you? There's something about Capello, especially when you're alone with him, that makes you feel small. He grows in stature. You shrink.

"Sit down," he said, and, okay, sure, of course I sat down. In front of me was an old TV with an even older VHS player, and Capello inserted a videocassette into it.

"You remind me of a player I coached at Milan," he said.

"I think I know who you mean."

"Do you?"

"I've heard it a lot of times."

"Excellent. Don't get stressed out by the comparison. You're not a new van Basten. You've got your own style, and I see you as a better player. But Marco van Basten moved more skillfully in the box. Here's a film where I've collected his goals. Study his movements. Absorb them. Learn from them."

Then Capello walked out, and I was left alone in the locker room and started watching, and, well, it really was all van Basten goals, from every angle and direction. The ball just thundered in and Marco van Basten came up again and again. I sat there for ten, fifteen minutes and wondered when I could go.

Did Capello have somebody keeping watch outside the door? It wasn't out of the question. I decided to watch the whole tape. It ran for twenty-five, thirty minutes, and then I thought, Okay. This ought to be enough. I left. I snuck out, and I have no idea whether I learned anything. But I got the message. It was the usual: Capello wanted to get me to score goals. I had to get that into my head, into my movements, into my whole system, and I knew it was serious.

We were leading the league, jockeying for the top spot with AC Milan, and in order to win I needed to keep scoring goals. That was the truth, nothing else, and I remember I was really working hard up there in the box. I was being marked as well. The opposing defenders were on me like wolves, and word had gotten around that I had a temper. The players and spectators tried to provoke me all the time with insults and abuse and shit. Gypsy, vagrant, stuff about my mom and my family—they'd shout all kinds of crap, and from time to time I blew up. There were some headbutts, or markings in that direction. I play best when I'm angry, though, and things really loosened up.

On April 17 I scored a hat trick against Lecce, and the fans went crazy and the journalists wrote, "They said he wasn't scoring enough goals. Now he's already scored fifteen."

I was the third-highest goal-scorer in the Italian League. People were saying I was Juventus's most important player. There was praise everywhere: it was all, "Ibra, Ibra." But there was something else in the air as well.

There were disasters lurking around the corner.

13

I had no idea the police and prosecutors were bugging Moggi's telephone, and that was probably a good thing. We and AC Milan were battling it out at the top of the league standings, and for the first time in my life I was living with someone. Helena had been pushing herself. She'd been working for Fly Me in Gothenburg during the daytime and in a restaurant in the evenings, while also studying and commuting to Malmö.

She'd been working too hard and her health was suffering, and I told her, "Enough now. You're moving down here with me," and even though it was a major adjustment, I think she thought it was nice. It was like she finally had time to breathe.

I'd moved out of Inzaghi's place into an amazing apartment with high ceilings in the same building on the Piazza Castello. It looked a little like a church, and there was a café called Mood on the ground floor where some guys who later became our friends worked. They sometimes served us breakfast, and although we didn't have kids yet, we had Hoffa the pug, and that chubby little guy was great. We'd buy three pizzas for dinner—one for me, one for Helena, and one for Hoffa, and he'd eat it all up, except for the crusts, which he'd just dribble on and fling around the apartment—thanks a lot! That dog was our fat baby, and we had a good time. Still, we were definitely from different worlds.

On one of our holidays with my family we flew business class to Dubai, and Helena and me knew all about how you're supposed to behave on flights and stuff. My family's a bit different, though, and at six in the morning my little bro wanted a whiskey. Mom was sitting in the seat in front of him, and Mom is great, of course, but she's not one for messing around. She doesn't like it when we drink alcohol, and you can understand that when you think about what she's been through. So she took off her shoe. That was just her way of dealing with the issue—she took her shoe and whacked Keki right over the head with it. Just bang, boff! and Keki went nuts. He hit back. There was a huge commotion in business class at six o'clock in the morning, and I looked at Helena. She wanted to sink down into the floor.

———

I usually headed to the training ground around a quarter to ten in Turin, but one day I was running late, and I was rushing around in the apartment, and we thought we could smell smoke. That's what Helena says, anyway. I dunno. What I do know is that when I opened the door to leave, there was a fire outside the front door. Somebody had gathered up some roses and set fire to them. We all had gas cookers in the building, and in the stairwell nearby there was a landing with a gas pipe along the wall. Things could have turned out really badly. There could have been an explosion. We fetched water in buckets and put out the fire, and I just wished I'd opened the door thirty seconds sooner. I would've caught that idiot red-handed and massacred him.

Starting a fire right outside our door? That's sick. And with roses too. Roses!

The police never found out who did it, and in those days the clubs weren't as careful about security as they are now, so we forgot about it. You can't go around worrying all the time. There are other things to think about. There was new stuff all the time, and lots had happened. Early on in Turin, I'd had a visit from two clowns from *Aftonbladet.*

That's when I was living at the Meridien hotel. *Aftonbladet* wanted to patch up our relationship, they said. I meant money to them, and Mino thought it was time to bury the hatchet. Remember, though: I don't forget. Stuff gets etched in my memory. I get my own back, even if it's ten years later.

When the guys from the paper arrived, I was up in my hotel room, and I think they'd been chatting with Mino for a while when I came down, and I immediately sensed: this isn't worth it. A personal ad! A fabricated police report! "Shame on You, Zlatan!" all across the country! I didn't even say hello. I got even more furious. What were they playing at? So I bossed them around, and I think I scared them out of their wits. I even chucked a bottle of water at their heads.

"If you were from my neighborhood, you wouldn't have survived," I said, and maybe that was harsh.

I was sick of it, and furious, and it's probably impossible to explain to all of you what kind of pressure I was under. It wasn't just the media. It was the fans, the spectators, the coaches, the club management, my teammates, the money. I had to perform, and if there weren't any goals I'd hear about it from every level, and I needed to vent. I had Mino, Helena, the guys on the team, but there was also other stuff, simpler things, like my cars. They gave me a sense of freedom. I got my Ferrari Enzo around this time. The car was part of my terms in the contract negotiations. There had been me, Mino and

Moggi and then Antonio Giraudo, the chief executive, and Roberto Bettega, the club's international guy, and we were sitting in a room discussing my contract when Mino said, "Zlatan wants a Ferrari Enzo."

Everybody just looked at one another. We hadn't expected anything else. Enzo was Ferrari's latest bad boy: the most awesome car the company had ever manufactured. Only 399 of them were ever made, and we thought we might have asked for too much. But Moggi and Giraudo seemed to view it as a reasonable request. After all, Ferrari is owned by the same corporate group as Juventus. It was, like, Of course the guy should have an Enzo.

"No problem. We'll get one for you," they said, and I thought, Wow! What a club!

Of course, they didn't get it. When we had signed, Antonio Giraudo said in passing, "And that car, that's the old Ferrari, right?" I was startled. I looked at Mino.

"No," he said, "the new one, the one they only made 399 of," and Giraudo gulped.

"I think we have a problem," he said, and we did.

There were only three cars left, and there was a long waiting list for them, with loads of heavyweight names on it. What were we going to do? We phoned the Ferrari boss, Luca di Montezemolo, and explained the situation. It was difficult, he said, virtually impossible. Finally, he gave in. I'd get one if I promised never to sell it.

"I'll keep it until the day I die," I replied, and honestly, I love that car.

Helena doesn't like to ride in it. It's too wild and bumpy for her liking. But I go nuts in it—and not just for the usual reasons. It's cool, awesome, fast: here I am, the guy who made it in life. The Enzo gives me a feeling that I've got to work harder in order to deserve it. It prevents me becoming complacent, and I can look at it and think:

If I don't make the grade, it'll be taken away from me. That car became another driving force, a trigger.

Other times when I needed a boost, I'd get a tattoo done. Tattoos became like a drug for me. I always wanted something new. They were never impulsive things, though. They were all thought through. Even so, I was against them in the beginning. Thought they were in bad taste. But I got tempted anyway. Alexander Östlund helped me find my way, and the first tattoo I got was my name across my waist in white ink. You can only see it when I have a tan. It was mainly a test.

Then I got more daring. I heard the expression, "Only God can judge me." They could write whatever they wanted in the papers. Scream anything at all from the stands. They still couldn't get at me. Only God could judge me! I liked that. You have to go your own way, so I got those words tattooed on me. I got a dragon as well, because in Japanese culture the dragon stands for a warrior, and I was a warrior.

I got a carp—the fish that swims against the current—and a Buddha symbol to protect against suffering, and the five elements: water, earth, fire, air, and wood. I got my family tattooed on my arms—the men on my right, because the right side stands for strength: Dad, my brothers, and later on my sons; and then the women on my left, closest to the heart: Mom, Sancla, but not my half-sisters who split with the family. It felt obvious then, but later I spent some time thinking about it: Who's family and who's not? That was later on, though.

I was focused on soccer. Often it's clear early in the spring who will become the league champions. There's some team that stands out. That year, though, it was a hard fight right to the end. We and AC Milan both had seventy points, and the papers wrote a ton about it. The stage was set for a drama. On May 18, we were going to meet at San Siro. It felt like the real league final, and most people thought

Milan would win, and not just because they had the home advantage. In the season opener against us at Stadio delle Alpi, we'd drawn 0–0. But AC Milan had dominated play, and many people considered them to be the best squad in Europe then, despite our strong team, and nobody was really surprised when AC Milan went to the Champions League final again. We had the odds stacked against us, they said, and things weren't exactly looking up after our match against Inter Milan.

It was April 20, just a few days after my hat trick against Lecce, and I was being praised everywhere, and Mino had warned me that Inter Milan would be marking me really tightly. I was a star. Inter Milan had to block me or psych me out.

"If you're going to survive, you've got to give it both barrels. Otherwise, you haven't got a chance," Mino said, and I responded the way I always do:

"That's no problem. Tough stuff gets me going."

I was definitely nervous. There's an old hatred between Inter Milan and Juventus, and that year Inter Milan had a really brutal defense. Marco Materazzi was one of them. To this date, nobody has been given more red cards in Serie A than him. Materazzi was known for playing dirty and aggressively. A year later, in the summer of 2006, he gained global notoriety when he said something really crude to Zidane during the World Cup final and got headbutted in the chest. Materazzi trash-talked and played rough. Sometimes, he was called "The Butcher."

Inter Milan also had Iván Córdoba, a short but athletic Colombian, and Siniša Mihajlović. Mihajlović was a Serb, so there was a lot written about that, how the match was going to be a mini–Balkan War. That was bullshit. What happened on the pitch had nothing to do with the war. Mihajlović and I later became friends at Inter Milan, and I've never cared where people come from. I don't give a damn about that ethnicity crap, and honestly, how could I do anything else? We're all mixed together in our family. My dad's Bosnian, my mom's Croatian, and my little brother has a father who's a Serb. No, it wasn't about that at all.

Mihajlović was really tough. He was one of the world's best free kickers, and he trash-talked a lot. He'd called Patrick Vieira *"nero de merda"* (you black shit), in a Champions League match, and that led to a police investigation and allegations of racist abuse. Another time, he kicked and spat on Adrian Mutu, who'd just started playing for us, and he got an eight-match ban for that. He could go off like a bomb. Not that I want to make a big thing of it, not at all. What happens on the pitch stays on the pitch. That's my philosophy and, to be honest, you'd be shocked if you knew what goes on out there. There are punches and insults, it's a constant fight, but to us players it's business as usual, and I'm just mentioning this stuff about the Inter Milan defenders to give you an idea that these guys were not to be taken lightly. They could play nasty and hard, and I realized immediately that this is brutal, this is no ordinary match. It's insults and hate.

There was a load of crap about my family and my honor, and I responded by striking back hard. There's nothing else you can do in that situation. If you waver, you'll be crushed. You've got to channel your rage to give even more on the pitch, and I played an extremely physical, tough game. It wasn't going to be easy to face Zlatan, not for a second, and at that time I'd been gaining in strength. I wasn't the skinny Ajax dribbler anymore. I was bigger and faster. I was no easy prey, not in any sense.

Afterward, Inter Milan's coach, Roberto Mancini said, "That phenomenon Ibrahimović, when he's playing at that level, he's impossible to mark."

God knows they tried. They gave me plenty of tackles, and I was just as tough in return. I was wild. I was *"Il Gladiatore,"* as the Italian papers put it, and, just four minutes in, Córdoba and I smashed our heads into each other, and we were both left lying on the pitch. I got up, groggy. Córdoba was bleeding heavily, stumbled off, and needed stitches. He returned with a bandage around his head, and nothing let up. Not at all. Instead, there was something serious brewing, and we cast dark looks at each other. This was war. It was nerves and aggression and, in the thirteenth minute, Mihajlović and I landed together after a collision.

For a moment we were confused—just wondering what had happened. Then we discovered that we were sitting on the grass next to each other, and the adrenaline rush came, and he made a gesture with his head. I responded by miming a headbutt. I'm sure it looked ridiculous; it was meant as a threat, but I just pushed my head against him. Believe me, if I'd really headbutted him, he wouldn't have gotten up. It was more of a touch, a way of showing: I'm not giving in to you, you bastard! But Mihajlović put his hand up to his face and dropped to the ground. Of course, it was all an act. He wanted to get me sent off. I didn't even get a warning, not then.

That came a minute later in a tackle with Favalli. It was an ugly match in general, but I was playing well and was involved in almost all our goal attempts, but Inter's goalkeeper, Francesco Toldo, was brilliant. He made one save after another, and we conceded one goal. Julio Cruz headed it in, and we tried everything to equalize. It was close, but we didn't manage it, and there was war and revenge in the air.

Córdoba wanted to get me back: he kicked me in the thigh and got a yellow card. Materazzi was trying to psych me out, and Mihajlović continued with his insults and his tackles and shit, and I was working hard. I powered my way through. I fought and had a good shot just before halftime.

In the second half, I shot from far away and hit the outside of the goalpost, right by the corner, and then I had a free kick, which Toldo saved with an incredible move.

There was no goal, and with just a minute left on the clock Córdoba and I clashed again. We collided and, reflexively, I gave him another whack, a punch to the chin or the throat. It was nothing serious, I thought, it was part of our fight on the pitch, and the referee never saw it. But it had consequences. We lost, and that was hard. The way things looked in the league standings, this match could cost us the Scudetto.

The Italian League's disciplinary committee examined video of my punch to Córdoba and decided to give me a three-match ban, and that was a minor disaster. I was going to miss the closing fight in the series, including the decisive match against AC Milan on May 18, and I felt I'd been treated unfairly. "I haven't been judged honestly," I told the journalists. All that shit I'd taken, and I was the one being punished?

That was hard, and, considering the significance I'd had for the team, it was a blow for the entire club, and the management appealed and called in Luigi Chiappero, the star lawyer. Chiappero had defended Juventus against the old doping charges, and now he maintained not only that my hit was part of a play for the ball, or at least in close connection with it, but that I'd also been subjected to attacks and insults throughout the entire match. He even hired a lip-reader to try to analyze what Mihajlović had yelled at me. But it wasn't easy. A lot of it was in Serbo-Croatian, so instead Mino went out and said that Mihajlović had said things that were too crude to repeat, stuff about my family and my mom.

"Raiola is nothing but a pizza chef," Mihajlović retorted.

Mino had never been a pizza chef. He'd helped out with other things in his parents' restaurant, and countered, "The best thing about Mihajlović's statement is that it now proves what everybody already knew, that he's stupid. He doesn't even deny that he was provoking Zlatan. He's a racist, he's shown us that before."

It was a mess. Accusations were flying back and forth, and Luciano Moggi, who was never afraid of anything, hinted at a conspiracy, a coup. The cameras that had caught my punch came from Mediaset, Berlusconi's media corporation, and of course Berlusconi was the owner of AC Milan. Hadn't the images been handed over awfully fast to the disciplinary committee? Even the minister of the interior, Giuseppe Pisanu, commented on the matter, and there were disputes in the papers every day.

None of it helped. The ban was confirmed, and I would be out for the decider against AC Milan. This had been my season, and I wanted nothing more than to be part of it and win the league. Now I'd have to watch the match from the stands, and that was tough. The pressure was terrible, and the bullshit continued to flow in from every direction, and now it wasn't just about my ban. It was about all sorts of things. It was a huge commotion.

This was Italy, and Juventus implemented a gag order: nobody was allowed to speak to the media. Nothing—no new arguments about my ban—could be allowed to disturb the final preparations. Everyone had to shut up and concentrate on the match, which was seen as one of the most important of the year in Europe. Both we and AC Milan had seventy-six points. It was a thriller. The match was the hot topic in Italy, and most people agreed, including the betting agencies: AC Milan was the favorite. There were eighty thousand tickets sold, AC Milan was on their home turf, and I was banned—me, who was seen as the key player. Adrian Mutu also had a ban. Zebina and Tacchinardi were injured. We didn't have our best gang together, while Milan had a brilliant lineup with Cafú, Nesta, Stam, and Maldini in defense, Kaká in the midfield, and Filippo Inzaghi and Shevchenko up front.

I had a bad feeling about it, and it was no fun at all when the papers wrote that my outbursts looked like they would cost us the league title. "He needs to learn to control himself. He needs to calm down." There was that kind of crap constantly, even from Capello, and it was awful that I couldn't be involved.

The team was incredibly motivated, though. The rage over what had happened seemed to fire everybody up, and twenty-seven minutes into the first half Del Piero was dribbling up the left side and was stopped by Gattuso, the Milan guy who works harder than anybody else, and the ball flew back in a high arc, with Del Piero rushing after it. He gave it a bicycle kick, and the ball flew into the penalty area and found David Trézéguet, who headed it into the goal. Still, there was a lot of time remaining in the match.

AC Milan put on an unbelievable amount of pressure, and, eleven minutes into the second half, Inzaghi broke free in front of the goal. He shot, and Buffon saved it, the ball bounced and Inzaghi got it back. He got a new chance, but was prevented by Zambrotta on the goal line and crashed into the goalpost.

Both teams had one chance after another. Del Piero hit the crossbar, and Cafú appealed for a penalty. There was stuff happening all the time. But the result stood. We won 1–0, and suddenly we were the ones who had the advantage, and not long after that I got to play again. A burden was lifted from my shoulders, and on May 15, 2005, we were meeting Parma at home at the Stadio delle Alpi, and there was huge pressure on me. Not just because it was my return after the ban. Ten leading soccer magazines had voted me the number-three striker in Europe after Shevchenko and Ronaldo, and there was even talk that I might win the European Golden Boot award.

I was going to have a lot of eyes on me in any case, especially since Capello had benched Trézéguet, the hero of the Milan match, and it felt like I had to perform. I had to be fired up—up to a certain point, that is. There couldn't be any new outbursts or bans; everybody made that absolutely clear to me. Every camera alongside the pitch would be on me, and as I entered the stadium I could hear the fans chanting "Ibrahimović, Ibrahimović, Ibrahimović."

It was thundering around me, and I was itching to play, and we scored 1–0, and later, in the twenty-third minute, after a free kick from Camoranesi, the ball came high toward me in the penalty area, and I'd been criticized for not heading well enough, despite my height.

Now I headed it for all I was worth into the net, and it was fantastic. I was back, and just a few minutes before the final whistle a message flashed up on the electronic scoreboard in the stadium: Lecce had drawn 2–2 against AC Milan, and it looked like the Scudetto was ours.

If we could just beat Livorno in the next round, we'd secure our victory. As it turned out, we didn't even need that. On May 20, AC Milan lost after leading Parma 3–1, and we were the champions. People were weeping in the streets of Turin, and we rode through the city in an open-topped bus. We could hardly get through. There were people everywhere, and everybody was singing and cheering and screaming. I felt like a little kid, and we went out and ate and partied with the whole team, and I don't drink that often. I've got too many unpleasant memories. Now, though, I just cut loose.

We'd won the championship title, and it was nuts. No Swede had done it since Kurre Hamrin won with Milan in 1968, and there was no disputing that I'd been a part of it. I was voted Best Foreign Player in the league and Best Player at Juventus. That was my personal Scudetto, and I drank and drank, and David Trézéguet kept egging me on. More vodka, more shots. He's a Frenchman and pretty uptight, but he wants to be an Argentinian—he was born in Argentina—and now he really cut loose. There was vodka flowing everywhere. It was no use resisting, and I got drunk as a skunk. When I got home to Piazza Castello, everything was swimming around me, and I thought, I'll take a shower, maybe that'll help. But everything kept spinning.

As soon as I moved my head, the whole world moved along with it, and finally I fell asleep in the bathtub. I was woken up by Helena, who just laughed at me. I've told her never to breathe a word about it.

14

Moggi was the way he was, but he garnered respect, and it was nice to talk with him. He made things happen. He got right to the point. He had power and he grasped things quickly. When I was renegotiating my contract the first time, of course it was an important thing to me. I was hoping for a better contract, and I really didn't want to antagonize him, I wanted to do the polite thing, treat him like the big shot he was.

The only thing was, I had Mino with me, and Mino doesn't exactly bow and scrape. He just strode into Moggi's office and sat down in his chair with his feet on the desk, without a care in the world.

"Goddamn," I said. "He'll be here soon. Don't wreck my contract. Sit over here with me."

"Go fuck yourself and be quiet," he said, and really, I hadn't expected anything else.

Mino's like that, and I knew the guy could negotiate. He was a master at it. Still, I was worried he'd ruin things for me, and I really didn't feel too good when Moggi walked in with his cigar and everything and growled, "What the hell, are you sitting in my chair?"

"Sit down and we'll talk." Of course, Mino knew what he was doing. They knew each other, him and Moggi.

They got a whole string of disrespectful stuff behind them, and I received a massive improvement in my contract. Above all, I got a promise of a new deal. If I continued to play well and remained just as important to the club, I'd become the highest paid on the team, Moggi promised, and I was happy. But then the fuss started, and that was the first sign that something wasn't right.

That second year, I often shared a room with Adrian Mutu in hotels and camps, and I didn't exactly have an opportunity to be bored. Adrian Mutu is Romanian, but he'd come to Italy and Inter Milan back in 2000, so he knew the language and everything, and he was a big help to me. That guy partied too. I mean, the stories he had! I'd lie there in the hotel room and just laugh at it all. It was crazy. When he was bought by Chelsea, he partied constantly. Of course, it couldn't last. He got caught with cocaine in his bloodstream and was sacked by Chelsea and got banned and caught up in a huge lawsuit. Later, when we were staying together, he'd been through treatment and was calm and clean again, and we could laugh at all the craziness. But, you understand, I didn't have much to contribute on that front. What did falling asleep in the bathtub one time amount to?

Patrick Vieira also arrived at the club then, and you sensed it straight away: this is a tough guy; and it was surely not by chance that we came to blows. I don't exactly go after the weaklings. With that type of guy, I give as good as I get, and at Juventus I'd got worse than ever. I was a warrior and, on this occasion, I ran onto the pitch, and Vieira had the ball.

"Give me the fucking ball," I yelled, and, of course, I knew exactly who he was then.

Patrick Vieira had been team captain at Arsenal. He'd won three Premier League titles with them and won the World Cup and the European Championship with France. He wasn't just anybody, not by a long shot, but I really screamed at him. I had reason to, and I mean, this was elite soccer, we weren't meant to be wiping each other's asses.

"Shut up and run," he hissed.

"Just pass me the ball and I'll be quiet," I answered, and then we went for each other, and people had to come and separate us.

Honestly, it was nothing, it was just proof that we both had that winner's mind-set. You can't be nice in this sport. If anybody knew that, it was Patrick Vieira. He's the type who gives a hundred percent in every situation, and I saw how he boosted the entire team. There aren't many soccer players I have that kind of respect for. There was a brilliant quality to his play, and it was amazing to have him and Nedvěd behind me in the midfield, and I got off to a good start in my second season with Juventus.

Against Roma, I got a ball from Emerson right on the center line, but I never brought it down. I backheeled it over Samuel Kuffour, the Roma defender. I backheeled it high and long, because I could see that Roma's end of the pitch was empty, and I rushed after it. I shot off like an arrow, and Kuffour tried to keep up. He didn't have a chance, he grabbed at my shirt and fell, and I brought the ball down on a half-volley, it bounced around my feet, and Doni, the goalkeeper, rushed out and I shot—bang—a hard shot that thundered up in the corner of the goal. "Mamma mia, what a goal!" as I said to the press afterward, and it looked like it was going to be a good year.

I won the Guldbollen in Sweden, the prize awarded to the best player of the year, and of course that was fun, but it wasn't without complications. The award ceremony was organized by that tabloid *Aftonbladet,* and I hadn't forgotten. I stayed at home.

The Winter Olympics were held in Turin the following year. There were people everywhere, with parties and concerts in the Piazza Castello, and in the evenings Helena and I would stand on the balcony and watch. We were happy together and decided to start a family—or rather, we just let it happen. I don't think you can really plan something like that. It should just happen. Who knows when you're ready? Sometimes we went back to Malmö to visit my family. Helena had sold her place in the country and we often stayed at Mom's, in the terraced house I'd bought her in Svågertorp, and occasionally I'd play a little soccer on her lawn. One day, I took a shot.

I really kicked it hard, and the ball went right through the fence. It made a big hole, and Mom was ready to kill me—she's got a temper, that woman. "Now get out of here and buy me a new fence. Go!" she roared, and of course in situations like that there's only one thing to do: you obey. Helena and I drove to the DIY center. Unfortunately, you couldn't buy just a few planks of wood. We had to buy a whole section of fencing the size of a shed, and it wouldn't fit in the car, no way. So I carried it on my back and on my head for two kilometers. It was like the time Dad carried my bed, and I got back absolutely wiped out, but Mom was happy, and that was the main thing, and like I said, we were having a nice time.

On the pitch, though, I was losing some of my flow. I started feeling too heavy. I was back up to 216 pounds, but now it wasn't all muscle. I was often eating pasta twice a day, and I discovered that was too much, and so I reduced the weight training and the food and tried to get back into shape. But there was some hassle. What was up with Moggi? Was he playing at something? I couldn't figure it out.

We were supposed to renegotiate my contract. Moggi kept stalling. He came up with excuses. He'd always been a tough guy, but now he was beyond the pale. Next week, he'd say. Next month. There was always something. It went back and forth, and finally I was fed up. I told Mino, "I don't give a damn. Let's sign now! I don't want to argue anymore."

We'd come up with an agreement that looked all right, and I thought, Enough is enough, I wanted it to be over and done with. Nothing happened then either, or rather, Moggi said, Fine, good, we'll sign in a few days' time. First we were going to play against Bayern Munich in the Champions League. That was at home in Turin, and during the match I encountered a center back called Valérien Ismaël. He was on me the whole time and, because he'd taken me down really badly, I kicked him and got a yellow card. It didn't stop there.

In the ninetieth minute, I was down in the penalty area and, sure, I should have kept my cool. We were ahead 2–1, and the match was nearly over. But I was annoyed with Ismaël and caught him with a scissor kick and got another yellow card. I was sent off, and, obviously, Capello was not happy. He chewed me out but good. That was only proper. What I'd done was unnecessary and stupid, and it was Capello's job to teach me a lesson.

Moggi, what did he have to do with it? He declared that my contract was no longer valid. I'd blown my chance, he said, and I went crazy. Was I supposed to miss out on my deal because of one mistake?

"Tell Moggi I'm never going to sign, no matter what he comes up with," I told Mino. "I want to be transferred."

"Think about what you're saying," Mino said.

I had thought about it. I refused to accept it, and that meant war, nothing else. This was it. This would have to do, so Mino went to Moggi and laid it on the line: Watch out for Zlatan, he's stubborn, crazy, you risk losing him. Two weeks later, Moggi finally turned up with the contract. We hadn't expected anything else. He didn't want to lose me. That still wasn't the end of it. Mino arranged meetings. Moggi postponed them, and came up with excuses. He had to travel, he had to do this, he had to do that, and I remember it clearly: Mino phoned me.

"Something's not right," he said.

"Huh? What do you mean?"

"I can't put my finger on it. But Moggi's behaving strangely."

———

Soon it wasn't just Mino who was sensing it. Something was up. Something was happening in the club, and it wasn't anything to do with Lapo Elkann, although that was a big enough thing. Lapo Elkann was the grandson of Gianni Agnelli. I'd met him a few times. We didn't really hit it off. A guy like that is on a different planet. He was a playboy and a fashion plate and had barely anything to do with the running of Juventus. It was Moggi and Giraudo who ran things, not the family who owned the club. It's true, the guy was a symbol of the club and of Fiat, and he was later included on lists of the world's best-dressed people, and all that. His scandal was a massive thing.

Lapo Elkann took an overdose of cocaine, and not just with anybody. He took it with transsexual prostitutes in an apartment in Turin, and was taken by ambulance to the hospital, where he lay in a coma, breathing on a respirator. It led all the news broadcasts in Italy, and Del Piero and some other players appeared in the media expressing their support. Of course, the whole thing had nothing to do with soccer. Afterward, though, it was still seen as the thing that sparked the catastrophe in the club.

I have no idea when Moggi himself found out about the suspicions. The police must have started questioning him long before the affair exploded in the media. As I understand it, everything started with the old doping scandal—where Juventus was actually cleared in the end. The police had bugged Moggi's phone in connection with that and got to hear a lot of stuff that had nothing to do with doping but which still seemed questionable. It seemed that Moggi was trying to get the "right" referees for Juventus matches, and so they kept him under surveillance, and, obviously, a load of shit came out—at least they thought so when everything was assembled, even though I don't set a lot of store by their evidence. Most of it was about Juventus being number one, I'm sure of it.

As always when somebody is on top, others want to drag them down into the dirt, and it didn't surprise me at all that the accusations emerged when we were about to claim the league title again. It looked bad, we realized. The media treated it like World War III. It was bullshit, like I said, most of it. Referees giving us preferential treatment? Come on! We'd struggled hard out there.

We'd risked our necks and didn't have any damn referees in our pockets—no way. I've never had them on my side. I'm too big for that. If some guy slams into me, I stand still, but if I crash into him, he goes flying several meters. I've got my body and my playing style against me.

I've never been buddies with the referees; nobody on our team had been. No, we were the best and had to be brought down. That was the truth, and there was also a load of suspicious stuff in that investigation. For example, it was conducted by Guido Rossi, a guy with close ties to Inter Milan, and Inter Milan emerged from the mess surprisingly unscathed.

A lot of things were either ignored or exaggerated in order to make Juventus out to be the big villain. AC Milan, Lazio, and Fiorentina, along with the Referees' Association also came off badly. Things were worse for us, though, because it was Moggi's telephone that was bugged and he was investigated from top to bottom. Still, the evidence was never that strong. Okay, things didn't look great either, that's true.

It seemed as though Moggi was putting pressure on the Italian referees to get good guys for our matches, and you can hear how he trashes the ones who've performed badly, including one called Fandel, who refereed Juventus's match against Djurgården. It was claimed that some other referees were held back in the locker room and given a dressing down after we lost to Reggina in November 2004, and then there was the thing with the pope. The pope was dying. No matches were supposed to be played then. The nation was supposed to mourn its Holy Father. Moggi was said to have phoned the minister of the interior, no less, and asked him to let us play anyway, according to the allegations, because our opponents, Fiorentina, had two players injured and two banned. I have no idea how much truth there is in that. That's probably the sort of stuff that goes on all over in this industry, and honestly, who the hell doesn't yell at referees? Who doesn't work on behalf of their club?

It was a mess—the scandal was often referred to as *"Moggiopoli"* in the Italian press, sort of like "Moggi-gate," and, of course, my name came up. I hadn't expected otherwise. Obviously, they were going to drag the top players into it as well. People were saying that Moggi had talked about my fight with van der Vaart and said something like I was heading in the right direction to leave the club. The guy's got balls, he'd said, or something to that effect. He was even alleged to have encouraged the fight, and people lapped that up, of course. That would be a typical Moggi thing, they thought, and a typical Ibra trick too, probably. It was bullshit, of course. That fight was a thing between me and van der Vaart, and nobody else.

In those days, though, people could say anything at all and, on the morning of May 18, 2006, I got a phone call. Helena and I were in Monte Carlo with Alexander Östlund and his family, and I heard over the phone that there were police outside my door. The police wanted to come in. They even had a warrant to search my apartment, so what could I do?

I left Monte Carlo immediately. I drove to Turin in an hour and met the police outside, and I have to say, they were gentlemen. They were just doing their job. Even so, it wasn't pleasant. They were going to go through all the payments I'd received from Juventus, like I was a criminal, and they asked me if I'd accepted anything under the table, and I told them the truth—"Never!"—and then they started poking around. Finally, I said to them:

"Is this what you're looking for?"

I handed over Helena's and my bank statements, and they were satisfied with those. They said, "Thanks," "Bye," "We like your playing," and stuff. Juventus's management, Giraudo, Bettega, and Moggi, resigned around that time, and it felt weird. They'd been landed right in the shit. Moggi told the papers, "I've lost my soul. It's been killed."

The next day, Juventus's share price crashed on the Milan stock exchange, and we had a crisis meeting in our weight room, in the gym, and I'll never forget that.

Moggi came down. On the surface, he looked the same as usual, well dressed and dominant. This was a different Moggi, though. Another scandal somehow involving his son had just emerged. This time, it was some kind of infidelity thing, and he talked about it, and about how insulting it was, and I remember I agreed with him. That was personal stuff that had nothing to do with soccer. But that wasn't what affected me most.

It was that he started to cry—him, of all people. I felt it in my gut. I'd never seen him weak before. That man always had control. He radiated power and strength. But now . . . how can I explain it? It wasn't long since he'd been throwing his weight around with me and declared my contract void, and all that. Now, suddenly, I was the one who was supposed to feel sorry for him. This world had been turned upside down, and maybe I shouldn't have been so bothered about him, and said something like You've only got yourself to blame. But I did really feel for Moggi. It hurt to see a man like him brought down, and I thought a lot about it afterward, and not just the same old stuff: you can't take anything for granted. I started to view certain things in a new light. Why had he kept postponing our meetings? Why had he made such a fuss?

Was it to protect me?

I started to think so. I didn't know for sure. That's just how I chose to interpret it. He must have known this was going to come out. He must have realized Juventus wouldn't be the same team as before, and that things would have been over for me if he'd tied me to the club. I would've had to stay at Juventus, no matter what happened. I believe he was thinking about stuff like that. Moggi maybe didn't always stop at red lights, or obey every rule and regulation. He was a talented businessman, and he took care of his players, I know that, and without him my career would have got stuck in a dead end. I thank him for that, and when the whole world is criticizing him, I'm on his side. I liked Luciano Moggi.

Juventus was a sinking ship, and people started saying the club was going to be relegated to Serie B, or even down to Serie C. That's how big a commotion it was. It wasn't possible to take in, not all at once. We'd built up such a team and won two league titles in a row— were we going to lose everything because of something that hadn't meant a thing to our game? That was just too much, and it seemed to take a while before the new club management grasped the seriousness of the situation. I remember an early phone call from Alessio Secco.

Alessio Secco was my old team manager. He was the one who used to call me to arrange training sessions: "We're starting tomorrow at ten-thirty. Be there on time." That type of stuff. Now he was suddenly the new director—completely crazy!—and I had a hard time taking him seriously.

In that first conversation, he gave me an opening: "If you get an offer, Zlatan, take it. That's my recommendation to you."

Then again, that was the last nice thing that was said to me. Afterward, things got tougher, and sure, I can understand that. One after another, the players left: Thuram and Zambrotta to Barcelona, Cannavaro and Emerson to Real Madrid, Patrick Vieira to Inter Milan, and all the rest of us who were still left were calling our agents, saying, "Sell us, sell us. What prospects are out there?" Uncertainty and desperation hung in the air. Things were buzzing everywhere, and there were no more remarks like the one Alessio Secco had made to me. Now the club was fighting for its life.

The management started doing everything it could to keep those of us who were still there, exploiting every loophole in our contracts. It was a nightmare. I was on my way up in my career. I was just starting to make a serious breakthrough. Was everything going to come crashing down now? It was an uncertain time, and with each day that passed I felt it more and more: I was going to fight. No way was I going to sacrifice a year in the second division. One year!—it would be more, I understood that. One year to get back up if we were relegated, and another year or two to get back to the top of the league and gain a place in the Champions League, and then we probably wouldn't have a team that could compete. My best years as a soccer player were in danger of being wasted, and I told Mino over and over:

"Do whatever it takes. Just get me out of here."

"I'm working on it."

"You better be!"

It was June 2006. Helena was pregnant, and I was happy about that. The baby was due at the end of September, but other than that I was in no-man's-land. What was going to happen? I knew nothing. During this time, I was preparing with the Swedish national team for the World Cup, which was being held in Germany that summer. My whole family was coming: Mom, Dad, Sapko, Sanela and her husband, and Keki; as usual, I was the one who was arranging everything—hotels, travel, money, rental cars, and all that.

It was already getting on my nerves, and at the last minute Dad decided not to come; it was the usual muddle, and there was a huge to-do with his tickets. What should we do with them? Who would get them instead? You can't say I was getting more balanced as a result of that, and then I started getting pains in my groin again, the same shit I had an operation for when I was at Ajax, and I spoke with the national team's management about it.

We decided I'd play. I have one fundamental principle: if things go badly, I don't blame my injuries. That's just ridiculous. I mean, if you're no good because of an injury, why are you playing? Whatever answer you give, it's wrong. You've just got to grit your teeth and go for it, but it's true, it was especially hard in those days, and on July 14, the verdict was finally handed down in Italy.

We were stripped of our two league titles and lost our spot in the Champions League, but, above all, we were relegated to Serie B and would start the season with a bunch of minus points, possibly as many as thirty, and I was still on that sinking ship.

15

Earlier, in September 2005, we'd played against Hungary in a World Cup qualifier at the Ferenc Puskás Stadium in Budapest. We basically had to win in order to qualify for the World Cup, and the pressure had been building for days before the match. It turned out to be an anticlimax. Nothing happened, and I never really got into the flow of the game. I was out of sorts and out of form, and when we'd played the full time the score was 0–0 and the spectators were just waiting for the final whistle.

Certain papers had clearly given me a failing mark. I was a disappointment, and I'm sure many people saw it as confirmation that I really was just an overhyped diva. Then I got a ball in the penalty area—I think it was from Mattias Jonson—and I didn't seem to know what to do with it either. I had a defender on me, and I dribbled out toward our half of the pitch without gaining anything from it. But then I turned, just like, bam!—because, don't forget, these are the kind of situations I play for, and that's why I seem to just wander around on the pitch so often. I save my energy so I can burst out with fast, aggressive moves, and now I took a few quick steps toward the baseline and the defender couldn't keep up, not at all, and I got a chance to shoot, not a good angle. It was too narrow, and the goalie was well positioned, and most people were expecting a cross or a pass.

I thundered on and, from that position, the ball doesn't usually go in. Chances are it'll go into the side netting, and the goalie didn't react. He didn't even raise his arms, and for a fraction of a second I thought I'd missed. I wasn't the only one. There was no eruption in the stadium, and Olof Mellberg was hanging his head as if to say, Shit! So close, and in injury time. He even turned his back. He was waiting for Hungary to kick it back in, and down in our goal Andreas Isaksson was thinking, It's too quiet, and Olof is shaking his head. The ball must have gone into the side netting. Then I raised my arms and rushed around the net, and the stadium came alive.

The ball hadn't gone into the side, not at all. It flew straight into the top corner from an impossible angle, and the goalie didn't even have a chance to lift a finger, and not much later the referee blew the final whistle, and nobody was giving me a failing mark anymore.

The goal became a classic, and we made it to the World Cup, and I really hoped it would be a success. I needed it, and, really, it felt good down there in our World Cup village in Germany, despite the concerns at Juventus. We had a new assistant coach since Tommy Söderberg had left, and it wasn't just anybody. It was Roland Andersson, the guy who'd told me, "Time to stop playing with the little kids, Zlatan," the guy who'd called me up onto the first team, and I was honestly touched. I hadn't seen him since he got the sack from Malmö FF, and it felt great that I was able to show him, You were right, Roland. It was worth it to invest in me. He'd taken some flak for it. But here we were now, Roland and me. Things had worked out for both of us and, in general, the atmosphere was good. There were loads of Swedish fans and, everywhere, you could hear the song that little guy sang, you know the one that goes, "Nobody kicks a soccer ball like him, Zlatan, I said 'Zlatan.'"

It had a good beat. My groin didn't feel good, though, and my family was making a fuss. It was crazy, really. It doesn't matter that I'm the little brother—only Keki is younger than me—I've become like a dad to all of them, and there was always something going on there in Germany. There was Dad, who'd canceled and his tickets were still unclaimed, and then there was the hotel that was too far away, or Sapko, my big brother, who needed money and then when he got some he couldn't get around to exchanging it into euros. And then Helena was seven months pregnant. She could look after herself, but she was surrounded by chaos and uproar. When she was getting off the bus before our match against Paraguay, all the fans swarmed around her like lunatics, and she didn't feel safe and flew home the next day. There was one thing after another, both big and small.

"Please, Zlatan, can't you straighten out this, and that?"

I was my family's travel coordinator in Germany, and I couldn't focus on my game. My phone was ringing constantly. There were complaints and everything you can imagine. It was completely nuts. I was playing in the fucking World Cup. Yet I was supposed to straighten out rental cars and shit, and I probably shouldn't have been playing at all. My groin was giving me trouble, like I said. But Lagerbäck was certain. I was going to be in, and our first match was against Trinidad and Tobago, and of course we were supposed to win, not just by one goal, but three, four, five. Nothing went our way. Their goalkeeper was in incredible form and we couldn't score, even when one of their guys was sent off. The only positive thing that came out of that match happened afterward. I said hello to the Trinidad and Tobago coach.

The coach's name was Leo Beenhakker. It was fantastic to see him. God knows, there are a lot of people who want to take credit for my career. Almost all of it is bullshit—ridiculous attempts by people to ride on my coattails—but there are a few guys who've really meant a lot. Roland Andersson is one, and Beenhakker is another. They believed in me when others doubted. I hope I can do similar things myself when I get older. Not just complain about those who are different and say, Look, now he's dribbling again, Now he's doing this and that; but think a step ahead.

There's a photo of that encounter with Beenhakker. I've taken off my match shirt and my face is beaming, despite the disappointment of the match.

Things never loosened up for me during the tournament. We managed a draw against England, and that was good. Then Germany destroyed us in the final game of the group stage, and my playing sucked, and I'm really not going to try to defend myself. I take full responsibility. Your family is your family. You've got to take care of them. Even so, I shouldn't have been their travel coordinator, and the World Cup was also a lesson for me.

Afterward, I explained it to them all, "You're welcome to come along, and I'll try to organize things for you, but once you're there you'll have to fix your own problems and look after yourselves."

———

I returned to Turin, and it no longer felt like home. Turin had become a place I needed to leave, and the atmosphere in the club hadn't exactly improved. There had been yet another disaster.

Gianluca Pessotto had been a defender on the squad since back in

1995. He'd won everything with the club and was identified with Juventus. I knew him pretty well. We'd played together for two years, and the guy was really not the cocky sort. He was incredibly sensitive and kind, and stayed in the background. Exactly what happened after that, I don't know.

Pessotto had just retired from playing and became the new team manager, replacing Alessio Secco, who'd been promoted to director, and maybe it wasn't easy to switch to an office job after life as a player. More than anything, the match scandal and the relegation to the second division had hit Pessotto really hard, and then some things had happened in his family.

One day, he was sitting as usual in his office, four floors up. He climbed up to the window with a string of rosary beads in his hand and threw himself backward out of it, landing on the asphalt between two cars. Absolutely unbelievable that he survived. He ended up in the hospital with fractures and internal bleeding, but he pulled through, and people were happy, despite everything. Of course, his suicide attempt was seen as yet another bad sign. It was a little like Who'll be the next one to lose it?

Things felt really desperate, and now the new club president, Giovanni Cobolli Gigli, issued a declaration: the club was not going to let any more players go. The management would fight to keep each and every one, and of course I talked to Mino about it. We discussed it all the time, and we both agreed there was only one way. We had to hit back. So Mino told the press:

"We are prepared to use all legal means to free ourselves from the club."

We weren't going to show any weakness, no way. If Juventus took a hard line, we'd come back just as hard. This was no simple battle. There was a great deal at stake, and I spoke to Alessio Secco again, the guy who was trying to be the new Moggi, and I could tell that his attitude had changed.

"You have to stay with the club. We demand it of you. We want you to show loyalty to the team."

"Before the off-season, you said the opposite. That I should take an offer."

"But the situation is different now. We're in a crisis situation. We will offer you a new contract."

"I'm not staying," I said. "Not under any conditions."

Every day, every hour, the pressure increased, and it was really unpleasant, and I fought with everything I had—with Mino, with the law, with everything I could. It's true, though: I couldn't be that pigheaded. I was still getting paid by the club, and the big question was: How far should I go? I talked it over with Mino.

We decided I would practice with the team, but not play any matches. Mino claimed there was a possibility of interpreting the contract that way, so, in spite of everything, I headed off to the pre-season camp in the mountains with the rest of them. The players on the Italian national squad hadn't arrived yet. They were still in Germany. Italy went on to win the World Cup. That was an incredibly impressive achievement, I thought, when you consider the scandals they had going on at home, and I had to congratulate them. Of course, it didn't help me. Our new manager at the club was Didier Deschamps. He was a former player as well, a Frenchman. He'd been the captain of the French national team when they won the 1998 World Cup, and now, in his new job, he'd been given the task of getting Juventus back into the top division again. The pressure on him was enormous, and on the very first day at camp he came up to me.

"Ibra," he said.

"Yeah?"

"I want to build the game around you. You're my key player. You're the future. You've got to help us get back."

"Thanks, but—"

"No buts. You've got to stay with the club. I won't accept anything else," he added, and even though it didn't feel nice—I mean, I heard how important I was to him—I stayed firm.

"No, no, no. I'm leaving."

I was sharing a room at camp with Nedvěd. Nedvěd and I were friends. We both had Mino as our agent. But we were in different situations. Just like Del Piero, Buffon, and Trézéguet, Nedvěd had decided to stay at Juventus, and I remember how Deschamps came up to us, maybe to play us off against each other, I dunno. He clearly had no intention of giving up.

"Listen," he said. "I'm expecting great things from you, Ibra. You were one of the main reasons I took this job."

"Don't give me that," I replied. "You took it for the club, not for me."

"I mean it. If you quit, I quit," he continued, and I couldn't help smiling, in spite of everything.

"Okay, pack your bags and I'll call for a taxi," I said, and he laughed, as if I was joking.

———

I'd never been so serious in my life. If Juventus was fighting for its life as a big club, I was fighting for mine as a player. A year in Serie B would make everything come to a halt. One day, Alessio Secco and Jean-Claude Blanc came up to me. Jean-Claude was a Harvard man, a bigwig the Agnelli family had brought in to save Juventus, and he'd been very thorough. He had his papers in order and had printed out a draft contract with various sums, and I thought, Don't even read it! Argue instead. The more you argue, the more they'll want to get rid of you.

"I don't even want to see it. I'm not going to sign," I replied.

"You can at least look at what we're offering, can't you? We've been damn generous."

"How come? It won't lead anywhere."

"There's no way you can know that if you haven't even looked at it."

"Of course I know. If you offered me 20 million euros, I wouldn't be interested."

"That's very disrespectful," Blanc hissed.

"You can take it however you want," I said, and walked off, and sure, I knew I'd insulted him, and that's always a risk, and in the worst case I could be without a club come September.

I had to play a high-stakes game. I had to keep it up, and sure, I realized I no longer held the best cards for negotiating. I'd played badly in the World Cup and hadn't been particularly good the past season at Juventus. I was too heavy and hadn't scored enough goals. I just hoped people recognized my potential. Only a year before, I'd been awesome and was voted Best Foreign Player on the team. There should be some interest among the other clubs, I thought, and Mino was also working hard behind the scenes.

"I've got Inter and AC Milan biting," he said early on, and that definitely sounded good. There was a light at the end of the tunnel.

It was still idle talk at that point, though, and we still didn't know what the situation looked like with my contract at Juventus. What chance did I have to get away from the club if they refused? I wasn't sure, and things were up and down every day. Mino was optimistic. It was his job to be, and I couldn't do anything but wait, and fight. It was already known in the press that I wanted to get out at any price. Now there were also murmurings that Inter Milan was after me, and the Juventus supporters hate Inter, and as a soccer player you're constantly surrounded by fans. They hang around with their autograph books and flags outside the gates of the training grounds, and they're often allowed to pay to come in and watch. There's business everywhere in this sport, and there in the mountains outside Turin at our preseason camp they were standing by the pitch, screaming at me.

"Traitor, swine," they roared, and other stuff like that, and sure, it wasn't nice.

Really, though, as a player, you get used to most of it, and those insults rolled off my back. We were going to play an exhibition match against Spezia, and what had I said about matches? I wasn't going to play them. So I stayed in my room and played on my PlayStation. Outside, the bus was waiting to take us to the stadium, and everybody was already down there, including Nedvěd, and, as I understand it, the bus was waiting with its engine running. They were massively impatient: Where the hell's Ibra? They waited and waited, and finally Didier Deschamps came up to my room. He was furious.

"Why are you sitting here? We're supposed to leave." I didn't even look up. I just carried on playing.

"Didn't you hear what I said?"

"Didn't *you* hear what *I* said?" I retorted. "I'll train, but I'm not playing any matches. I've told you that ten times."

"You goddamn well will play. You belong to this team. Now come on, right now. Get up."

He came over and stood right next to where I was sitting, but I continued playing.

"What the hell kind of respect is this, sitting here and playing?" he growled. "You're going to get a fine for this, you hear me?"

"Okay."

"What do you mean, okay?"

"Go ahead and give me a fine. I'm staying here."

He finally left. He was absolutely furious, and I sat there with my PlayStation while all the rest of them drove off in the bus, and if the situation hadn't been tense before, it certainly was now. The story was reported up the chain of command, of course. I got a fine, thirty thousand euros, I think. It was all-out war and, as in any war, you had to think tactically. How was I going to strike back? What was the next move? My thoughts were bubbling away inside me.

I had secret visitors. Ariedo Braida, a bigwig from AC Milan, came to meet me during the camp. I just snuck out and met him at another hotel nearby, and we talked about what it would be like to belong to AC Milan. I didn't like his style. There was a lot of: Kaká is a star. You're not. But Milan can make you into one. It was like I needed AC Milan more than AC Milan needed me, and I didn't feel particularly respected or sought after, and I would have been happy to say Thanks, but no thanks, but my negotiating position wasn't exactly ideal. I was too desperate to get away from Juventus. I had no trump card, and I was forced to return to Turin with no concrete offers.

It was hot. It was August, and Helena was heavily pregnant, and she had some stress symptoms. The paparazzi were after us all the time, and I supported her as best I could. I was in my no-man's-land. I didn't know anything about the future, and nothing was easy. The club had a new training facility. Everything from Moggi's era was going to be cleaned out, including his crummy old locker rooms, and I continued to go to practice sessions. I had to stick to my line. It was strange. Nobody saw me as a part of the team anymore, and I noticed at least one good thing: Juventus was no longer fighting for me as hard as before.

Who wants a guy who doesn't give a damn and just plays on his PlayStation?

———

There was still a long way to go, and the question was still: AC Milan or Inter? It should have been an easy choice. Inter hadn't won the league title in seventeen years. Inter wasn't really a top team any-more. AC Milan was one of the most successful clubs in Europe, in every respect. "Of course you should go to AC Milan," Mino said. I wasn't so sure. Inter was Ronaldo's old team, and the club seemed to really want me, and I thought about what Braida had told me up there in the mountains. "You're not a real star yet!" AC Milan had the strongest team. I was still leaning toward Inter. I wanted to join the underdogs.

"Okay," Mino said. "But remember, Inter will be a totally differ-ent challenge. You won't get any championship titles for free there." I didn't want to get anything for free. I wanted challenges and re-sponsibility. That feeling kept growing stronger, and even then I real-ized what it would mean if I went to a club that hadn't won the league in seventeen years and made sure they did it with me. It could raise everything to a completely different level. Like I said, though, noth-ing was set yet, not at all, and first of all we had to get lined up. We had to get off the sinking ship, and we'd have to take whatever came along.

AC Milan was qualifying for the Champions League then. That was a consequence of the whole scandal. The club was really a shoo-in in the tournament, but because the court had penalized the team with minus points, AC Milan was forced to play a qualifier against Red Star Belgrade. The first match was at San Siro in Milan. It was an important match for me too. If Milan made it into the tour-nament, the club would get more money to buy players, and Adriano Galliani, the vice president of AC Milan, had told me, "We'll wait and see the result, and then we'll be in touch again."

Up until then, Inter had been more interested—not that they had been easy to deal with either. Inter was owned by Massimo Moratti. Moratti is a big shot. He's an oil magnate. He owns the club, and, of course, he could also sense my desperation. He had reduced his offer on four separate occasions. There was always something, and on August 18 I was sitting in our apartment on the Piazza Castello in Turin.

Kickoff for AC Milan's match against Red Star Belgrade at San Siro was at a quarter to nine. I wasn't watching it. I had other stuff to do. Clearly Kaká played it right up to Filippo Inzaghi, who scored 1–0, and that eased some of the tension on the club. Soon after that, my cell phone rang. It had been ringing all day, and it was usually Mino. He was telling me about every stage in the process, and now he informed me that Silvio Berlusconi wanted to meet me, and that made me sit up, of course. Not just because it was him, but because it showed they really were interested. Still, I wasn't sure. Inter was my first choice. I realized, though, that this conversation couldn't exactly hurt us.

"Can we exploit this?" I asked.

"You bet we can," Mino replied, and he immediately phoned Moratti, because if there's anything that gets that man going, it's a chance to give AC Milan a smack in the face.

"We just wanted to let you know that Ibrahimović is going to be having supper with Berlusconi in Milan," Mino told him.

"Huh?"

"They've booked a table at Ristorante Giannino."

"Like hell they will," Moratti spluttered. "I'll send a guy over at once."

Moratti sent Branca. Marco Branca was sports director at Inter Milan. He was a really young, skinny guy, but when he knocked on our door just a couple of hours later, I learned another thing about him. He was one of the heaviest chain-smokers I'd ever seen. He paced back and forth in our apartment and filled a whole ashtray with butts in no time at all. He was stressed. He'd been tasked with getting the deal tied up before Berlusconi had a chance to do up his tie and head out for supper at Giannino. So of course he was worked up. He was going to screw the most powerful man in Italy out of a deal, no less, and Mino took advantage of that. He likes it when his opponents are under pressure. It softens them up, and there were various phone calls and figures being tossed back and forth. This was my contract. These were my terms, and during that time the clock was ticking, and Branca kept on smoking and smoking.

"Do you accept?" he asked. I checked with Mino. Mino said, "Go for it!"

"Okay, definitely."

Branca started smoking even more, and he contacted Moratti. I could actually hear the excitement in his voice.

"Zlatan's accepted," he said.

This was good news. This was big. I could tell from his tone of voice. It wasn't finished yet, though. Now the clubs had to negotiate their terms. How much would I be sold for? This was a new game, and sure, if Juventus lost me, at least they'd get a hefty sum. Before anything was settled, Moratti phoned.

"Are you happy?"

"I'm happy," I said.

"Then I'd like to welcome you," and I'm sure you can understand I let out a sigh of relief.

All the uncertainty of that spring and summer vanished in an instant, and the only thing left was for Mino to call the management of AC Milan. Berlusconi would hardly want to eat supper with me now. We weren't exactly going to chat about the weather, and if I understood correctly, the AC Milan crew had just had the rug pulled out from under them and were wondering what the hell happened. Is Ibra going to Inter now?

"Things can happen fast sometimes," Mino said.

———

In the end, I was bought for 27 million euros. It was the biggest transfer fee that year in Serie A, and I even got out of paying the fines leveled against me for playing on my PlayStation at the training camp. Mino magicked them away, and Moratti was quoted in the press saying my transfer was just as significant as when the club had bought Ronaldo, and of course that went straight to my heart. I was ready for Inter. First, though, I had to go to a meeting for the Swedish national team in Gothenburg, and I was expecting a nice, easy trip before things got serious.

16

We played against Latvia and won 1–0. Kim Källström scored for us, and then we had a day off. It was September 3, 2006, and Olof Mellberg's twenty-ninth birthday. He was captain at Aston Villa. We'd met on the national squad, and at first I thought he was really uptight, a little like Trézéguet, but he loosened up and we got to be friends. Now he wanted me and Chippen to hang out and celebrate his birthday—sure, why not?

We ended up in a place with photos on the walls on Avenyn, which is the main drag in Gothenburg. The papers called it a trendy hangout. Every bar I go to becomes a trendy hangout. Not here, though. The place was nearly empty. We were virtually the only ones there, and we sat and had a drink, totally relaxed. It didn't get much more exciting than that, and soon it was 11 p.m. We were supposed to be back at the hotel by eleven, according to the rules of the national squad. But we thought, What the hell. They can't be that strict, can they? We'd come back late before without getting into hot water.

Besides, it was Olof's birthday and we were sober and well behaved. At a quarter past midnight, we got back to the hotel and went to bed like good boys. That's all there was to it. My pals from Rosengård would hardly have bothered to listen if I'd told them about it. It was nothing, honestly.

The only problem is, I can't even go out and buy milk without the papers getting wind of it. I've got spies on my trail wherever I go. People send texts and photos—"I saw Zlatan at such and such a place, woo-hoo!"—and in order to make it not sound too dull they exaggerate, and then their buddies tell, and exaggerate a little more. It's got to be cool, at least a tiny bit. That's part of the deal, and most of the time I've got people who stick up for me—they'll say, "What kind of crap is that? Zlatan hasn't done a damn thing." This time, though, the papers were cleverer.

They turned the tables and phoned our team manager, asking not about us and what time we got back to the hotel, but about what sort of rules the national squad had. He told them the truth: everybody was supposed to be at the hotel by eleven o'clock.

"Zlatan, Chippen, and Mellberg got in later than that. We've got witnesses," the journalists said, and sure, the team manager is a good guy, normally he defends us. This time, he wasn't quick enough on the uptake, and I suppose you can't blame him. Who says the right thing every single time?

If he'd been clever and done what the guys in the Italian clubs do, he'd have asked if he could get back to them and then called and given them a good explanation for why we'd been out a bit later, like saying we'd had permission to be out, something along those lines. That's not to say that we'd get out of being punished—not at all. The basic principle should always be that you maintain a united front. We're a team, we're a unit, and then they can punish us internally as much as they like.

The team manager told them that nobody was allowed to stay out past eleven, and we must have broken the rules. All hell broke loose. People called me in the morning, saying, "You've been summoned to a meeting with Lagerbäck," and, of course, I don't like meetings. Then again, I knew the ropes. I'd been getting summoned in ever since nursery school. It was business as usual for me. It was my life, and this time I knew what it was about. It was nothing, and I didn't get worked up about it. I phoned one of the security guys I knew, who usually knew what was going on.

"How's it looking?"

"I think you can pack your bags," he said, and I didn't understand what he meant.

Pack my bags? Because I got in a little late? I refused to believe it. Eventually, I accepted the situation. What else could I do? I packed my stuff and didn't even invent any excuses. The whole thing was too ridiculous for that. The truth would have to do for once. I wasn't even going to blame my brother. I just strolled in, and there was Lagerbäck with the whole crew, and then Mellberg and Chippen. They weren't as cool about it as me; they weren't used to it the way I was. I felt right at home. It was almost like I'd been missing this, like I'd been too well behaved and should've been living more on the edge.

"We have decided to send you home immediately," Lagerbäck began, and everybody cringed. "What have you got to say to that?"

"I apologize," said Chippen. "It was a really stupid thing to do."

"I apologize as well," said Mellberg. "So . . . what are you going to say to the media?" he added, and there was some discussion about that. I was silent through the whole thing. I had nothing to say about it, and maybe Lagerbäck thought that was odd. Most of the time, I don't exactly hold my tongue.

"And how about you, Zlatan? What do you say?"

"I've got nothing to say."

"What do you mean, 'nothing'?"

"Just that. Nothing!"

That made them worried. I'm sure they'd have been more at ease if I'd come out all cocky. That would've been my style. This was something new. It was stressing them out—they were thinking, What's Zlatan planning now? And the more confused they got, the calmer I felt. It was strange, in a way. My silence was upsetting the balance. I got the upper hand. Everything felt so familiar. It was Wessels department store again. It was school. It was the Malmö FF youth squad, and I was listening to Lagerbäck's little lecture on how clear they'd been about the rules with the same level of interest I'd listened to the teachers at school, thinking, You just go ahead and yak, I don't give a shit. There was one thing that pissed me off, though. It was when he said, "We've decided that the three of you will not play against Liechtenstein."

Now, don't think I cared about that—I'd already packed. Lagerbäck could have sent me up to Lapland and I wouldn't have kicked up a fuss, and really, who cares about Liechtenstein? It was the word "we" that got my back up. Who the hell was this?

He was the boss. Why was he hiding behind other people? He should've been man enough to say, "I've decided." I would've respected him then, but this—this was cowardly. I fixed him with a really hard stare but still said nothing, and then I headed back up to my room and phoned Keki. In situations like this, you need your family.

"Come and pick me up!"

"What have you done?"

"Got in too late."

Before I cleared out, I spoke to the team manager. He and I have always been on good terms. He knows me better than most on the national team and he knows about my background and the way I am.

He knows that I don't forget things easily. "Look, Zlatan," he said, "I'm not worried about Chippen and Mellberg. They're regular Swedish guys, they'll take their punishment and come back, but with you, Zlatan . . . I'm worried Lagerbäck is digging his own grave."

"We'll see" was all I said, and an hour later I was gone from the hotel. Me and my little bro took Chippen along with us. It was him, me, Keki, and another of my friends in the car, and we stopped off at a gas station. Then we saw the tabloid headlines.

It must have been the biggest fuss ever made about a broken curfew. It was basically as if a flying saucer had landed—and things would just get worse. The whole time, I was in touch with Chippen and Mellberg.

I became a bit like a father to them, saying, "Calm down, guys. In a while, this'll just be an advantage. Nobody likes nice boys."

I was getting more and more annoyed about the whole thing. Lagerbäck and the rest were playing this us-against-them business. It was just ridiculous. Not that long ago, I had been in a fight with a guy at Milan—Oguchi Onyewu is his name. I'll tell you about it later; it was really brutal. Of course, nobody thought that punch-up was a good idea. The management did defend me publicly, saying I was fiery and keyed up, something along those lines. They kept a united front. That's what they do in Italy. They defend their own in public and criticize in private. Here in Sweden, though, it became bad guys and good guys. It was handled really badly, and I said so to Lars Lagerbäck.

"It's water under the bridge to me," he said. "You're welcome to come back."

"Am I? Well, I'm not coming. You could've given me a fine. You could've done anything. But you went to the media and hung us out to dry. I'm not standing for that"—and that was that.

I said no to the national team, and dismissed the whole thing from my mind. Well, sort of. I was reminded about it constantly, and, if I'm honest, there was one thing I regretted. I should've taken that scandal up a notch, since I was out of the squad anyway. What the hell was the problem, sitting in a place that was practically empty, with just one drink, and coming in an hour late? I should've smashed up a bar and crashed a car into a fountain up there on Avenyn and staggered back in nothing but my pants. That would've been more like a scandal on my level. This was a farce.

It's easy to feel little when you're new at a club. Everything is new, and everybody's got their roles and their places and their talk. It's easiest to take a step back and get a feel for the mood of the place. But then you lose your initiative. You lose time. I came to Inter Milan to make a difference and make sure the club won the league title for the first time in seventeen years. In those circumstances, you can't hide, or play it safe, just because the media is criticizing you and because people have preconceived opinions: Zlatan's a bad boy. Zlatan's got problems with his temper, all that stuff. It's easy to let it get to you and try to show you're the opposite—a nice guy. Then you're letting yourself be controlled.

It wasn't exactly ideal that the events from Gothenburg were being trotted out in all the Italian papers right then. It was like, Look, this guy doesn't care about the rules, that one who was so expensive. Isn't he overrated? Or an outright mistake? There was a lot of that. The worst was a so-called expert from Sweden, who said:

"The way I see it, Inter Milan has always made some strange purchases, they just invest in individualists. . . . Now they've acquired another problem."

Like I said, I thought about what Capello had said. It's about respect. It was like setting foot in a new yard in Rosengård. You can't back down or worry that somebody might have heard something or other about you. Instead, you've got to step up, and I gave it all that attitude I'd picked up at Juventus: All right, guys, here I come, now we're gonna start winning!

I gave dirty looks at practice sessions. I had my winner's mindset, all that wild attitude and willpower. I was worse than ever. I went ballistic if people didn't give a hundred percent on the pitch. I screamed and made noise if we lost or played a poor match, and I took on a leading role in a totally different way to how I had done it previously in my career. I could see it in people's eyes: it was up to me now. I was going to lead them onward, and I had Patrick Vieira by my side again. A lot of things are possible when you've got him there with you. We were two winning fiends who gave all we had to increase the motivation of the team.

There were problems on the club. Moratti, the president and owner, has done loads for Inter Milan. He's spent over 300 million euros on acquiring players. He's invested in guys like Ronaldo, Maicon, Crespo, Christian Vieri, Figo, and Baggio. He's taken an amazingly aggressive line. He also had another quality. He was too generous, too kind. He'd give us hefty bonuses after winning a single match, and I reacted against that. Not that I've got anything against bonuses and benefits. Who does? But these bonuses weren't handed out after league titles or Cup trophies. It could be after just one match, and not even an important one.

It was sending the wrong signals, I thought, and sure, as a player, you don't just go up to Moratti. Moratti comes from a ritzy family with old money. He is power. He is money. By this time, though, I'd acquired a certain standing at the club, so I did it anyway.

Moratti isn't a difficult person. He's easy to talk to, so I said to him, "Hey!"

"Yes, Ibra?"

"You've got to take it easy."

"How do you mean?"

"With the bonuses. The guys could get complacent. Hell, one match won, that's nothing. We get paid to win, and sure, if we bring home the Scudetto, go ahead and give us something nice if you want, but not after just one win."

He got it. There was an end to that, and don't get me wrong, I didn't think I could run the club better than Moratti, not at all. If I saw something that could have a negative impact on the team's motivation, though, I'd point it out, and that stuff with the bonuses was really just a little thing.

The real challenge was the cliques. That bothered me right from day one, and it wasn't just because I was from Rosengård, where everybody just got along in one big jumble—Turks, Somalis, Yugos, Arabs. It was also because I'd seen it clearly in soccer, both at Juventus and at Ajax: every team performs better when the players are united. At Inter Milan, it was the opposite. The Brazilians sat in one corner, the Argentinians in another, and then the rest of us in the middle. It was so superficial, so lazy.

Okay, sure, sometimes you sort of get cliques forming in clubs. It's not good when that happens, but at least people usually choose their friends and stick with the ones they get along with. Here, it was according to nationality. It was so primitive. They played soccer together, but otherwise they lived in separate worlds, and that drove me crazy. I knew right away that that had to change or we wouldn't win the league title. Some might say, What does it matter who we eat lunch with? Believe me, it matters. If you don't stick together off the pitch, it shows in your game.

It impacts on motivation and team spirit. In soccer, the margins are so small that those kinds of things can be the deciding factor, and I saw it as my first big test to put an end to that stuff. I realized it wasn't enough just to talk the talk.

I went around saying, What is this crap? Why are you sitting in these groups like schoolkids? And sure, a lot of them agreed with me. Others got a little embarrassed, but nothing happened. Old habits die hard. Those invisible barriers were too high. So I went up to Moratti again, and this time I made it as clear as I could. Inter hadn't won the league title for ages. Was that going to continue? Were we going to be losers just because people couldn't be bothered to talk to one another?

"Of course not," said Moratti.

"So we need to break up these groups. We can't win if we don't work as a team."

I don't think Moratti had really grasped how bad things were, but he did understand my reasoning. It was totally in line with his philosophy, he said.

"We need to be like one big family at Inter. I'll speak to them," he said, and it wasn't long before he went down to speak to the team, and you could see the kind of respect everyone had for him.

Moratti *was* the club. He didn't just make decisions. He owned us as well. He gave a little speech. He was all fired up, talking about unity, and everybody was glaring at me, of course. It sounded like what I'd been saying. Is Ibra the one who snitched? I guess most of them were convinced of that. I didn't care. I just wanted to get the team together, and the atmosphere actually improved, a bit at a time. The cliques were broken, and everybody started to spend time with one another.

We were more fired up and united, and I went around and talked to everybody, trying to get everyone together even more. Of course, that in itself won't win you the league title. I remember my first match. It was against Fiorentina, in Florence. It was September 19, 2006, and of course Fiorentina wanted to beat us at any price. Their team had also been dragged into the Italian soccer scandal and started the season on minus fifteen points, and the spectators at the Artemio Franchi were seething with hatred.

Inter had emerged from the scandal completely unscathed, and many people thought that stank. Both teams were dead set on winning: Fiorentina to regain their honor, and us to get some respect in order to finally aim for the Scudetto.

I played from the start alongside Hernán Crespo up front. Crespo was an Argentinian who'd come from Chelsea, and we got off to a good start together, at least on the pitch, and a little way into the second half I received a long pass inside the penalty area and scored with a half-volley—and you can just imagine. It was such a relief. That was my debut, and following that I became increasingly integrated into the team and it felt completely natural to say no to the Swedish national team's qualifiers for the European Championships against Spain and Iceland in October. I wanted to focus entirely on Inter and my family. Helena and I were counting the days. We were going to have our first baby, and we'd decided the birth would be in Sweden, at the university hospital in Lund. We trusted Swedish health care more than any other system, in spite of everything. It wasn't that easy, though. There were issues.

There was the media, and the paparazzi. There was the whole hysteria, and we took security staff along with us and notified the hospital's management, who closed off Ward 44 in the maternity hospital. Everyone who entered was security-checked. There were police patrolling outside, and we were both nervous. There was that peculiar hospital smell in there. People were running down the corridors, and we could hear shouts and voices. Have I mentioned that I hate hospitals? Well, I hate hospitals. I'm well when other people are well. If people are ill around me, then I get ill myself, or at least that's how it feels. I can't explain it. Hospitals give me a stomachache. There's something in the atmosphere, and I usually get out of there as soon as I can.

Now, though, I was determined to stay put and be there for everything, and it made me tense. I get loads of letters from all over the world, and usually I don't open them. It's a question of fairness. Since I can't read and answer them all, I often leave them unopened. Nobody should be singled out for special treatment. Sometimes Helena can't help herself, and we hear the most awful stories, like there's a sick child with a month left to live who idolizes me, and Helena asks, "What can we do? Can we send some tickets for a match? Send an autographed shirt?" We really try to help. But it's an awkward feeling. It's a weakness of mine, I admit, and now I was supposed to spend the night at the hospital, and I was worrying about that—but it was worse for Helena, of course. She was all worked up. It's not easy being chased while you're giving birth to your first child. If anything goes wrong, the whole world will find out about it.

Would anything go wrong? I had all kinds of thoughts like that. It went fine, and afterward I felt joy, of course—happiness. He was a lovely little boy, and we'd done it. We were parents. I was a dad, and there was no question in my mind that anything could be wrong with him, not when we'd made it through this ordeal and all the doctors and nurses seemed so happy. It wasn't on the map, but the drama wasn't over—not even close.

We named the boy Maximilian. I don't really know where we got the name from. It sounded great. Ibrahimović was great in and of itself. Maximilian Ibrahimović was even more so. It sounded both good and powerful, and of course we ended up calling him Maxi, but that was fine too. Everything felt so promising, and I left the hospital almost immediately. Not that it was easy, exactly. Outside, there were journalists all over the place. The security guy put a white coat on me—I became Dr. Ibrahimović. Then they put me in a laundry basket—completely nuts, a massive great basket—and then I curled up in there like a ball and was pushed down passageways and corridors into the underground parking garage, and only once we were down there did I hop out and get changed, and then I headed off to Italy. It fooled everybody.

Things didn't go so well for Helena. It wasn't easy for her. It had been a difficult birth, and she wasn't as used to the commotion as I was. I hardly even thought about it any longer. It was just a part of my life. Helena got more and more stressed, though, and she and Maxi were smuggled out in separate cars to my mom's terraced house in Svågertorp. We thought she'd be able to take a breather there. We were naïve. It only took an hour before the journalists started gathering outside, and Helena felt as if she was being hunted and trapped, and soon afterward she flew to Milan again.

I was already there, set to play a match against Chievo at San Siro. I was on the bench. I hadn't slept much. Roberto Mancini, our manager, didn't think I'd be able to focus properly, and I'm sure that was sensible. My thoughts were all over the place, and I looked out toward the pitch and up toward the spectators. The Ultras, Inter's hard-core fans, had hung a huge white banner from the stands. It looked like a giant sail flapping in the wind, and there was something written, or spray-painted, on the cloth in blue and black letters. It said "Benvenuto, Maximilian," which means "Welcome, Maximilian," and I wondered, Who the hell is Maximilian? Have we got a player by that name?

Then I realized. It was my son. The Ultras were welcoming my little boy to the world! That was so beautiful I wanted to cry. Those fans are not to be messed with. They're tough dudes, and I'd end up in fierce fights with them in the future. But at that moment . . . what can I say? This was Italy at its best. It was their love for soccer and their love for children, and I took out my cell and took a photo and sent it to Helena, and there are few things that have touched her heart like that. She still gets tears in her eyes when she talks about it. It was as if San Siro was sending them its love.

———

We'd also got a new puppy. We called him Trustor, after some Swedish financial affair where some people had cleared all the money out of a company. So now I really had a family. I had Helena, Maxi, and Trustor.

I was playing my Xbox constantly in those days. I went completely overboard. It was like a drug. I couldn't stop, and I'd often sit with little Maxi on my lap and play.

We were living in a hotel in Milan then, while we waited for our own apartment to be ready, and when we called the kitchen to order food, we could tell they were tired of us, and we were tired of them. The hotel was getting on our nerves, so we moved to the Hotel Nhow on the Via Tortona, and that was better, but still chaotic.

Everything was new with Maxi, and we noticed that he was vomiting a lot and wasn't putting on weight—the opposite, in fact. He was getting thinner. Neither of us knew how things were supposed to be. Maybe that was normal. Somebody said that infants sometimes lose weight for a while after they're born, and he seemed strong, didn't he? But the milk came back up, and his vomit seemed really thick and looked strange. He was spitting up all the time. Was it supposed to be like that? We didn't have a clue, and I phoned my family and my friends, and they all reassured me, saying they were sure it was nothing serious, and that's what I thought too—or at least that's what I wanted to think, and I tried to come up with explanations for it.

It's all right. He's my boy. What could go wrong? My worry didn't go away; it just became increasingly obvious that he couldn't keep anything down, and he lost even more weight. He'd weighed six pounds, ten ounces when he was born. Now he was down to six pounds, two ounces, and I felt in my gut that this was not good, not at all, and I couldn't keep it inside any longer.

"Something's not right, Helena."

"I think so too," she replied, and how can I explain it? What had previously been a suspicion, a hunch, I was now totally convinced of, and the room started to sway. My whole body was in knots. I'd never felt anything like it, not even close. Before I had a kid, I was Mr. Untouchable. I could get angry and furious, have every emotion possible. Everything could be solved if I just fought harder. Now there was nothing like that. Now I was powerless. I couldn't even make him healthy by training. I couldn't do anything.

Maxi got weaker and weaker, and he was so small you could really see it, he was just skin and bones. It was as if the life force was leaving him. We called around in a panic, and a doctor, a woman, came up to our hotel room. I wasn't there at the time. I was supposed to be playing a match. But I think we were lucky.

The doctor smelled his vomit. She looked at it, and recognized what it was a symptom of, and said immediately, "You've got to get him to the hospital right now." I remember it very clearly. I was with the team. We were up against Messina at home, and my phone rang. Helena was hysterical. "They're going to operate on Maxi," she said. "It's urgent." And I thought, Are we going to lose him? Is that really possible? My head was buzzing with every conceivable question and worry, and I told Mancini about it. Like so many others, he was a former player, and he'd begun his coaching career under Sven-Göran Eriksson at Lazio. He understood; he had a heart.

"My boy is sick," I said, and he could see in my eyes that I was feeling like shit.

I no longer had only winning on my mind. I had Maxi there—nothing else, my little boy, my beloved son—and I had to decide for myself: Was I going to play or not? I'd scored six goals so far that season, and I'd been awesome in a lot of matches. But now . . . what to do? It wouldn't make anything better with Maxi if I sat on the bench, that much was true. Would I be able to perform? I didn't know. My brain was fizzing.

I got reports from Helena every so often. She'd rushed to the hospital and, apparently, everybody was screaming around her and nobody spoke English, and Helena barely knew a word of Italian. She was totally lost. She didn't understand anything, other than that it was urgent, and that a doctor was asking her to sign some document. What kind of document? She didn't have a clue. There was no time to think. She signed. In situations like that, people will sign anything, I guess. Then there were more documents. She signed them as well and Maxi was taken away from her, and that hurt, I can really understand that.

It was like, What's happening? What's going on? She was in an absolute state, and Maxi was getting weaker and weaker. Helena gritted her teeth. There was nothing else she could do. She had to deal with it and hope, while Maxi was taken away into another room with doctors and nurses and all that stuff, and only gradually did she start to grasp what was wrong. His stomach wasn't working properly, and he had to have surgery.

As for me, I was there at the San Siro Stadium with all the crazy fans, and it wasn't easy to focus on anything. But I'd decided to play. I was in from the start. At least I think so. Everything's a little vague, and I guess I wasn't playing too well. How could I? And I remember

Mancini was standing on the sideline, and he gestured to me—I'm taking you out in five—and I nodded. Definitely, I'll go out. I'm no use here.

A minute later, though, I scored a goal, and I thought, To hell with you, Mancini! Try and take me out now. I played on, and we won big. I was playing on pure rage and worry, and afterward I headed off. I didn't say a single word in the locker room, and I barely remember the drive. My heart was pounding. But I do remember the hospital corridor and the smell in there, and how I rushed up and asked, "Where? Where?," and how I finally found my way to a big ward where Maxi was lying in an incubator alongside a load of other children. He was smaller than ever, like a tiny bird. He had tubes going into his body and his nose. My heart was ripped out of my chest, and I looked at him and then at Helena, and what do you think I did? Was I the tough guy from Rosengård?

"I love you two," I said. "You're everything to me. But I can't handle this. I'm gonna freak out. Phone me, the tiniest little thing that happens," and then I got out of there.

That wasn't a nice thing to do to Helena. She was on her own with him. I just couldn't deal with it. I started to panic. I hated hospitals more than ever, and I went back to the hotel and, probably, I played on my Xbox. It usually calms me down in that type of situation, and the whole night I lay with my cell phone right next to me. Sometimes I woke up with a start, as if I were expecting something terrible.

It went well, though. The operation was a success, and Maxi is doing great these days. He's got a scar on his tummy. Otherwise, he's just as healthy as all the other kids, and sometimes I think about that episode. It gives me a little perspective.

We actually won the Scudetto that first year at Inter Milan and, later, in Sweden, I was nominated for the Jerring Prize. There's no panel of judges to select the winner. It's chosen by the Swedish public. People in Sweden vote for the Swedish athlete or sports team they think has performed the best that year, and sure, that type of prize almost always goes to figures in individual sports, like Ingemar Stenmark in alpine skiing, Stefan Holm in athletics, or Annika Sörenstam in golf, although I should say that, a couple of times, an entire team has won it as well. The Swedish national soccer squad got it in 1994. Then, in 2007, I was nominated for the award on my own. Helena and I were there together at the gala award ceremony—I was in a tuxedo and bow tie. Before the prize was announced, I was working the room a little and bumped into Martin Dahlin.

Martin Dahlin is a former player, one of the greats. He was on the national team that won third place in the World Cup and got the Jerring Prize in 1994, and he'd been a pro with Roma and Borussia Mönchengladbach and scored tons of goals. It's the same as ever, though: it's one generation against another. The older ones want to be the greatest of all time. So do the younger ones. We don't want to have the old stars waved in our faces, and we really don't want to hear things like You should've been there in our day, and garbage like that. We want soccer to be at its best right now, and I remember hearing a sneer in Martin's voice:

"Oh, are you here?"

Why wouldn't I be there?

"And you too?" I said, with the same sneer, as if I was amazed he—of all people—had been let in.

"We did win the prize in '94."

"As a team, yeah. I'm nominated as an individual," I replied, and smiled. It was nothing, just a bit of cocky banter.

Just then, a sensation went through my whole body, and I was thinking, I want that award. I said to Helena when I got back to my table, "Please, cross your fingers for me!" I've never said anything like that, not even about winning the league or the Cup. It just came out. That award was suddenly important, as if something really depended on it. I can't really explain it. I'd gotten every kind of award and prize, but I'd never been affected in that way. Maybe, I dunno, I realized it could be a confirmation, a sign that I was really accepted, not just as a soccer player but as a person, in spite of all my outbursts and my background. So I was on edge while they were up on stage going through the nominees.

There was me and that girl who does the hurdles, Susanna Kallur, and the skier Anja Pärson. I had no idea how things would turn out. Before my Guldbollen awards I usually found out in advance— I don't want to go up there for no reason. This time, I knew nothing, and the seconds were ticking away. Goddamn it already, say it. And the winner is . . .

My name was announced. I almost welled up, and, believe me, I don't start crying easily. I never got much practice in that sort of thing when I was growing up, but now I got all emotional, and I stood up. Everybody was yelling and applauding. There was a roar surrounding me, and I passed Martin Dahlin again, and I couldn't stop myself from saying to him:

"Pardon me, Martin, I'm just going to go up and collect an award."

Up on the stage, I received the award from Prince Carl Philip and took hold of the microphone. I'm not someone who prepares acceptance speeches ahead of time, not at all. I just start talking, and suddenly I started thinking about Maxi and everything we'd been through with him, and I started to wonder . . . it was really strange, in fact. I'd gotten the award for helping Inter bring home their first Scudetto in seventeen years, and I asked myself whether Maxi had been born during that season, so not that same year but during the actual season we'd won the title.

It was like I suddenly didn't know, and when I got down I asked Helena, "Was that the season Maxi was born?" and I looked at her, and she could barely manage a nod.

She had tears in her eyes, and believe me, I will never forget that.

17

Maybe I was growing up and becoming an adult—or maybe not. I've talked about getting a buzz. I need buzzes. I've needed them ever since I was a kid, and sometimes I go off the rails. It still happens. I've got an old friend who used to own a pizzeria in Malmö. He weighs about 265 pounds, and I'd driven from Båstad on the west coast of Sweden down to Malmö in my Porsche with him, and, to be honest, a lot of people don't like to ride along with me. Not because I'm a bad driver, not at all. I'm awesome. I've got a lot of adrenaline, and that time I got it up to 300 km an hour. It felt slow, so I stepped on the gas: 301, 302—and after a while the road narrowed. I just kept on, and when the speedometer read 325 my friend burst out, "Zlatan, slow down, for Christ's sake, I've got a family!"

"And what about me, you fat bastard, what have I got?" I replied. Then I slowed down, probably reluctantly, and we gave a sigh of relief and smiled at each other. We did have to look after ourselves, after all. It wasn't easy to be sensible, though. I got a buzz out of stuff like that, and even though I've never taken drugs, maybe I've got something of an addictive personality. I get wrapped up in certain things. These days, it's hunting. Back then, it was my Xbox, and that November there was a new game out.

It was called *Gears of War,* and I was completely obsessed with it. I locked myself in. I turned one of our rooms into a gaming room and sat there for hours on end—it could be three or four in the morning, and I really should have been sleeping and looking after myself and making sure I wasn't a wreck in practice. Still I kept going. *Gears of War* was like a drug—*Gears of War* and *Call of Duty.* I was playing them all the time.

I needed more and more. I couldn't stop, and I'd often play online with other people—Brits, Italians, Swedes, anybody, six or seven hours a day, and I had a gamertag. I couldn't be known as Zlatan online. So, of course, nobody knew who was concealed behind my online tag.

I promise you, I impressed people even under a false name. I'd been playing videogames my whole life, and I'm an extremely competitive person. I'm focused. I crushed everybody. Sure, there was another guy who was good as well. He was online constantly, all night long, just like me. His gamertag was D-something, and I'd hear him talking sometimes. We all had headsets on, and people would talk between and during rounds of play.

I tried to hold my tongue. I wanted to be anonymous. It wasn't always easy. I had adrenaline flowing through my body, and one day people were talking about their cars. D— had a Porsche 911 Turbo, he said, and I couldn't stop myself. I'd given away one of those to Mino after that lunch at Okura in Amsterdam. So I started to talk, and people noticed almost instantly. They were suspicious. "You sound like Zlatan," somebody said. "Nah, nah, I'm not." "Come on," they went, and they started asking different questions. I wriggled out of it, and then we got talking about Ferraris instead, but that was no better.

"I've got one," I said. "A really special one, in fact."

"What model?"

"You wouldn't believe me if I told you," I replied, and of course that made D— curious.

"Ah, come on. What is it?"

"It's an Enzo." He was silent.

"You're making that up."

"No, I'm not!"

"An Enzo?"

"An Enzo!"

"Then you can only be one guy."

"Who's that?" I ventured.

"The one we were talking about."

"Maybe," I said, "maybe not," and we continued playing, and when we weren't playing we talked, and I interrogated that guy a bit and found out he was a stockbroker.

It was easy to talk to him; we liked the same stuff. He didn't ask any more about who I was. We talked about other stuff, and sure, I noticed he liked soccer and fast cars. He was no tough guy, though, not at all, more of a sensitive, thoughtful guy, and one day we got talking online about watches. Watches are another thing I'm interested in. D— wanted to get this very particular, very expensive watch, and somebody else online said, "There's a huge waiting list for it," and maybe there is, but not for me. Things are good if you're a soccer player in Italy. You can jump all sorts of queues and get a discount on anything, so I interrupted again and said:

"I can get ahold of one for you for such and such amount."

"Are you joking?"

"No way!"

"And how is that supposed to happen?"

"I'll just phone a guy," I said, thinking, What have I got to lose? If D— didn't want the watch or if he was just talking shit, I could keep it for myself. It was no big deal, and the guy seemed trust-worthy, and sure, he talked about Ferraris and expensive stuff. He didn't seem like a show-off, though. He just seemed to like those things, so I said, "Listen, I'm coming to Stockholm soon and I'll be staying at the Scandic Park Hotel."

"Okay," he said.

"And if you're sitting in the lobby at four o'clock, you'll get your watch."

"Are you serious?"

"I'm a serious guy!"

Afterward, I phoned my contact and got ahold of that unique watch, a nice little thing, and then texted my bank details to D— via my Xbox account. Not long after that, I flew to Stockholm. We were playing a qualifying match for the European Championship and, as usual, we were staying at the Scandic Park Hotel. Lagerbäck and I had reconciled, and I arrived at the hotel and said hello to the guys on the team. I had the watch in a box in my bag, and that afternoon I went down to the lobby with it, like we'd agreed. I felt totally relaxed. I did have Janne Hammarbäck, the security guard, with me, though, just to be on the safe side.

I had no idea what D— looked like or who he was. No matter how nice he sounded, he could've been anyone, a screwball with ten aggressive cronies—not that that's what I believed. But you never know, and so I looked around down there, left and right, and the only person I noticed was a slight, dark-haired guy sitting in a chair, look-ing shy.

"Are you here to collect a watch?" I asked.

"Er, yeah, I—"

He got up, and I saw it right away. He was confused. I think he'd already realized who I was, but still, only then did it finally hit home: It's *you*! I'd seen it before, of course. People feel awkward around me, and in those kinds of situations I become more open and friendly, so I asked a load of questions about the guy's job and where he usually went out, that sort of thing. Eventually, he loosened up too, and then we started talking Xbox. What can I say? It was nice. It was something new.

My friends from Rosengård are from the street: they've got buckets of attitude and adrenaline, and there's nothing wrong with that, not at all, that's what I grew up with. Still, this guy, he was intelligent and cautious, he had a different way of thinking. He wasn't macho at all, didn't need to play it cocky, and, normally, I don't let people get too close. I've learned the hard way that people often want to use me for their own ends—like, I know Zlatan, I'm so cool.

I felt though that things just clicked with me and this guy, and I said to him, "I'll leave the watch at the reception desk, and as soon as I've got the money in my account you can pick it up."

Half an hour later, he'd transferred the cash, and we stayed in contact. We texted, we talked on the phone, and he came down to visit us in Milan. He was a well-brought-up Swedish guy who says things like "Nice to meet you." He didn't fit in with my Rosengård guys. He did get along with Helena, though. He was more her type—finally, a guy who doesn't chuck firecrackers into hot dog stands. He became a new figure in my life, and Helena likes to call him my Internet date.

Remember the Mile at Malmö FF, the running route I used to goof off on by taking the bus or swiping a bike? That wasn't all that many years ago, and I'd think about all that stuff sometimes, not only because it was when I'd just been taken up onto the first team. So many things were different now. Take those fancy houses on Limhamnsvägen. They'd seemed so unattainable, especially that one pink house that was as big as a castle. In those days, I couldn't even imagine what kind of people lived like that. They must be amazingly well off.

I still sort of thought like that. I didn't feel awkward around that sort of people anymore, quite the opposite, but I remembered the pain—the pain of standing outside that world, knowing that you don't live on the same terms. You don't forget those sorts of feelings, and I still dreamed of revenge—of showing them all that I was no longer the kid with Fido Dido in Rosengård. That I was someone who could own the wickedest house—and Helena and I really needed a home in Malmö.

We couldn't stay with Mom in Svågertorp any longer. We had another baby on the way. I wanted a fence of my own to wreck, so Helena and I would drive around here and there and rate the houses. It was this fun thing we did. We made top-ten lists, and which house do you think came in at number one? The pink one on Limhamnsvägen, of course, and it wasn't just because of my old dreams. That house was really marvelous. It was the nicest one in Malmö, but, of course, there was one problem.

There were some people living there, and they didn't want to sell, and what can you do? That was the question. We decided not to give up. Maybe give them an offer they couldn't refuse. Not that I was going to send some Rosengård guys their way, exactly. This had to be handled with style, but, even so, we decided to go on the offensive. One day, Helena was at IKEA.

She bumped into a friend there, and they got to talking about the pink house.

"Oh, some good friends of mine live in that pile," her friend said.

"Set up a meeting. We want to speak to them," Helena told her.

"Are you joking?"

"Not at all," and so she did.

The friend called and explained the situation, and was told that the couple really didn't want to sell, no way. They liked living there and the neighbors were so nice and lovely and the grass was green, and the view toward Ribersborg Beach and the Øresund Strait was terrific, blah blah blah. The friend had been given her instructions and told them that we weren't going to take that as an answer from her. If they wanted to stay there, no matter what we were willing to pay, they'd have to tell us to our faces, and wouldn't it be fun to meet Zlatan and Helena over a cup of coffee? Not everyone got to do that.

They clearly thought that would be fun, so Helena and I went over, and I knew right away that I had the upper hand. I am who I am, but even so, I was of two minds. As I walked through those gates, I felt big and small at the same time, both the kid who gawked at those houses during the Mile and the guy who was a huge star. At first, I just went with Helena and checked it out, "Very nice, very nice, what a lovely place you've got here." I behaved and was polite, and all that. Over coffee, I couldn't restrain myself any longer.

"We're here because you're living in our house," I said, and the man started laughing, as if to say, How funny, and sure, I had a gleam in my eye. It was a sort of joke, a line from a movie.

Then I continued, "You can take it as a joke if you want. But I'm serious. I intend to buy this house, I'll make sure you're happy, but we're going to have it," and then he went on, saying it wasn't for sale, not under any conditions.

He was adamant—or rather, he pretended to be, but now I could hear it. It was just like on the transfer market. It was a game. The house had a price for him. I could see it in his eyes and I could sense it in the atmosphere, and I explained my thinking: I don't want to do things I don't know how to do. I'm a soccer player. I'm not a negotiator. I'll send a guy to do a deal.

Not Mino, if that's what you're thinking. There's got to be a limit somewhere. I sent a lawyer, and don't think I'm a fool who just pisses his money away. I'm a tactician. I'm careful. There was no, Get it at any price, none of that. It was, Make sure you get it for as little as possible.

Afterward, we sat at home waiting. It was a bit of a drama. Then the call came. "They'll sell for thirty mil"—and there was nothing to discuss. We bought it for 30 million kronor (around $3.5 million), and honestly, for that kind of money I bet that couple went skipping out of the house.

I'd done it. Sure, it wasn't free. We'd paid to be able to kick them out. This was just the beginning. We went mad renovating the place. We didn't cut any corners. We couldn't make the garden wall higher. The council said no. What could we do? We wanted a higher wall so no fans or stalkers could stand out there and look in on us. So we dug ourselves deeper instead. We lowered the level of the plot. There were loads of things like that. We really went to town, and that wasn't always popular.

The houses in that neighborhood are usually passed down as inheritances. Daddy's money pays, and nobody from my sort of background had moved in before. It's all ritzy people, and there's nobody who speaks like me, who says stuff like "the wickedest house," and that. Here they use words like "distinguished" and "extraordinary."

I wanted to show that a guy like me could get in here with his own money. That was important to me right from the start, and I hadn't expected everybody to give me a round of applause. Even so, I was still surprised at the neighbors: What, they're going to do this and that? They carried on like that constantly. They moaned. We didn't care, though, and we made that house just the way we wanted it.

It was Helena who worked at it. She was incredibly thorough and got help from various museums and whatever. I wasn't as involved as she was. I don't have the same instinct for those things, but there was one thing I contributed. On the red feature wall in the foyer, I hung a big picture of two dirty feet. When my friends came by, they were all like, Awesome, wicked, cool place you've got here.

"But what are these disgusting feet doing here? How can you have this shit on your wall?"

"You idiots," I said. "Those feet have paid for all of this."

18

I remember when I saw him at the training ground. It was pretty nice, I have to say—a sense that something was still the same, even after all the changes from one club to another. Even so, I couldn't come up with anything better than yelling, "Hey, you following me or something?"

"Of course. Somebody's got to make sure you've got cornflakes in the fridge."

"I refuse to crash on a mattress on your floor this time."

"If you're nice, you won't have to."

It felt good to have Maxwell there at Inter. He'd arrived a few months before me, but then he injured his knee and had to go through physio, so it was a while before I saw him. I don't think I know of a more elegant player. He's the aggressive Brazilian defender who dares to play beautifully deep in defense, and I often enjoy just watching him play. Sometimes, though, I'm surprised he got to be so good. Guys that nice don't usually make it in soccer. You've got to be tough and hard, and I felt that was how I'd become after my years at Juventus, and now I'd been in the thick of things more than ever and contributed to the league title my first year at Inter. Not just in matches, but generally, as a result of my attitude.

All that nonsense with the Brazilians in one corner and the Argentinians in the other was over, and every month my status on the club increased, and of course Moratti noticed that. He was good to me and made sure my family was doing well, and I continued to shine on the pitch. We were at the top of the league standings again. The miserable nineties, when Inter never really succeeded, were gone. Things had turned out the way I'd hoped. The whole team got a boost when I came, and of course Mino and I realized we were in a good bargaining position.

It was time to renegotiate my contract, and nobody does that better than Mino. He used all his tricks on Moratti. I've no idea how their discussions went. I was never there for the negotiations, but there was talk that Real Madrid wanted me then, and he drove at that one hard and put pressure on Moratti. Really, it wasn't all that necessary. The situation was different now. When I signed with Inter, I was so desperate to leave Juventus that Moratti could easily exploit that. In this business, you always aim for your opponent's weak points. That's part of the game. You put a knife to their throat. During the negotiations, he reduced my pay four times. Now we were going to get even with him. Mino and I were agreed on that, and Moratti was no longer as strong. Given how important I'd become to the team, he couldn't afford to lose me, and it didn't take long for him to say, "Give the guy what he wants." I got a fantastic deal. Later, when the details filtered out, there was even talk of me being the world's highest-paid soccer player. At the time, nobody knew about it yet. One of Moratti's stipulations was that the negotiations had to remain secret for six or seven months, but we knew that, sooner or later, it was going to explode, and really, the big thing wasn't the pay in itself but the hype it generated.

If you're seen as the highest paid in the world, people look at you differently. Another spotlight gets switched on. The public, other players, the supporters and sponsors start to view you in a new light—and what is it they say? Whoever has, will be given more. As you approach the top, you carry on upward. It's pure psychology. Everybody's interested in the one who's number one. That's how the market works, and even though I don't think anybody's worth that kind of money, I knew my value on the market, and it was in my blood now: never get screwed over again like in the Ajax deal. It's true, though, with high salaries there comes a load of other stuff— more pressure. You've got to deliver and continue to shine.

I liked it too. I wanted the pressure on me. It got me going, and midway through the season I'd scored ten goals for the team, and there was hysteria everywhere. It was all "Ibra, Ibra!," and in February it looked as if we'd secured the league title again. People thought nothing could stop us. Then I started having trouble with my knee. I tried to ignore it, thinking, Oh, never mind, it's nothing. But it kept coming back, and it got worse every time. We'd finished top of our group in the Champions League, and things were looking promising there as well.

In the first knockout stage match we were up against Liverpool, and in that first match at Anfield I could feel the injury was restricting me. Our playing was a disaster, and we lost 2–0. I was in real pain afterward, and I couldn't put it off any longer. I went for an examination, and pretty soon the diagnosis came back. I had an inflamed knee tendon.

The knee tendon extends from the quadriceps, the thigh muscle. I sat out the league match against Sampdoria. That was no big deal, I thought, either for me or the team. Sampdoria wasn't Liverpool. The guys ought to be able to manage without me. We'd had an incredible run of victories in the league. We'd even broken the record for the number of consecutive matches won in Serie A. It didn't help, though.

Play was deadlocked against Sampdoria. That was one of the first signs that something had started to go wrong, and it looked as if we were going to lose. Hernán Crespo rescued it for us with a header in the final minutes. We ended it 1–1 by the skin of our teeth, and things continued like that. After my injury—whether that was the cause of it or not—we lost our flow. We drew 1–1 against Roma as well and lost to Napoli, and I listened to Mancini and the others. They sounded worried. I had to play again. We couldn't lose our advantage in the league, and so I was sent for treatment. I needed to get fit quickly, and soon thereafter, on March 18, 2008, I was put in against Reggina.

Reggina was second from the bottom in the league, and it's really debatable whether it was necessary to have me on the pitch. I was in pain. I was playing on painkilling injections, and Reggina shouldn't have been a problem. The nerves had spread throughout the team, though. Their confidence had vanished while I was away, and Roma and AC Milan had been creeping up on us week by week in the league standings, so I guess Mancini didn't want to risk it. We'd gone from being a winning machine to feeling unsure whenever we faced the bottom teams in the league. I couldn't say no, especially not when the doctor said it was okay, even though he'd said it under pressure. In a way, that knee didn't belong to me.

The management owned my flesh and bones, in a sense. A soccer player at my level is a bit like an orange. The club squeezes it until there's no juice left, and then it's time to sell the guy. That might sound harsh, but that's how it is. It's part of the game. We're owned by the club, and we're not there to improve our health, we're there to win, and sometimes even the doctors don't know where they stand. Should they view the players as patients or as products on the team?

After all, they're not working in a general hospital, they're part of the team. And then you've got yourself. You can speak up. You can even scream, This isn't working. I'm in too much pain. Nobody knows your body better than you yourself.

The pressure is intense, and usually you want to play and not give a damn about the consequences. It's a risk you run. I might be able to be useful today, but might ruin things both for myself and the club in the longer term. Those questions come up all the time. What should you do? Who should you listen to? The doctors, who are still more cautious, or the manager who wants to play you and is often just thinking about the match at hand: who cares about tomorrow, make sure we win today!

I played against Reggina, and Mancini was proved right—at least in the short term. I scored my fifteenth goal in that match and led us to victory, and sure, that was a relief. But it also meant that the club wanted me to play the next match and then the next, and I went along with it. What else could I do? I got more injections and more pain-killers, and all the time I heard it, sensed it: We've got to have Ibra in there. We can't afford to let him rest, and I don't really blame any of them. Like I said, I wasn't a patient. I was the one who'd been leading the team ever since I started at the club, and it was decided that I would also play in our second leg against Liverpool in the Champions League, which was really important, both to me and the team.

The Champions League had become something of a fixation. I wanted to win that damned tournament. Because we'd lost the first leg, we were fired up for a big win in order to go through, and, of course, we tried everything. We worked hard. Our game still didn't really gel now either, and I wasn't in top form at all. I missed a load of chances, and in the fiftieth minute Burdisso got sent off.

It was hopeless. We had to struggle even harder. It wasn't helping, and I was feeling it more and more: this isn't working. I'm in too much pain. I'm destroying myself; and finally I limped off with pain shooting up my knee, and I will never forget that.

The away fans booed and jeered me, and, you know, when you're injured you're constantly asking yourself, Should I play or go off, and how much am I prepared to sacrifice for this match? Not because you know—there's no way of knowing. It's like roulette. You have to place your bet and hope you don't lose everything: an entire season, anything. I'd stayed on the pitch a long time because that's what the manager wanted and because I thought I could do something for the team. The only things that happened were that my injury got worse and we lost 1–0. I'd put my health on the line and hadn't gotten a damn thing in return, and the English fans were screaming at me. I've never really got along with the English spectators or the press, and now I was being called a "whingeing prima donna" and "Europe's most overrated player." Normally, that kind of stuff just gets me going. It's like when those parents signed a petition to get rid of me—I just fight harder to show those bastards. Now, though, I didn't have a body to fight back with. I was in pain, and the mood on the team was miserable. Everything had changed. All the harmony and optimism were gone. Something is wrong at Inter, the journalists wrote, and Roberto Mancini announced that he was leaving the club. He was getting out, he said. Later, he retracted it. Suddenly, he wasn't leaving at all, and people started to mistrust him. What did he want? As a manager, you can't flip-flop like that: I'm not staying; I'm staying. It's unprofessional, and we kept losing points.

We'd had a big lead at the top of the league standings, but it was shrinking all the time. We only managed a 1–1 draw against Genoa and lost at home to Juventus. I was there for that one as well. I was such an idiot, I couldn't say no. Afterward, I was in so much pain I could hardly walk, and I remember coming into the locker room and wanting to tear every damn thing off the walls, and I screamed at

Mancini and went absolutely nuts. Enough was enough. I needed rest and some physio. Never mind the drama in the league—I couldn't help them. I had no choice. I was forced to step down. Believe me, it wasn't easy. It was shit.

You're sitting there. The others go out and practice. You trot off to the gym, and from the window you can see your teammates on the pitch. It's like watching a film you should be in, but you're not allowed. That hurts. That feeling is worse than the actual injury, and I decided to escape the whole circus. I headed to Sweden. It was spring, and beautiful. I didn't enjoy it, though—not in the slightest.

I had only one thought in my head, and that was to get fit again, and I had myself examined by the doctor for the Swedish national squad, and I remember he was shocked. How had they let me play for so long on painkillers? There were only two months until the European Championships, hosted by Switzerland and Austria, and now my participation in that tournament appeared to be hanging by a thread.

I'd worked myself too hard, it was shit, and I had to do everything I could to get fit again. I phoned Rickard Dahan. He was a physiotherapist at Malmö FF, and we'd known each other since my time at the club. We started working hard together, and somebody told me about a doctor.

He was up north in Umeå, so I flew there and got some injections that killed some cells in my knee tendon, and I improved. Even so, I was far from fit, and I still couldn't play. It was hopeless, and I was furious and irritable and no fun to be around, and the lack of flow continued in the league. The team could secure the Scudetto against Siena, just one win and everything would be over. Patrick Vieira made it 1–0, and the fans in the stands started dancing and singing. It looked as if it would hold, in spite of everything, and Mario Balotelli, a young talent who'd gone in instead of me, scored another goal. Things simply couldn't go wrong, not against a club like Siena.

Then Siena scored one goal, then another. It was 2–2 and incredibly tense, with only ten minutes left on the clock. Then Materazzi was brought down and the whistle went for a penalty, and people were trembling. We just had to score. Everything was at stake and, in those times, Julio Cruz, an Argentinian, normally took our penalties. But Materazzi—that guy is temperamental and has authority, everybody on the pitch knows it, and he was thinking, I don't give a damn. I'm taking the penalty. I guess people were comfortable with that, anyway. Materazzi was thirty-four. He was a veteran; he'd been part of a World Cup final and decided it. This time though, it was a terrible penalty. The goalkeeper saved it, and the supporters screamed in anguish and fury, as I'm sure you can understand. It was a feeling of complete disaster, and sure, if anybody could handle that, I guess Materazzi could. He's like me. Hatred and revenge are what get him going. It can't have been easy.

The Ultra fans were furious and aggressive, and the press coverage was full of outrage, and nobody at the club was doing too well. While we'd missed our chance, Roma had beaten Atalanta and were closing in on us. Roma seemed to be on a roll now, and there was only one more round of matches in the league, and of course we were worried. Damn straight we were worried!

The Scudetto had been within our grasp. Most people had thought it was all over. Then I was injured and our nine-point lead had shrunk to just one, and it was no wonder so many people thought the odds were against us, and probably the gods as well. There were a lot of misgivings around. That didn't feel good. "What had happened to Inter? Why isn't it working?" That kind of talk was everywhere.

The fact was that if we lost or drew against Parma, and Roma beat Catania, which they definitely would do because Catania was at the bottom of the standings, we'd fall at the finishing line and lose everything we thought we'd had sewn up. I was back in Milan then, still not recovered. That didn't help; I was hearing all that stuff again, more than ever: Ibra has to play, we've got to have him in there. The pressure on me was insane. I'd never experienced anything like it. I'd been away for treatment for six weeks and I was not match fit. The last match I'd played had been on March 29. Now it was mid-May, and everybody knew there was no way I'd be in brilliant form.

Nobody took any notice of that—and I'm not blaming anyone, not at all. I was seen as Inter's most important player, and in Italy soccer is more important than life itself, especially in situations like this. It was years since there'd been so much excitement in the league right down to the wire, and it was Milan against Rome, the two major cities, facing each other, and people barely talked about anything else. If you switched on the TV, it was wall-to-wall sports programs, and my name was mentioned constantly. Ibra, Ibra. Is there any chance he'll play? Will he manage it? Is he fit, even after being away? Nobody knew. Everybody was talking about it, and the fans were screaming, "Help us, Ibra!"

It really wasn't easy to think about my health and about the up-coming European Championship. The match against Parma was going around and around in my head all the time, and if I went out, I saw myself on the front pages of the newspapers with headlines like "Do it for the team and for the city"—and I remember Mancini coming up to me. It was only a few days before the team was due to head out. Roberto Mancini is a bit of a snob. He likes flash suits and hand-kerchiefs and that sort of thing, and I'd never had anything against him, not at all. Since his U-turn about his job, though, his status at the club had crumbled. I mean, either you're leaving or you're not. You don't say, "I want to go," and then stay. That annoyed a lot of people. The club needed stability, not uncertainty about where the hell the coaches were going. Now Mancini was fighting for his place.

He damn well had to. The most important day in his life as a manager was approaching, and nothing could go wrong. So it wasn't exactly surprising that he was looking grave.

"Yeah?" I said.

"I know your injury isn't completely better."

"No."

"I don't give a damn, to be honest," he said.

"I suppose that's the right thing."

"Good. I intend to put you in against Parma, no matter what you say. Either you play from the start, or you start off on the bench. But I've got to have you there. We've got to bring this home."

"I know. I want to play too."

That's what I wanted, more than anything. I didn't want to be out when the Scudetto was going to be decided. That's the kind of thing you wouldn't want to live with. Better to be in pain for weeks and months than miss a fight like that. It was true that I didn't know anything about my form. I didn't know how my knee would respond in a match situation or if I'd be able to give it my all, and maybe Mancini sensed my doubts, and he didn't want his message to be misunderstood.

He sent Mihajlović after me as well. You remember him. Me and him had had it out between us when I was playing at Juventus. I'd headbutted him, or mimed a headbutt, and he'd yelled all kinds of shit at me. But all that was ancient history. What happens on the pitch stays on the pitch, and often I've gone on to become pals with guys I've fought with, maybe because we're similar, I dunno. I like being around warriors, and Mihajlović was a bruiser. He always did everything to win. Now he'd retired from playing and was an assistant coach under Mancini, and honestly, there are few guys who've taught me as much about taking a free kick as Mihajlović.

He was a master at it. He'd scored upward of thirty free kick goals in Serie A. He was a good guy. He was big and rumpled and came straight to the point.

"Ibra," he said.

"I know what you want," I said.

"Okay, but there's one thing you need to know. You don't need to practice. You don't need to do a damn thing. But you're going to be there against Parma and you're going to help us bring home the Scudetto."

"I'll try," I said.

"You won't try. You'll do it," he said, and then we headed out on the bus.

19

Sometimes, things cast a long shadow. There are memories within clubs that can be toxic, like the entire decade of the nineties at Inter Milan. Even though the team had Ronaldo then, they didn't win a single league cup. The club always stumbled at the finish line. Take the 1997–98 season, for example.

I was sixteen, seventeen years old and knew nothing of Ravelli and the gang, or anything much about Sweden in general. I did know all about Inter Milan, though. I knew all about Ronaldo. I studied his feints and his acceleration. A lot of us did, like I said. But nobody took it as far as I did. I didn't miss a single detail. Without him, I believe I would've been a different kind of player, and I'm not a guy who's easily impressed. I've met all kinds of people. I once sat next to the king of Sweden at a dinner in Barcelona, and, okay, maybe I did think, Am I holding my fork wrong?, or, Am I saying "you" when I should be saying "Your Majesty"? But it was cool. I'm me. I just go for it. It was different with Ronaldo, though. When I was with Inter he was playing for AC Milan, and there's a video on YouTube where I'm chewing some gum and just watching him and watching him, as if I can't believe that he and I are on the same pitch.

He had such gravity. Such an eye for the game. There was quality in every single movement, and in that 1997–98 season he and Inter were absolutely amazing. They won the UEFA Cup, and Ronaldo scored twenty-five goals and was voted Best Player in the World for the second year in a row. They dominated Serie A. And yet they lost it in early spring, same as us now in the run-up to the fight against Parma. Inter had bad luck and troubles and shit, and they played a classic match against Juventus at the Stadio delle Alpi in Turin in the spring of 1998. There was only one point, maybe two, between the teams. This was a real season finale, with incredible tension in the air, and Ronaldo was dribbling in the penalty area, on the left side. Then he got a brutal block, and the entire stadium started screaming. People went crazy. The stadium was at the boiling point. But the referee never blew his whistle. He let play continue, and Juventus won the match 1–0 and later the league title, and it was in that moment that everything was decided. That's how it's usually seen. It was Inter's tragic second. People still talk about it. It was considered to be a blatant penalty. But nothing happened, and there were protests and anger throughout Italy, and talk that the referee had taken a bribe, or that all referees were on the take and corrupt and stupid in general. All the older players at the club had clear memories of all that, especially as a number of similar things had happened to the club around the same time. They'd had the Scudetto within their grasp the previous season as well, but lost it in the final stretch in an awesome match against Lazio, and, the year after that, Ronaldo was injured. Everything went to hell, as though the team had lost its engine and its drive, and Inter finished eighth in the league—their worst-ever finish, I think.

Nobody said it out loud. Nobody wanted to unleash a bad omen. Still, a lot of people were thinking about it before our match against Parma. There were bad premonitions. People remembered and obsessed over it, and then there was that penalty that Materazzi had missed. The guys had had several chances to clinch the league title, but they'd blown every one. It was little things all the time, bad luck, mistakes. It was all kinds of crap, and sure, everybody was gunning for Parma, ready to give their all. That in itself could also be a problem. There were mutterings about it. There was a risk that the pressure could become too much. Things could get deadlocked, and the club's management banned all of us from speaking to the press. We had to maintain total concentration, and even Mancini, who always held a press conference before matches, kept his mouth shut, so the only one who said a word was Moratti.

He turned up at our hotel the evening before the match and said nothing to the journalists other than, "Wish us luck. We're going to need it." It didn't help that Parma was geared up to beat us in order to retain their place in the league. Things were just as deadly serious for our opponents as they were for us. We weren't going to be handed anything for free, and just before we went to the stadium, the decision came in that we weren't going to have the support of our own fans.

It was an issue of fairness. For security reasons, the Roma supporters hadn't been allowed to travel to their away match against Catania, and so we wouldn't be able to have our fans there in Parma. Quite a few did manage to get in, though. They were scattered around. Every little thing was scrutinized and discussed, and I remember Mancini. He went nuts when he heard that Gianluca Rocchi would be refereeing.

"That bastard's always got it in for us," he fumed, and there were dark clouds gathering on the horizon.

It looked like rain, and I started off on the bench. I hadn't played in a long time, and Mancini started with Balotelli and Cruz in front. "But be ready," he told me. "Be ready to jump in," and I nodded. We all sat there under a canopy and heard the first raindrops fall. Soon the rain was pattering over us and the match got under way, and the spectators were booing. The pressure was terrible, but we dominated. We kept pressing them, and Cruz and Maicon had some incredible chances, but it didn't work out. It looked hopeless, and of course those of us on the bench were following the game on the edge of our seats. We yelled and swore and hoped and feared, but we always kept one eye on the giant scoreboard in the stadium.

Because it wasn't just about our match. There was Roma's to think of as well, and it was still 0–0 there too, and that was cool. We'd still top the league. The Scudetto would be ours. Then it flashed up. The whole team sat up. Please, no goal for Roma! That would be too cruel. You can't lead the league all season and then lose at the last minute. That should damn well be outlawed. But yes, Roma had made it 1–0 against Catania and suddenly we were second in the league. It was unreal, and I looked at everyone on the bench, the physios, the doctors, the equipment guys—everybody who'd been there in the nineties, they remembered. They went pale. Is it happening again? Is the old curse back?

I've never seen anything like it. The color drained out of them, and out on the pitch as well. We're talking pure terror, nothing less. This couldn't happen. It was terrible, it was a disaster, and the rain just kept falling. It was bucketing down, and the home supporters were shouting with joy. The result was to their advantage, because if Catania lost, Parma would remain in the league. To us, it felt like nothing short of death, and the players got more and more tense. I could see it in them. They were bearing crosses on their backs, and I can't say I was particularly upbeat myself—of course not—but, still,

I already had three Scudettos and I didn't feel any of that old curse. I was too young for it, and with every minute I became more focused and more up for it. It was like there was a fire inside me.

I was going to go in and turn this around, no matter how much pain I was in. I refused to accept anything else, and at halftime when it was still 0–0 and the league title was in Roma's hands, I got the order to warm up. I remember it so clearly: everybody was looking at me—Mancini, Mihajlović, everybody; the equipment guys, the physio, everybody—and I could see it: they were counting on me. I could see it in their eyes. They stared pleadingly at me, and, obviously, it was impossible not to feel the pressure.

"Get this for us," they said, one after another.

"I will, I will!"

I didn't go in after halftime, either. It took another six minutes, and then I stepped onto the pitch. The grass was wet. Running was heavy and I wasn't completely match fit, and the pressure was ridiculous. Still, I'd never been so fired up in my life, and I remember I attempted a shot almost right away from the midfield, outside the penalty area.

It didn't go in. A few minutes later, I tried it again. I missed that one too. It felt like I kept ending up in the same position over and over without getting anything out of it and, in the sixty-second minute, it happened again. I got the ball in the same spot. It was Dejan Stanković who passed it, and I drew a guy who threw himself toward me and ran toward the goal, and every time I nudged the ball, a little stream of water went up, and then I saw an opening and shot—not a thundering kick, by any means.

It was a shot along the ground, and it struck the left goalpost and went in, and, instead of doing a wicked goal celebration, I just stood there and waited, and they all came from the bench and the pitch: first was Patrick Vieira, I think, and then Balotelli, then the whole gang—the equipment guys, the guys from the supply store, each and every one, all of them who'd given me those pleading looks, and I saw: the fear had subsided. Dejan Stanković threw himself down on the wet pitch, and it looked like he was thanking the gods. There was complete hysteria and, way up in the stands, Massimo Moratti was cheering, he was almost dancing in his VIP spot, and we all felt it, everybody in the club, every single one.

A millstone had been released from around their necks. The color returned to people's faces. It was much more than a goal. It was almost as if I'd saved them from drowning, and I looked toward the spectators. The cheers from our supporters emerged from behind the booing, and I made a gesture with my hand up to my ear, as if to say, What's that I hear? And then the stadium was even more electric, and when the commotion finally died down the match continued.

Nothing was certain yet. A single goal by Parma and we'd be back to square one, and the nerves came back, but not the old fear. Still, nobody dared to exhale. Worse things than a draw have happened in soccer. Then, in the seventy-eighth minute, Maicon dribbled along the right side, past one, two, three guys, and then he put in a cross and I rushed up. I got there at the same time as a defender, but I got my foot on the ball and shot a half-volley into the goal, and you can just imagine. I'd been away for two months, and the journalists had been writing shit about me and about the team.

They'd been saying all kinds of crap, that Inter had lost its winning instinct and everything was going to slip through our fingers and that I wasn't a true great, not like Totti or Del Piero, and even that I wasn't good when it really mattered. Now I'd shown them, and I sank down to my knees on that rain-sodden pitch and just waited for all of them to pile on top of me again, and I could feel it throughout my whole body: this was big, and it wasn't long before the whistle went and the Scudetto was ours.

Inter Milan hadn't won it in seventeen years. They'd had a long, hard spell, filled with suffering and bad luck and shit. Then I came, and now we'd brought home the league title two years in a row, and the whole place was a three-ring circus. People ran onto the pitch and grabbed us, and inside in the locker room everybody was screaming and jumping around. But then people grew silent. Mancini came in. He hadn't always been so popular, especially after he'd flip-flopped about his future with the club and not done too well in the Champions League. Now, though, he'd won the league trophy, and the players went up, one by one, kind of formal, shook his hand and said, "Thank you so much, you did it for us." Then Mancini came up to me, completely filled with victory and all the congratulations. The only thing was, he didn't get a thank-you from me. I said, "You're welcome," and everyone laughed, as if to say, Fucking Ibra!, and afterward, when I was speaking to the journalists, several of them asked, "Who do you dedicate this victory to?"

"To you," I replied. "To the media. To everybody who doubted and dissed me and Inter."

That's how I roll. I'm always planning my revenge. It's been with me ever since Rosengård, it's what drives me, and I'll never forget what Moratti told the media.

"All of Italy was against us, but Zlatan Ibrahimović was the symbol of our struggle."

I was voted Best Player of the Year in Serie A, and not long afterward that stuff about me possibly being the world's highest-paid soccer player came out, and everything went completely crazy. I could barely go out, and wherever I went there was a commotion. Of course, everybody thought I'd negotiated the contract after the match against Parma. In fact, the deal had been agreed upon seven or eight months earlier, and I thought, My God, there's no way Moratti could have any regrets now, not after that finish. I felt as if things had turned around. The clouds had cleared up. I'd been able to strike back. There were definitely signs for concern, though. I noticed right after the Parma match.

My knee had swollen up again. I hadn't been completely fit, and I think it came as a shock to a lot of people when I was forced to sit out the Italian Cup final, and of course that was no fun. We'd had a chance of the double, to bring home both the Cup and the league title. Without me, Roma got its revenge in the final, and the Euro 2008 tournament was approaching. I had no idea whether my knee was going to hold out. I'd worked myself too hard that season.

I was going to have to pay a heavy price.

20

I didn't go out that often anymore. I stayed at home with my family, and at that time I'd just become a father for the second time. Now we had little Vincent as well. Vincent! He was so lovely, and his name comes from the Italian word for "winner," and of course I liked that. He'd been born amidst a whole circus as well. But he was number two, and the media was a bit more relaxed about it.

Really, two boys! That's no picnic. I started to realize how things had been for Mom when I was younger, with all her kids and her cleaning job—no other parallels besides that, of course. We were very well off, me and Helena—shamelessly well off. At least I had some sense of how tough it must have been for Mom, and, after the drama with Maxi, I'd become really paranoid: What kind of rash is that? How come Vincent's breathing is so heavy? Why's his belly so swollen? All that.

We had a new girl to help with the kids then. Our previous nanny had met a guy while she was living with us in Malmö and had handed in her notice, and we went into a bit of a panic. We needed help, and we wanted a Swedish girl for the sake of the kids, so Helena phoned the foreign department of the employment agency to discuss the issue. How should we do it? I mean, we couldn't just put out an ad: Zlatan and Helena are looking for a babysitter. That would hardly attract the right people.

Helena pretended we were ambassadors or something. "Swedish diplomatic family seeks nanny," she put in the ad, and we got over three hundred replies. Helena read them all. She was thorough, as ever, and I guess she expected it to be difficult. She picked one out immediately. It was a girl from a little village in Dalarna in central Sweden, and apparently that alone was a point in her favor. Helena wanted somebody from the countryside. She comes from a small community herself, and this girl was a qualified nursery school teacher and could speak foreign languages and liked to keep fit, just like Helena, and generally seemed nice and hardworking.

I didn't get involved. Helena phoned up that girl without telling her who she was. She was still pretending to be an ambassador's wife. The girl seemed interested and easy to talk to, and Helena sent her an email, saying, "Come and have a week's trial with us."

They decided they'd take Helena's rental car to the airport in Stockholm and fly to Milan together with the boys, so the girl was going to meet up with Helena in Lindesberg. Her dad drove her. Before they set off, Helena sent over the travel documents, and that made the girl wonder. According to the tickets, this diplomatic family's children were called Maximilian and Vincent Ibrahimović, and that was a little odd. Maybe there could be diplomats' families with names like that as well, couldn't there? There could be lots of Ibrahimovićs in Sweden, for all she knew. She asked her dad about it.

"Have a look at this," she said.

"It looks like you're going to be nanny to Zlatan's children," he told her, and that made her want to back out. It was like, Help!

She was scared. I'm sure it sounded daunting. Then again, it felt too late to back out now. The tickets were booked and everything, so they set off, she and her dad, and now she was really nervous, she told us later. But Helena . . . what can I say about Helena? She's the *Evilsuperbitchdeluxe* when she gets all dressed up. It takes some courage to go up to a woman like that. But honestly, she's incredibly laidback. She's an expert at making people feel comfortable, and during that journey she and the girl had a long time to get to know each other—far too long, in fact.

The problems started at Arlanda Airport. They were going to fly easyJet, because only easyJet had a flight to Milan that day. But there was something wrong with the plane. The flight was delayed an hour, then two, three, six, twelve, eighteen hours. It was ridiculous. It was an absolute scandal, and everybody was tired and irritated and climbing the walls, and, finally, I went nuts. I couldn't stand it. I phoned a pilot I know, the guy who flies the private plane I have access to.

"Go and fetch them," I told him, and that's what happened. Helena and the girl collected their bags and were taken to the private plane, and I'd made sure there was catering on board, with strawberries dipped in chocolate and all that stuff, and I hoped they'd enjoy it. They deserved it after that ordeal, and then I finally got to meet the girl. She was really nervous then too, from what I understand. We got on well, and she's helped us and lived with us ever since. She's part of the family, you could say, and we wouldn't manage for a day without her. The kids are crazy about her, and she and Helena are like sisters, and exercise and study together. At nine o'clock every morning, they work out together. We gained some new routines and habits in general.

One year, we went off to St. Moritz. Do you think I felt at home there? Not exactly! I'd never skied in my life. The thought of going to the Alps with Mom and Dad was like going to the moon.

St. Moritz was for ritzy people. They drank champagne with breakfast. Champagne? I sat around in my pants and wanted cereal. Olof Mellberg was there as well and tried to teach me to ski. It was no use. I was all over the place like an idiot, while Mellberg and the others in our gang danced down the slopes. I looked completely ridiculous, and, to be on the safe side, I put on one of those balaclavas and some massive sunglasses. Nobody would know who I was. One day, though, I was on a chairlift and there was an Italian kid sitting next to me with his dad, and the kid started staring. No worries, I thought. He won't recognize me in this outfit. No way.

Then after a while the kid said, "Ibra?"

It must have been my damn nose. I flat-out denied it. Ibra, what? Who's that? But what did I get? Helena started laughing. That was about the funniest thing she'd ever experienced, and the kid carried on with his "Ibra? Ibra?" Finally, I said, "*Si,* it's me," and then there was a bit of a pause. The guy was well impressed. But that was a problem. He wasn't going to be so impressed when he saw me ski, and I thought about what I was going to do. I was the sports star. I couldn't reveal myself to be a clown on the slopes. Then things got even worse than I feared. Word got around. A whole crowd turned up, and they all stood there to watch me ski. I had issues with my gloves. Paid special attention to how they fit around my fingertips.

I was thorough with my jacket as well, and my ski pants and bindings—especially those, because that was something I'd seen. People were constantly fiddling with their bindings, fastening them and undoing them, and for all anybody knew, maybe I was an extremely thorough pro who needed to have everything done up just so before I went zooming off like Ingemar Stenmark. It was annoying, obviously: the longer I kept it up, the greater their expectations grew. They were thinking, Is he gonna do some tricks? Shoot off out of a cannon on those soccer legs?

I was forced to adjust my scarf and my cap and my hair, and finally they got tired. They went away, thinking, We're not bothering about him. I was definitely Ibra, but that doesn't mean you can stare at me forever. I could ski down in peace and quiet like the newbie I was, and Olof Mellberg and the others were all wondering, "Where have you been? What were you doing?"

"I had to adjust a few things," I said.

———

Most of the time, it was hard work. The summer after our match against Parma and the second league victory with Inter, I was supposed to play in the Euro 2008 tournament in Switzerland and Austria, and I was still concerned about my knee. A lot was being written about my injury, and I spoke to Lagerbäck about it, and neither I nor anybody else knew whether I'd be able to give a hundred percent. We had Russia, Spain, and Greece in our group, and that didn't look very easy.

I've got a contract with Nike. Mino was against that deal, but I stood my ground, and sure, it's been fun a lot of the time. We've made some fun videos together, like when I do tricks with a piece of chewing gum and kick it up into my mouth, and Dad's even there pretending to be worried I'm going to choke on it—and, above all, Nike was there and helped me build Zlatan Court in Cronmans Väg in Rosengård, where I'd played as a kid.

That was great. The pitch was made out of the soles from old sneakers. There was a nice rubber underlay, and lighting and stuff. The kids wouldn't have to stop playing the way we did because it got too dark, and we put up an inscription there: *My heart is here. My history is here. My game is here. Take it further. Zlatan.* It felt fantastic to be able to give something back, and I was there and officially opened the pitch, and you can just imagine. "Zlatan, Zlatan!" the kids were screaming. It was a complete circus. It was a homecoming, and I was really touched, honestly, and I played with the kids in the dark and felt like, Wow, you didn't think this would happen to the snotnosed kid from Cronmans Väg!

At the Euro 2008 tournament, though, I was pissed off with Nike. Nike had made a strict rule that all of us who had a contract had to wear the same color shoes, and I thought, Okay then, go for it, I don't care. Then it emerged that another guy was still going to get his own color. I took it up with Nike: How come you're talking shit? Everybody was supposed to have the same. That's what we decided, they replied, and then I told them what I thought of that, and then they changed their minds. Suddenly, I was getting my own color too. It wasn't fun any longer, though. You shouldn't have to talk your way into stuff like that, and I kept my old shoes. Maybe it all sounds kind of silly. But people need to be able to talk straight.

Our first match was against Greece. I had Sotirios Kyrgiakos on me. Kyrgiakos is a talented defender. He had long hair, which he wore in a ponytail. Every time I jumped or made a move, I got his hair in my face. I practically got hair in my mouth. He was marking me hard. He did a good job, no doubt about that. He locked me in. Then he let up for a couple, three seconds, and that was all I needed. I got a throw-in and started to dribble, and suddenly Kyrgiakos was far away, and then I got some space. I shot straight up into the top corner.

That was a perfect start to the European Championship tournament. We won 2–0, and my family, who were there, looked after themselves. We'd all learned our lesson from the World Cup in Germany. I was playing soccer. I couldn't be their travel coordinator as well. Everybody took care of their own stuff, and that felt good. My knee was hurting, though, and it was swollen, and we had Spain in our next match. Spain was one of the favorites to win the tournament. They'd beaten Russia 4–0 in their first match, and we knew it was going to be tough, and there was a lot of talk about my injury. Should I play or not? I wasn't sure. It was painful, but yeah, I was happy to ignore the pain.

It was the European Championship, and I would have gone out there with a knife in my leg. Like I said, though, in soccer, there's always a short-term and a long-term perspective. There's the match today, and then there are the matches tomorrow and the next day. You can sacrifice yourself in a fight and make a big effort, but then be out of commission. We had Spain now and Russia after that, and then the quarterfinal if we made it through, and there was talk that I was going to play on painkilling injections. I'd done it many times in Italy. The doctor for the Swedish national team was opposed to that, though. Pain is the body's warning signal. You can relieve the pain temporarily, but then you risk serious damage. It's a bit like gambling. Gaming with injuries. How important is this match? How much should we risk to make the guy fit for today? Is it worth the risk that he might be out for weeks or months afterward? It's those kinds of considerations, and, traditionally, the doctors in Sweden are more cautious than those elsewhere on the Continent. They see the guy more as a patient than as a soccer playing machine. It's never simple, and as a player you often put pressure on yourself. There are matches that seem so crucial you want to say, Fuck the future! I don't give a damn about the consequences. The only thing is, you can't escape the future, and if you're playing on your national squad, your club is always in the background.

They're the ones who are paying the big money, and I was a huge investment. I wasn't allowed to break. It wouldn't do to sacrifice me for an international match that had nothing to do with Inter, and Sweden's doctor got a phone call from the club's doctor. Those conversations can get heated. Two opposing interests are at odds. The club wants their player for the league, and the national team needs the same guy for the European Championship.

There was also just a month to go before the preseason would get under way, and I was Inter's most important player. Both doctors were reasonable people. It was a totally calm discussion, I think, and they came to an agreement. I wouldn't play on injections, and I got hours of treatment from a sports osteopath, and it was decided that I would play against Spain after all.

It was me and Henrik Larsson in front, and that felt good. But Spain was skillful. They got a corner early on. Xavi made a short pass to David Villa, who played it diagonally back to David Silva, who was free and crossed to Fernando Torres. Torres fought for the ball with Petter Hansson, but Torres was one step ahead and nudged it, almost pushed it in to make it 1–0, and of course that was tough. It's not easy to equalize against Spain. Then the Spaniards backed off and tried to secure their win and their place in the quarterfinal, and they provided us with chance after chance, and I forgot all about my knee. I went for it. I worked hard and, in the thirty-fourth minute, I got a nice long ball from Fredrik Stoor in the penalty area, and I was on my own with Iker Casillas, the goalkeeper, and I tried to kick the ball straight into the net. That was the sort of position van Basten had talked to me about and Capello and Galbiati had trained me for, because you've got to be able to exploit those sorts of situations. But I missed—I didn't get good contact with the ball and a half-second later I had Sergio Ramos in front of me, the young star defender at Real Madrid.

Even so, I damn well had no intention of giving up. I blocked it, I kept away and shot again through a little gap between him and another defender, and the ball went into the net. It was 1–1, and the

match was in full swing and I was definitely in form. I'd made a
brilliant start to the tournament, but still, it didn't help. When the
referee blew the whistle for halftime and my adrenaline subsided, I
realized I was in pain. My knee was not good at all. What should I
do? It wasn't an easy decision. I'd been crucial for the team, but I had
to last. There was at least one match to go, and our prospects looked
good. We had three points from the match against Greece, and even
if we lost this one, we could play our way into a place in the quarterfinal in the last group match against Russia. So I went over to Lars
Lagerbäck during the break.

"I'm really in pain," I said.

"Damn."

"I think we'll have to make a choice."

"Okay."

"Which is more important to you: the second half now, or the
Russia match?"

"Russia," he said. "We've got more of a chance against them."

So I was put on the bench for the second half. Lagerbäck put
Markus Rosenberg in instead, and that seemed promising. Spain had
a lot of chances in the second half. We managed to keep them away,
and sure, you could tell I was out. There was a quality that had gone
from the game, some intangible momentum. I'd been in fine form,
and I was cursing my knee. Goddamn. But the guys fought on and,
when ninety minutes were over, the score still stood at 1–1. It looked
as if things would turn out all right, and we nodded encouragingly to
one another on the bench. Were we going to pull this one off after
all? Then, two minutes into injury time, someone took the ball off
Markus Rosenberg in a really nasty tackle, far down on our side of
the pitch. Lagerbäck stood up and was furious. Fucking idiot referee!

It was a blatant free kick, he thought. The referee let play continue, and there were agitated gestures. Many on the bench had al-

ready taken the view that the referee was against us, and people were screaming and ranting—but not for long. Disaster struck. Joan Capdevila, who'd taken the ball from Rosenberg, hit a long cross, and Fredrik Stoor tried to stop it. But he was totally exhausted. Everybody had worked themselves into the ground. David Villa rushed past him, and past Petter Hansson as well, and scored 2–1, and almost immediately after that the referee blew the final whistle. I can safely say that was a difficult loss.

In our next match against Russia, we were crushed. I was in pain, and it felt like Russia was better at everything. We were out of the tournament and incredibly disappointed. What had started so well came to nothing. It was terrible. And, as always, as soon as one thing is done, something new comes along, and just before the European Championship I'd heard that Roberto Mancini had been sacked as coach of Inter.

He would be replaced by a guy called José Mourinho. I hadn't met him yet. But he'd already surprised me. He formed an attachment to me even before we met. He would become a guy I was basically willing to die for.

21

I still didn't have a real handle on him. Of course, Mourinho was the "Special One" even then, and I'd heard a lot about him. People said he was cocky, and that he put on a show at his press conferences and said exactly what he thought. I didn't really know anything, though, and just thought, I bet he's like Capello, a really tough leader, and that's good for me. I like that style. It turned out I was wrong—partly, at least. Mourinho is Portuguese, and he likes to be at the center of things. He manipulates players like no one else. But that's still not saying anything.

The guy had learned a lot from Bobby Robson, the old England captain. Robson was coaching the team Sporting Clube de Portugal in those days and needed a translator, and Mourinho happened to be the guy they took on. Mourinho was good at languages. Robson soon noticed that the guy could do other stuff as well. He had a quick mind, and it was easy to toss ideas around with him. One day, Bobby Robson asked him to write a report on an opposing team. I've no idea what he was expecting. Like, what does a translator know? But Mourinho's analysis was first-class, apparently.

Robson was just amazed. Here was a guy who'd never played soccer at a high level, but he still came up with better material than Robson had ever received. It was like, Shit! I must have underestimated that translator. When Bobby Robson went to a different club, he took the guy with him, and Mourinho kept learning, not just facts and tactics but psychological stuff as well, and finally he became a manager himself at Porto. That was in 2002. He was a complete unknown back then. He was still "the translator" in the eyes of many people, and maybe Porto was a good team in Portugal.

Come on, it was no big club. Porto had finished in the middle of their league the previous year, and the Portuguese League—I mean, what was that? Not much, by comparison. Nobody paid attention to Porto in the European tournaments, especially not in the Champions League. But Mourinho came to the club with something totally new: complete knowledge of every single detail about the opposing teams, and sure, I was clueless about that stuff. I'd find out later on, that's for certain. In those days, he used to talk a lot about conversions in soccer, when one team's offensive was smashed and the players had to regroup from attacking to defending mode.

Those seconds are crucial. In situations like that, a single unexpected maneuver, one little tactical error, can be decisive. Mourinho studied that more thoroughly than anybody else in soccer and got his players to think quickly and analytically. Porto became experts at exploiting those moments, and, against all the odds, they not only won the Portuguese League title, they also made it into the Champions League and came up against teams like Manchester United and Real Madrid, clubs where a single player earned as much as the entire Porto squad combined. Mourinho and his guys still won the Champions League trophy.

That was a massive upset, and Mourinho became the hottest manager in the world. This was in 2004. Roman Abramovich, the Russian billionaire, had bought Chelsea and was pouring money into the club, and the key thing he did was to bring in Mourinho. But do you think Mourinho was accepted in England? He was a foreigner. A Portuguese. A lot of snobs and journalists expressed doubts about him, and at a press conference he said, "I'm not some guy coming from nowhere. I won the Champions League with Porto. I am a special one"—and that last bit stuck.

Mourinho became the "Special One" in the British media, but I suppose it was said as much out of scorn as respect—at least at first. That guy got up people's noses. Not just because he looked like a movie star. He said cocky things. He knew what he was worth, and sometimes he really went at his competitors. When he thought Arsenal's Arsène Wenger was obsessed with Mourinho's Chelsea squad, he talked about Wenger like he was some sort of voyeur, a guy who sits at home with binoculars to spy on what other people are doing. There's always some uproar around Mourinho.

He didn't just talk the talk, though. When he came to Chelsea, the club hadn't won a league title in fifty years. With Mourinho, they won two seasons in a row. Mourinho *was* the "Special One," and now he was headed our way, and, considering his reputation, I was expecting harsh commands right from the start. Already during the European Championships I was told that Mourinho was going to phone me, and I thought, Has something happened?

He just wanted to chat. To say, "It'll be nice to work together, looking forward to meeting you"—nothing remarkable, not then, but he was speaking in Italian. I didn't get it. Mourinho had never coached an Italian club. But he spoke the language better than me. He'd learned the language in no time at all—in three weeks, people said—and I couldn't keep up. We switched to English, and already then I could sense it: this guy cares. The questions he asks are different, somehow, and after the match against Spain I got a text message.

I get a ton of texts all the time. But this one was from Mourinho. "Well played," he wrote, and then gave me some advice, and I promise you, I stopped in my tracks. I'd never had that before. A text message from the coach! I mean, I'd been playing with the Swedish squad, which had nothing to do with him. Still, he got involved, and I replied and got more messages. It was like, Wow! Mourinho's checking me out! I felt appreciated. Maybe that guy wasn't so tough and harsh after all.

Sure, I understood he was sending those texts for a reason. It was like a pep talk. He wanted my loyalty. I liked him right off. We clicked. We understood each other, and I realized, This guy works hard. He works twice as hard as all the rest. Lives and breathes soccer 24/7 and does his analyses. I've never met a manager with that kind of knowledge about the opposing sides. It's not just the usual stuff—Look, they play like this or like that, They've got this or that tactic, You've got to look out for him. It was everything, every little detail, right down to the third-string goalkeeper's shoe size. It was everything. We all sensed it immediately: this guy knows his stuff.

It was a while before I met him. This was during the European Championships and then the summer closed season, and I don't really know what I was expecting. I'd seen loads of photos of him. He's elegant, he's confident, but, well, I was surprised. He was a short man with narrow shoulders, and he looked small next to the players.

I sensed it immediately: there was this vibe around him. He got people to toe the line, and he went up to guys who thought they were untouchable and let them have it. He stood there, only coming up to their shoulder, and didn't try to suck up to them, not for a second. He got straight to the point, and he was absolutely cold: From now on, you do it like this and like this. Can you imagine! And everybody started to listen. They strained to take in every shade of meaning in what he was saying. Not that they were frightened of him. He was no Capello, like I said. He created personal ties with the players with his text messages and his emails and his involvement and his knowledge of all our situations with wives and children, and he didn't shout. People listened anyway, and everybody realized early on, This guy does his homework. He works hard to get us ready. He built us up before matches. It was like theater, a psychological game. He might show videos where we'd played badly and say, "Look at this. So miserable! Hopeless! Those guys can't even be you. They must be your brothers, your inferior selves," and we nodded, we agreed. We were ashamed.

"I don't want to see you like that today," he would continue. No way, we thought, no chance. "Go out there like hungry lions, like warriors," he added, and we shouted, "Definitely! Nothing else is good enough."

"In the first battle you'll be like this—" he went on. He pounded his fist against the palm of his open hand. "And in the second battle—"

He gave the flip chart a kick and sent it flying across the room, and the adrenaline pumped inside us, and we went out like rabid animals. There were things like that all the time, unexpected things that got us going, and I felt increasingly that this guy gives everything for the team, so I want to give everything for him. It was a quality he had. People were willing to kill for him. It wasn't all just pep talks, though. That guy could take you down with a few words.

For instance, he'd come into the locker room and say in an icy-cold voice: "You've done zero today, Zlatan, zero. You haven't achieved a damn thing," and in those situations I didn't shout back.

I didn't defend myself—not because I was a coward or had excessive respect for him, but because I knew he was right. I hadn't achieved a thing, and it didn't mean jack shit to Mourinho what you'd done yesterday or the day before that. Today was what counted. It was right now: "Go out and play soccer."

I remember one match against Atalanta. The following day I was supposed to receive the award for Best Foreign Player and the Best Player Overall in Serie A, but we were down 2–0 at halftime and I'd been pretty invisible, and Mourinho came up to me in the locker room.

"You're gonna get an award tomorrow, eh?"

"Huh? Yeah."

"Do you know what you're going to do when you get that award?"

"Er, what?"

"You're going to be ashamed. You're going to blush. You're going to know that you haven't won shit. People can't get awards when they play so terribly. You're going to give that award to your mom, or somebody who deserves it more," he said, and I thought, I'll show him, he'll see I deserve that honor, just wait until the second half, never mind if I can taste blood in my mouth, I'll show him. I'm going to dominate again.

There were things like that all the time. He pumped me up and cut me down. He was a master at manipulating the team, and there was just one thing that really bothered me: his facial expression when we played. No matter what I did, or what goals I scored, he looked just as ice-cold. There was never any hint of a smile, no gestures, nothing at all. It was as if nothing had happened, sort of like there was a motionless game in midfield, and I was more awesome than ever then. I was doing totally amazing things, but Mourinho had a face like a wet weekend.

One time we were playing Bologna and, in the twenty-fourth minute, Adriano, the Brazilian, was dribbling along the left side and made it down toward the goal line. He put in a cross, a hard shot that came too low to head and too high to catch on the volley, and I was crowded out in the penalty area. I took a step forward and backheeled it. It looked like a karate kick, just bam! straight into the net. It was absolutely insane. That was later voted Goal of the Year, and the spectators went nuts, people stood up and screamed and applauded—everybody, even Moratti in the VIP section. But Mourinho, what did he do? He stood there in his suit with his hands by his sides, completely stone-faced. What the hell is it with that man? I thought. If he doesn't react to a thing like that, what does get him going?

I talked it over with Rui Faria. Rui is Portuguese as well. He's the fitness coach, and Mourinho's right-hand man. The two of them have followed each other from club to club and know each other inside and out.

"Explain one thing to me," I said to him.

"Okay, sure!"

"I've scored goals this season that I don't even know how they happened. I can't believe Mourinho has seen anything like them. And yet he just stands there like a statue."

"Take it easy, fella," said Rui. "That's how he is. He doesn't react like the rest of us."

Maybe not, I thought. Even so . . . then I'm damn well going to make sure I liven him up, even if I have to achieve a miracle.

One way or another, I was going to make that man cheer.

22

I had kind of a fixation about the Champions League. We'd started the league season and my knee was better, and I scored one incredible goal after another, so early on we had a feeling that we were going to bring home the Scudetto that year as well. Let's get this straight: that wasn't such a huge thing anymore. I'd already won the Italian League title four times and been named Best Player of the Season. The Champions League felt like the crucial thing. I'd never made it very far in that tournament, and we were due to play Manchester United in the first round.

United was one of the best teams in Europe. They'd won the Champions League trophy the previous year and had players like Cristiano Ronaldo, Wayne Rooney, Paul Scholes, Ryan Giggs, and Nemanja Vidić, but none of them carried the game, none of them was the deciding factor for the club—quite the opposite: you really got a sense that United was a team. No player was bigger than the club. No manager drove that philosophy harder than Alex Ferguson—

Sir Alex Ferguson, I suppose I should say. Everybody knows Sir Alex. He's like a god in England, and he never wears out his stars. He rotates them.

Originally, Ferguson was a working-class kid from Scotland, and when he joined United as manager in 1986, there wasn't much going on with the club. United's glory days seemed to be behind them. Everything was in a mess, and the players used to go out and get drunk. That was considered a cool thing? Ferguson waged war on all that. Goddamn, drinking beer! He put discipline into those guys. He brought home twenty-one titles with the club and was knighted in 1999 when United won the Premier League title, the FA Cup, and the Champions League all in the same year. So you can imagine the rivalry between a guy like that and Mourinho. There was endless talk about it.

There was Mourinho versus Sir Alex, and there was Cristiano Ronaldo versus Zlatan. There was loads written about us. We were the two poster boys for Nike and we'd filmed a commercial together, a duel where we did tricks and scored goals—a fun thing, with Eric Cantona as a TV presenter. I didn't know him, though. We never met during the filming. Everything was done separately, and I wasn't too bothered about that media stuff either. But I felt up for it. I believed our chances were good, and of course Mourinho had prepared us thoroughly. The first match at San Siro was a disappointment. We'd only managed a 0–0 draw, and I didn't really get into the game, and of course the British papers wrote loads of shit afterward. That was their problem, though, not mine. They could go ahead and write all the nonsense they wanted, I didn't give a damn. But I really wanted to win the second leg at Old Trafford and progress in the Champions League. It was something that was growing inside me, and I remember when I ran out onto the pitch and heard the applause and the boos.

The air was crackling with nerves, and Mourinho was dressed in a black suit and a black overcoat. He looked serious, and as usual he didn't sit down. He stood right by the sideline, following the game, like a general on the battlefield, and several times the spectators sang or chanted, "Sit down, Mourinho!," and he often waved his hands. He roared, "Get in there and help Ibra!" I was too alone up front, and I was being marked really hard. A lot depended on me. That's how it had been all season, and Mourinho also played 4–5–1 with me up front. I felt pressure to score goals, and sure, I liked it. I wanted the responsibility.

United was sharper, though, and I became too isolated and crowded out up there, and I cursed the situation. Worst of all, just three minutes in, Ryan Giggs took a corner and Vidić headed it in 1–0. That was a bucket of cold water.

All of Old Trafford stood up and roared, "You're not special anymore, José Mourinho."

Mourinho and I were the ones who got the worst boos. Then things loosened up more and more, and the fact was, we only needed one goal to progress. If we just made it 1–1, victory would be ours, and I started to shine. Things kept improving, and after thirty minutes I got a long cross in the penalty area and headed it hard, straight down on the goal line. The ball bounced up, onto the crossbar, and out. It was so close, and I had a growing sense that we were going to take this one yet, and we had one chance after another. Adriano struck the goalpost with a volley. But no, it didn't go in. Instead, Wayne Rooney dribbled the ball outside the penalty area and sent in a cross to Cristiano, who headed it in 2–0, and that felt awful. It was tough, the minutes ticked away, and we weren't managing to reduce their lead. Toward the end of the match, the entire stadium was singing, "Bye, bye, Mourinho. It's over." I wanted to kick up the turf and smash something valuable, and I remember coming into the locker room. Mourinho tried to cheer us up, saying, "Now we're going to focus on the league." He's as hard as a rock before and during matches, and sometimes, after a few days have passed and he's analyzed our defeat, he can attack us so we don't repeat our mistakes. In situations like this, though, there was no reason to lay into us. It wouldn't serve any purpose. We were upset enough as it was.

It felt as if everybody wanted to commit murder, and I think that's when the thought started to sprout inside me. I wanted to move on. I'm a restless sort. I've always been on the move. I changed schools, homes, and clubs even as a kid. I kind of got addicted to it and now, as I sat there and looked down at my legs, I started to suspect it: I was never going to win the Champions League with Inter. I didn't think the team was good enough, and already in the first interviews after the match, I gave some hints about that. Or rather, I just answered honestly, instead of the usual, Oh sure, we'll win it next year.

"Can you win the Champions League if you stay at Inter?" the journalists asked.

"I dunno. We'll see," I replied, and I'm sure the fans suspected something already.

That was the start of the tensions, and I talked to Mino. "I want to move on," I said. "I want to go to Spain." He understood exactly what I meant, of course. Spain meant Real Madrid or Barcelona, the two top clubs, and Real was tempting. They had brilliant traditions and had had players like Ronaldo, Zidane, Figo, Roberto Carlos, and Raúl. But I was leaning toward Barça more and more. They played brilliantly and had guys like Lionel Messi, Xavi, and Iniesta.

How should we approach things? It wasn't easy. I couldn't say, I want to go to Barça. Not only because it would be a disaster for my reputation at Inter but because it would be like declaring, I can play for free. You can't go offering yourself around like that. Then the directors realize they can get you cheap. No, the club has to come to you. The management has to feel like they want you at any price. That wasn't the real problem, though.

The problem was my status and my terms in Italy. I was seen as too expensive. I was the player who couldn't leave. I heard that a lot. There was me at Inter, and Kaká at AC Milan, Messi at Barça, and Cristiano Ronaldo at Man United. It was thought that nobody could match our contracts. Our price tags were too high. Even Mourinho talked about it. "Ibra's staying," he said. "No club can pay the sums that are required. Nobody can bid 100 million euros," and that sounded absurd.

Was I too expensive for the market? A fucking *Mona Lisa* that couldn't be sold? I didn't know. The situation was difficult, and maybe it was stupid to be so open about it in the media, after all. I suppose I should've come out with the same crap as a lot of other stars: I'll always stay with my club, blah blah blah.

I can't do that. I couldn't lie. I was uncertain about the future and I said so, and of course that annoyed a lot of people, especially the fans. They saw it as a betrayal, or at least something like it, and many started to worry. Would I lose my motivation on the team? Especially when I mouthed off with stuff like "I'd like to try something new. I've been in Italy for five years now. I like technical soccer, and that's what they play in Spain." There was loads of talk and speculation.

That was no tactic, no trick to get out of the club, it was just honest, but nothing was simple, not for a player at my level. I was the most important guy at Inter, and nobody wanted me to leave. There was an uproar every time I said something about it, and maybe the whole thing was a waste of time. We didn't have any offers, and I wasn't exactly getting any cheaper. Sure, I longed to go somewhere new. It wasn't affecting my game, though, not at all. I was free of injury now, and better than ever, and I continued to do everything to get Mourinho to react.

For example, I made a nice breakaway against Reggina, a dribble almost from midfield. I made it past three defenders, and honestly, that was a performance in itself. The spectators were probably expecting me to finish it off with a hard shot. But I saw that the goalie was standing too far out, and I got an image, an idea. With my left foot, I chipped the ball over the guy, and it couldn't have been more perfect. The ball sailed in a beautiful arc into the top corner, and the entire stadium cheered—everybody except Mourinho, of course, who stood there in his gray suit, chewing his gum with a little frown. Same as usual, in other words. Still, that was better than most of my other goals, and it brought me up to joint first position with Bologna's Marco Di Vaio in the league's goal-scoring standings. It's a big thing in Italy to be the leading goal-scorer, and I started to focus on that more and more. That was a challenge I needed. I became more aggressive than ever in front of the goal, and nobody loves goal-scorers more than the Italian fans.

Nobody hates goal-scorers who want to leave their club more either, and it didn't help matters when I announced after the match, "I'm completely focused on winning the league title this year, but as for next season, we'll have to see."

It goes without saying that the tension was ratcheted up: What's up with Ibra? What's going on? There was still a long way to go until the silly season, and we had nothing concrete. The papers were already speculating. It was me and Cristiano Ronaldo at Manchester United. Would Real Madrid purchase either of us? And could they afford it? There were constant rumors. For example, people were speculating whether Real Madrid would do a trade and swap their star Gonzalo Higuaín for me.

That way, the club wouldn't have to pay so much. Higuaín would become part of the price. Like I said, though, that was just talk, or rather, nothing in the media is just talk. It has an impact, no matter how false it is, and a lot of people wanted to put me in my place. There was a lot of stuff like Nobody is bigger than the club, and Ibra's ungrateful and a deserter—all that stuff. But I didn't care.

I kept up the pace and, against Fiorentina in injury time, I hit an amazing free kick that was clocked at 109 km an hour and just slammed into the net from far away, and it looked like we were going to clinch the league title, and like I said, it went hand in hand. There was a good and a bad side to everything. The better I was, the more agitated the supporters got about my wanting to leave the club, and before our match against Lazio on May 2, 2009, the mood was explosive. The Ultra fans had written, "Welcome, Maximilian," and that kind of thing. They could show love. They could also show hate—not just toward the opposing side but to their own players as well, and I sensed it as soon as I came in. San Siro was at the boiling point.

All week, there had been things in the papers about how I wanted to leave Italy and try something new. Nobody could have missed it. Early on in the match, I worked my way into the penalty area. I struggled, but couldn't get the ball, and in those situations the supporters usually applaud. Like, Good try. Now I was getting boos and jeers from the Ultra fans. I was thinking, What the hell, we're working hard down here and we're at the top of the league standings, and this is what you bring? Who are you? I shushed them. Put my finger up to my mouth. But things didn't get any better, and just before halftime the score was still 0–0, even though we'd kept up a lot of pressure, and then they started booing the whole team, and that made me bear down, or, more accurately, I got pumped up with adrenaline.

I'd show them, and, like I said, I play better when I'm angry. Remember that—if you see me when I'm furious, don't worry. All right, I might do something stupid and get a red card. Most of the time, though, it's a good sign. My entire career has been built on the desire to strike back, and in the second half I got the ball about fifteen meters outside the penalty area. I turned. I rushed in. I feinted, and scored with a shot between two defenders. It was a shot of pure rage, a nice goal. But it wasn't the goal people talked about.

It was my gesture, because I didn't celebrate. I ran backward into our half of the pitch with my face turned toward the Ultra fans, and all the time I was shushing them with my finger to my mouth again. It was like, Shut your mouths. Here's my reply to your shit. I score goals, and you boo. That became the big thing in that match—like, Did you see it? Did you see it? It was something totally new.

It was a public battle between the fans and the team's biggest star, and over on the sideline stood Mourinho—no victory gesture from him, of course. Who would've expected it? He obviously agreed with me, though. Shit, booing your own team. He pointed at his head, as if to say, You're morons, up there in the stands.

Of course, you understand, if things were tense before, they were even worse now. There was a rumbling in the stadium. But I continued to play well. I was running on pure rage, and made a forward pass to make it 2–0. I dominated, and was happy when the referee blew the final whistle. That wasn't the end, though, no way. As I left the pitch, I got word that the Ultras' leaders were waiting for me down in the locker room. I have no idea how they got in there.

There they were down in the passage, seven or eight of them, and not the kind who say things like Excuse me, could we have a quick word? They were guys from the kind of streets I came from, guys brimming with aggression, and everybody around me got nervous. My pulse went up to 150. I was really stressing out, honestly. But I told myself, You can't chicken out now. Where I come from, you don't back down. So I went up to them and I saw right away that made them uneasy, but they played it cocky, like, What the fuck? Ibra's stepping up to us?

"Are there people who have some sort of beef up there?" I asked.

"Yeah, well, a lot of them are angry—" they began.

"Well, tell them to come down onto the pitch and we'll settle it right here!"

Then I walked away, and my heart was pounding. It felt good, though. I'd coped with the stress. I'd stood up for myself, but the shit carried on. The supporters' club demanded an official meeting. Come on. Why should I meet them again? What was in it for me? I was a soccer player. The fans might be loyal to their club. That's nice. But a soccer player's career is short. He's got to look after his own interests. He moves around to different clubs. The fans knew that. I knew that, and I told them: Apologize on your website for your boos and your jeers, and I'll be happy. We'll forget about this. But nothing happened—or rather, the Ultra fans decided they'd neither boo nor cheer me. They'd pretend I didn't exist. Good luck with that, I thought.

I wasn't easy to ignore, not then, not later. I was in form, and the talk continued. Is he leaving? Is he staying? Can anybody afford to pay? It was a tug-of-war, and I was afraid of ending up in a dead end. Of becoming one of those players who stay at a club with their tail between their legs. It was a game of nerves, and I phoned Mino. Were there any offers? Was anything happening? Nothing happening, and it was becoming increasingly obvious that it was going to take a record sum to get me out, if even that, and I tried to shut my eyes and ears to all the stuff in the media. It wasn't easy. Not when you're in that situation. I was in constant contact with Mino, and my hopes were resting more and more with Barcelona. Barça won the Champions League that season. They beat Manchester United 2–0 with goals by Eto'o and Messi, and I thought, Wow! that's the club for me, and I kept phoning Mino.

"What the hell are you doing? Napping?"

"Go fuck yourself," Mino said. "You're shit. Nobody wants you! You'll have to go back to Malmö FF."

"Fuck you!"

Obviously he was doing everything he possibly could to make it happen, not just because he was always fighting in my corner. This was the deal we'd both been dreaming of. Sure, it could all go belly up, with us not achieving anything other than pissing off the Ultras and the directors. Then again, it could also be the greatest thing ever, and we were prepared to play for high stakes.

Meanwhile, I kept playing. We'd already secured the Scudetto. But I really wanted to win the goal-scoring title. Winning the Capocannoniere means getting a place in the history books, and no Swede had done it since Gunnar Nordahl won in 1955. Now I had a chance, though nothing was sure yet. It was even at the top. Marco Di Vaio at Bologna and Diego Milito at Genoa were tied, and of course, it had nothing to do with Mourinho, not really. He coached the team.

Still, he stood up in the locker room and said, "Now we'll make sure Ibra wins the goal-scoring title as well," and that became a thing. Everybody would help me. They all said it publicly.

But Balotelli, that bastard—in one of the last matches, he got the ball in the penalty area, and I came running. I was completely un- marked. I was in the perfect position. Balotelli just kept dribbling, and I gave him a look. What are you doing? Aren't you going to help me? I was furious, but okay, the guy was young. He'd scored goals. I couldn't start yelling at him there. But I was angry, the whole bench was angry—damn it, running there and scoring while Zlatan's in a good position—and I thought, If this is how it's going to be, then fuck the goal-scoring title. Thanks for that, Balotelli. I got over it, though.

I scored a goal in the next match, and with one match left to play, it was set to be a nail-biting finish. Marco Di Vaio and I had both scored twenty-three goals, and Diego Milito at Genoa was right behind us with twenty-two. That was on May 31. All the papers were writing about it. Who would win?

It was hot that day. The league title had been decided. We'd clinched it long ago. There was tons of nerves in the air. With a bit of luck, this would be my farewell to the Italian League. That's what I was hoping. I had no idea. Regardless of whether this was my swan song or not, I wanted to play a brilliant match and win the Capocannoniere. Damn it, I had no intention of finishing with a scoreless draw.

Of course, it wasn't just down to me. It depended on Di Vaio and Milito too, and they were playing at the same time. Di Vaio with Bologna was facing Catania, while Milito and Genoa were up against Lecce, and I had no doubts that those bastards were going to score goals. I was dead set on replying. I had to get it in there, and that's not easy to do to order. If you try too hard, things seize up. Every striker knows that. You can't think about it too much. It's all about instinct. You've just got to go for it, and I could tell right away it was going to be an eventful match against Atalanta. The score was 1–1 after just a few minutes.

In the twelfth minute, Esteban Cambiasso hit a long ball just outside our own penalty area, and I was standing up there on the line with the defenders. I set off, I was just onside, and the defenders couldn't keep up. I ran like lightning and reached the goalkeeper on my own. But the ball bounced. It bounced and skittled, and I bumped it ahead with my knee and was about to collide with the goalie. Just before then I shot to the right, and it was a goal 2–1, and as of that point I was on top of the goal-scoring table. People were shouting that at me, and I started to hope. Maybe it would work out. But things were happening, and I never really got it. Sure, people were shouting from the sideline: "Milito and Di Vaio have scored!"—something like that. I didn't believe it, though. It sounded like some of the guys on the bench were just coming out with crap. There's a lot of that in soccer—trash talk to get people worked up and to annoy them—and I kept playing. I blocked out everything else, and I guess I thought one goal would be enough. There was real drama going on in the other battles.

Diego Milito was in third place in the standings. He's an Argentinian. He had a fearsome scoring record. Only a few weeks before, he had been cleared to join Inter Milan. So if I didn't get out of the club, we'd be playing together. Now, against Lecce, his flow was incredible. He scored two goals in just ten minutes and now had twenty-four goals, same as me, and there was a definite sense that a third goal could come at any time. But it wasn't just Milito. Marco Di Vaio had also scored. I knew nothing about that one. Now the three of us were level at the top, and that's no way to win. You can't share it. You have to bring it home alone, and even though I didn't know for sure, it started to dawn on me that I needed another goal. I could tell by the mood. I read it in people's faces on the bench, in the pressure in the stands. The minutes passed. Nothing happened. It looked like it was going to be a draw. The score was 3–3 with just ten minutes remaining. Mourinho sent on Hernán Crespo. He needed new blood.

He wanted to go on the offensive, and he was waving his arms, as if to say, Move up and go for it! Was I about to lose my chance at the goal-scoring trophy? That's what I feared, and I worked hard. I screamed for the ball. A lot of the players were tired. It had been a close match. But Crespo still had strength. He dribbled on the right side and I ran toward the goal. I got a long cross, and there was an immediate struggle for the ball. I pushed one guy away and ended up with my back to the goal while the ball bounced around, and I saw a chance. Like I said, I was facing the wrong way, so what do you do? You backheel it. I backheeled it at a backward angle, and sure, I'd made a lot of backheel goals in my career—the one against Italy in the European Championship, of course, and that karate move against Bologna. But this one, in this situation, this was just too much.

It couldn't go in. This was a performance, like in Mom's old neighborhood, and you don't win the goal-scoring trophy with a move like that in the very last match. That just doesn't happen. But the ball rolled into the goal. The score was 4–3, and I tore off my shirt, even though I knew it would earn me a yellow card. My God, this was big, and I went and stood down by the corner flag with my shirt off, and of course everybody was piling on top of me, Crespo and everybody. They were pressing down on my back. It looked almost aggressive, and they were all shouting at me, one after the other: "Now you've won the Capocannoniere!"

Slowly, it started to sink in—this is historic, this is my revenge. When I came to Italy, people said, "Zlatan doesn't score enough goals." Now, I'd won the goal-scoring trophy. There could be no more doubt. But I still played it cool. I strolled back toward the pitch, and there was something completely different that really made me stop short.

It was Mourinho, the man with the face of stone. The man who never batted an eyelid had woken up. He was like a madman. He was cheering like a schoolboy, jumping up and down, and I smiled: So I got you going, after all. But it took some doing.

I was forced to win the Capocannoniere with a backheel.

23

On June 3, 2009, Kaká went to Real Madrid for 65 million euros, and later on Cristiano Ronaldo was sold to the same club for 100 million. That said a lot about what level we were talking about, so I went up to Moratti. Moratti was pretty cool, after all. He'd been around for a while. He knew the business.

"Listen," I said. "These years have been incredible, and I'm happy to stay, and I don't care whether United or Arsenal or anybody else comes along. But if Barça should happen to turn up—"

"Yes?" he said.

"Then I want you to at least talk to them. Not that you should sell me for such and such a figure, definitely not. It's up to you. Just promise me you'll speak to them," I added, and he looked at me with his glasses and his ruffled hair, and sure, he understood there was money to be made, no matter how unwilling he was to let me go.

"Okay," he said, "I promise."

We headed to training camp in Los Angeles soon after that. It was the start of the preseason. I was sharing a room with Maxwell, and that was promising, just like old times. We were tired and jet-lagged, though, and the journalists were out of control. They crowded around the hotel, and the big thing of the day in the media was that Barça couldn't afford me. They were planning to take on David Villa instead—not that the papers knew a damn thing about it, but still, I had misgivings. Things had been up and down the last few weeks. I despaired. I'd hoped, and now things seemed to be going down the tubes again, and that goddamn Maxwell wasn't helping matters.

Maxwell is the nicest guy in the world, like I said. Now, though, he was driving me around the bend. We'd been following in each other's footsteps ever since our first days in Amsterdam, and now we were in the same situation yet again. We were both heading for Barcelona. But he was one step ahead—or worse, he was already on his way, while the door might be about to close for me. And he couldn't sleep. He just kept talking on the phone: Is it straightened out? Is it? It was getting on my nerves. It was nonstop, Barça this, Barça that. He kept it up all the time, day and night, or at least that's what it felt like. I was surrounded by this droning while I wasn't hearing a thing about my own deal—well, not much anyway. It was driving me mad. I went at Mino—goddamn Mino, setting it up for Maxwell and not for me, so I called him.

"So you can work for him but not for me?" I said.

"Go fuck yourself," Mino said, and it wasn't long before Maxwell really was set for Barça.

Unlike me, where every single step in the process was followed in the media, he'd managed to keep the negotiations secret. Nobody believed Maxwell would go to Barcelona. That day when we came into the locker room and everybody was sitting in a circle waiting for us, he told them what was going on.

"I'm set for Barcelona!"

People leapt up: You're going? It's true? The talk started. Things like that set people off. Inter Milan wasn't Ajax. The guys were more laid-back, but, even so, Barça had won the Champions League. Barça was the best team in the world. Sure, some guys got jealous, and Maxwell looked almost embarrassed when he started to pack his gear and his shoes.

"Take my shoes as well," I said in a loud voice. "I'm coming with you," and everybody started laughing, saying, Good joke. I was too expensive to be sold, they thought. Or I had it too good at Inter. Nope, Ibra's staying. Nobody can afford him. That's what people thought.

"Sit down! You're not going anywhere," people yelled, and I joked around a little with them, but honestly, I was uncertain myself.

I only knew that Mino was doing the best he could, and it was going to be all or nothing. One day around that time we played Chelsea in a practice match, and I got tackled by John Terry. My hand hurt afterward, but I ignored it. My hand? I wasn't too bothered about that. You play with your feet, and I had other things to think about. Barça was whirling around in my head, and I rang Mino again and again. It was like a fever in my body. Instead of good news, though, I got another kick in the teeth.

Joan Laporta was the president at Barcelona. He really was a big shot. It was during his time that the club had started to dominate again in Europe, and I'd heard he had flown to Milan in a private plane to have dinner with Moratti and Marco Branca, the sports director. I'd had high hopes for that meeting, of course. But nothing came of it.

Laporta had barely come in the door before Moratti said, "If you're here for Zlatan, you can turn around and go home. He's not for sale."

I went nuts when I heard about that. What the fuck? They'd promised! So I phoned Branca and asked him, "What's Moratti playing at?" Branca refused to take responsibility. The meeting wasn't about you, he said. That was a lie. I knew that from Mino, and I felt betrayed. Sure, I also understood it was a game. At least it could be. "Not for sale" could be another way of saying "expensive." But I didn't have a clue what was really going on, and the damned journalists were like rabid dogs.

They were constantly asking, "What's going to happen? Are you set for Barça? Are you staying at Inter?" I had no answers to give. I was in a new no-man's-land, and even Mino, who was working like crazy, was starting to sound a little pessimistic:

"Barça is fired up, but they can't get you out of here," he said.

I was on tenterhooks, and L.A. was hot and noisy. There were a few things that happened which seemed to confirm I'd be staying. I was going to have the number-ten shirt for the next season at Inter, the same number Ronaldo had when he was on the squad. There were a few things like that, PR stuff and other things I was involved in. Everything was uncertain. The mood was unsettled.

I heard that Joan Laporta and Txiki Begiristain, Barça's sports director, were in their private plane again. This trip had nothing to do with me. They were on their way to Ukraine to purchase Dmytro Chygrynskiy, one of the key players at FK Shakhtar Donetsk, who'd stunned everyone by winning the UEFA Cup that year. Their trip still had implications for us. Mino's a sly one. He knows all the tricks. He'd just had yet another meeting with Moratti and sensed an opening, in spite of everything. So he phoned Txiki Begiristain, who was on the plane with Laporta. They were on their way back to Barcelona.

"You should land in Milan instead," Mino said.

"Why?"

"Because I know Moratti's sitting at home right now, and if you go and knock on his door, I think you can put together a deal for Ibrahimović."

"Okay, wait a minute. I need to discuss it with Laporta."

The minutes dragged by, and the stakes were high. Moratti hadn't promised anything, and he had no idea anyone might come knocking on his door. Now everything was happening at once. Txiki Begiristain phoned back. "Okay," he said, "we'll turn around. We'll land in Milan instead," and, of course, I got word about that right away.

Mino rang me. There were calls and texts going back and forth. Phones were ringing off the hook. Moratti was told, "Barça's managers are on their way!" He might have thought it was a bit out of the blue, I don't know, or that those guys could at least have booked a meeting ahead of time. Of course, he let them in. He had style. He didn't want to lose face, and in that situation I didn't hesitate. I had to do whatever I could.

I texted Marco Branca. I wrote, "I know Barça's management are on their way to Moratti. You've promised me you'll talk to them, and you know I want to join their club. Don't mess this up, and I won't mess things up for you," and I waited a long time for a reply. I didn't get any. I'm sure they had their reasons. It's a game, like I said. Now, though, I could sense it in the air: it's serious. It's happening! Or the door will shut. It was one or the other, and the minutes passed. What were they talking about in there? I didn't have a clue.

I knew what time they were meeting and I watched the clock, expecting it to take hours. After twenty-five minutes, Mino rang, and of course it made me jump. What now? Had Moratti sent them on their way again? My pulse was racing. My mouth went dry.

"Yeah," I said.

"It's set," he replied.

"What do you mean, 'set'?"

"You're going to Barcelona. Pack your bags."

"You can't fucking joke about stuff like this."

"I'm not joking."

"How the hell could it have happened so fast?"

"No time to talk now."

He hung up, and I couldn't quite take it in. My head was whirling. I was at the hotel. What should I do? I went out into the corridor. I needed to talk to someone. Patrick Vieira was standing there, and he's a guy you can trust.

"I'm set for Barça," I said. He looked at me.

"No way," he replied.

"Yeah, I promise."

"How much are we talking about?"

I didn't know. I had no idea, and I could tell he had his doubts. He thought I was too expensive, and that made me unsure. Could it really be true? Soon Mino called me again, and the pieces of the puzzle began to fall into place. Moratti had been surprisingly cooperative.

He'd had just one condition—though it wasn't just any condition, that's for sure. He wanted to give AC Milan one in the eye and sell me for more than Real Madrid had paid for Kaká, and that was no small potatoes: it would mean the second-most-expensive transfer in history, and Joan Laporta clearly had no problem with that. He and Moratti had reached an agreement quickly, and it took a while to sink in when I heard the sums involved. My old 85 million kronor in the Ajax deal—what was that? Small change, by comparison. Now we were talking more like 700 million Swedish kronor (around $82 million).

Inter was getting 46 million euros for me, and along with that they'd receive Samuel Eto'o as partial payment—and Samuel Eto'o was not just anybody. He'd scored thirty goals the previous season. He was one of the top goal-scorers in Barcelona's history and was valued at 20 million euros. That amounted to 66 million euros in all, a million more than what AC Milan had sold Kaká for, and you can just imagine. There was a huge uproar when it came out. I'd never experienced anything like it.

It was 104 degrees. It was as if the air was boiling. Everybody was after me, and it felt . . . honestly, I don't know. It was impossible to think straight. We were playing a practice match against a Mexican team, and I had that number-ten shirt at Inter for the first time—and the last, for that matter. My years with the club were over. It was starting to sink in. When I arrived, Inter hadn't won a league title in seventeen years. Now we'd triumphed three years in a row, and I'd won the Capocannoniere goal-scoring title. It was unbelievable, and I looked at Mourinho, the guy I'd finally got to react to a goal, and of course I noticed he was furious and upset.

He didn't want to lose me, and he put me on the bench for that practice match, and I was feeling it too: no matter how happy I was to be going to Barça, it was sad to leave Mourinho. That guy is special. The following year, he left Inter for Real Madrid, and at the same time he and Materazzi parted ways. Materazzi is about the world's toughest defender. As he hugged Mourinho, though, he began to cry, and I can understand him in a way. Mourinho arouses feelings in people, and I remember when we bumped into each other the next day at the hotel. He came up to me:

"You can't leave!"

"Sorry, I've got to take this opportunity."

"If you leave, I will too."

My God, what can you say to that? That really hit me.

"Thanks," I said. "You've taught me a lot."

"Thank you," he said.

We chatted for a bit, and it was nice. But that guy, he's like me. He's proud, and he wanted to win at any price, and of course, he couldn't help himself. He had a little dig at me as well.

"Hey, Ibra!"

"Yeah?"

"You're going to Barça to win the Champions, huh?"

"Yeah, maybe."

"But we're the ones who're gonna bring it home—don't forget. It's gonna be us!"

Then we said goodbye.

———

I flew to Copenhagen and got back home to our house on Limhamns-vägen and saw Helena and the kids. I'd really been looking forward to having a chance to tell them about everything and get a bit grounded, but our home was practically under siege. There were journalists and fans sleeping outside our house. They were ringing our doorbell. People were yelling and singing out there. They waved Barcelona flags. It was completely crazy, and my whole family got stressed out: Mom, Dad, Sanela, Keki—nobody dared to go out. People were after them as well, and I was rushing around, and sure, I noticed that my hand was hurting, but I didn't pay much attention to it.

Things were happening all the time—details in my contract being ironed out, Eto'o being difficult and wanting more money, Helena and I discussing where we were going to live—all that stuff. There was no way I'd be able to get grounded or think things through properly, so after just two days I headed off to Barcelona. In those days, I was used to flying on private planes. It might sound snooty, but it's not easy for me on regular commercial flights. Everybody's after me. It's chaos, both in the airport and onboard.

This time, I did take an ordinary flight. I'd spoken to the Barça gang on the phone, and as you know, Barcelona and Real Madrid are at war with each other. They're archrivals, and a lot of it has to do with politics—Catalonia against the central power in Spain, all that stuff—but the clubs also have different philosophies. "At Barcelona, we've got our feet on the ground. We're not like Real. We travel on regular planes," they told me, and sure, that sounded reasonable. I flew with Spanair and landed in Barcelona at a quarter past five in the afternoon, and if I hadn't understood how big a deal this was before, I did now.

It was chaos. Hundreds of fans and journalists were waiting for me, and the papers wrote pages and pages about it. People were talking about "Ibramania." It was crazy. I wasn't just Barcelona's most expensive purchase ever; no new player had attracted this level of attention. I was going to be introduced at the Camp Nou stadium that evening. It's a tradition at the club. When Ronaldinho arrived in 2003, there were thirty thousand people there. Just as many had welcomed Thierry Henry. But now . . . there were at least twice that many waiting for me, and it gave me chills, honestly, and I was taken out through the rear exit of the airport and driven to the stadium in a security vehicle.

We were holding a press conference first. Several hundred journalists were crammed into the room. It was jam-packed and people were restless: Why isn't he coming? We still couldn't go in. Eto'o kept making things difficult for Inter Milan right down to the wire, and Barcelona was waiting for a final confirmation of the deal, and time was ticking and the voices in the room kept getting more agitated and worried; there was a riot brewing. We could hear it just as clearly as if we'd been in the middle of it. Me, Mino, Laporta, and the other bigwigs sat behind the scenes and waited, wondering what was going on. How long are we going to have to keep sitting here?

"I've had enough," said Mino.

"We need confirmation . . ."

"Screw that," he said, getting the others onboard, and then we finally went in. I'd never seen so many reporters, and I answered their questions, but the whole time I could hear the roar out in the stadium. Everything was nuts, I'm telling you, and afterward I got out of there and changed into my Barça jersey. I'd been given number nine, the same number Ronaldo had when he was at the club, and now things were getting really emotional. The stadium was at the boiling point. There were sixty or seventy thousand people out there. I tried to take a few deep breaths, and then I went out. I will never be able to describe it.

I had a ball in my hand, and I went out to that stand they'd set up, and the crowd was roaring all around me. Everybody was screaming my name. The entire stadium was cheering, and the press guy was running around saying stuff to me all the time like "Say '*Visca, Barça!,*'" which means "Go, Barça!" I did what he said, and I did some tricks, up and down, on my chest, on my head, backheels, all that stuff, and the spectators were screaming for more so I kissed the club's badge on my shirt. I have to tell you about that. I got a lot of shit for that—people were saying, How could he kiss the club's badge when he'd only just left Inter? Didn't he care about his old fans? All kinds of people grumbled about that. There were comedy sketches on TV and crap. The press guys had asked me to do it. They were going crazy, saying, "Kiss the badge, kiss the badge," and I was like a little boy. I obeyed. My whole body was vibrating, and I remember I wanted to go back into the locker room and calm down.

There was too much adrenaline. I was shaking, and when it was finally over I looked at Mino. He'd never been more than ten meters away. At times like that, he's everything to me, and together we went into the locker room and looked at all the names on the wall: Messi,

Xavi, Iniesta, Henry, and Maxwell, all of them, and then mine, Ibra-himović. It was already there, and I looked at Mino again. He was blown away. It was like he'd become a parent. Neither of us could take it in. It felt bigger than we could have imagined, and just then a text pinged on my phone. Who was it? It was Patrick Vieira. "Enjoy," he wrote. "This doesn't happen to many players." Honestly, you can hear all kinds of things from all kinds of people, but when a guy like Vieira sends you a message like that, you know you've been involved in something incredible. I sat down to catch my breath.

Afterward, I told the journalists, "I'm the happiest guy in the world!"; "This is the greatest thing that's happened since my sons were born"—the sort of things I'm sure other athletes have said before in similar situations. But I really meant it. This was big, and I went to the Princesa Sofia Hotel, which was also besieged by fans, who thought it was a massive deal just to have a chance to see me drinking coffee in the lobby.

That night, I had a hard time getting to sleep—no wonder, really. My whole body was jumping, and sure, I did feel that my hand wasn't all right. I didn't give it much thought then, either. There was so much other stuff going around in my head, and I didn't think there would be any problems at my medical exam the next day. When you join a club it's routine that they give you a thorough checkup. How much do you weigh? How tall are you? What's your body-fat percentage? Do you feel match fit?

"My hand hurts," I said during the exam, and the doctors did an X-ray.

I had a fracture in my hand. A fracture! That was insane. One of the most important things when you join a new club is that you get to be there in the preseason and get to know the guys and their game. Now that seemed to be out of the question, and we had to make a quick decision. I spoke to Guardiola, the manager. He seemed nice and said he was sorry he hadn't been there to welcome me. He'd been in London with the team, and just like everyone else he declared that I needed to get match fit as quickly as possible. They couldn't take any chances, so they decided to operate on me immediately.

An orthopedic surgeon implanted two steel pins in my hand to hold the fracture in place and help it heal faster. The same day I headed back to the training camp in Los Angeles. It seemed absurd, somehow. I'd just been there with Inter Milan. Now I was arriving with a new club and a huge plaster cast around my hand. It would take at least three weeks before it healed up.

24

We were going to be playing against Real Madrid at home at Camp Nou. This was in November of 2009. I'd been out again for fifteen days. I'd been having pains in my thigh and would be starting on the bench, which of course was no fun. There are few things like El Clásico. The pressure is enormous. It's war, and the papers produce special supplements that are about sixty pages long. People talk about nothing else. These are the big teams, the archenemies facing each other.

I'd had a good start to the season, despite the fracture in my hand and all the upheaval. I'd scored five goals in my first five league matches and was praised to the skies. That felt good, and it was clear La Liga was the place to be. Real and Barça had invested the equivalent of nearly 2.5 billion Swedish kronor (around $300 million) in Kaká, Cristiano, and me, and the Italian Serie A and the Premier League were both worse off. La Liga was on top now. Everything was going to be fantastic. That's what I thought.

Even in the preseason when I was running around in a plaster cast with pins in my hand, I'd become part of the gang. It wasn't easy with the language, of course, and I hung around a lot with the ones who spoke English—Thierry Henry and Maxwell. I got on well with everybody, though. Messi, Xavi, and Iniesta are good, down-to-earth guys, awesome on the pitch and easy to deal with—there's none of that, Here I come, I'm the biggest and best, not at all, and none of the fashion parades in the locker room that so many of the players in Italy were into. Messi and the guys showed up in warmups and kept a low profile—and then, of course, there was Guardiola.

He seemed all right. He'd come up to me and talk after every training session. He really wanted to bring me onto the team, and sure, the club had a special atmosphere. I'd sensed that right off. It was like a school, like Ajax. But this was Barça, the best team in the world. I'd been expecting a little more of an attitude. Here, everybody was quiet and polite and a team player, and sometimes I'd think, These guys are superstars. Yet they behave like schoolboys—and maybe that's good, what do I know? I couldn't help wondering: How would these guys have been treated in Italy? They would've been like gods.

Now they toed the line for Pep Guardiola. Guardiola is a Catalan. He's an old midfielder. He won the La Liga title five or six times with Barcelona and became team captain in 1997. When I arrived, he'd been managing the club for two years and had been very successful. He definitely deserved respect, and I thought the obvious thing to do was to try to fit in. That wasn't exactly something I was unfamiliar with—I'd switched clubs several times and never just barged straight in and started ordering people around. I sound out my surroundings. Who's strong? Who's weak? What's the banter like? Who tends to stick together?

At the same time, I was aware of my qualities. I had concrete evidence of what I could mean for a team with my winner's mind-set, and I was usually back to taking up a lot of space quickly, and I joked around a lot. Not long ago, I gave Chippen Wilhelmsson a playful kick at a session with the Swedish national team, and I couldn't believe it when I opened the paper the next day. People saw it as this fierce attack. It was nothing, though, nothing at all. That's just what we do. It's both a game and deadly serious at the same time. We're a bunch of guys who are together all day long and pull little stunts to keep ourselves going. Nothing more to it than that. We joke around. But at Barça I got boring. I became too nice, and I didn't dare to yell or blow up on the pitch the way I need to do.

The newspapers writing that I was a bad boy and stuff was definitely part of it. It made me want to prove the opposite, and of course it went too far. Instead of being myself, I was trying to be the super-nice guy, and that was stupid. You can't let the garbage from the media get you down. It was unprofessional. I admit it. That wasn't the main thing, though.

This was: "We keep our feet on the ground here. We are *fabricantes*. We work here. We're regular guys."

Maybe that doesn't sound so strange, but there was something peculiar about those words, and I started to wonder, Why is Guardiola saying this to me?

Does he think I'm different? I couldn't put my finger on it, not at first. But it didn't feel quite right. Sometimes it was like on the youth squad at Malmö FF. Was this another coach who saw me as the kid from the wrong neighborhood? I hadn't done anything, hadn't headbutted a teammate, hadn't stolen a bike—nothing. I've never been such a wimp in my life. I was the opposite of what the papers were saying. I was the guy who tiptoed around and always weighed things up beforehand. The old, wild Zlatan was gone. I was a shadow of my former self.

That had never happened before but, for now, it wasn't a major thing. Things will work out, I thought, I'll soon be myself again. Things will loosen up, and maybe it's just my imagination, some kind of paranoia. Guardiola wasn't unpleasant, not at all. He seemed to believe in me. He saw how I scored goals and how much I meant to the team, and yet . . . that feeling wouldn't go away: Did he think I was different?

"We keep our feet on the ground here!"

Was I the guy who didn't keep his feet on the ground? Is that what he thought? I didn't get it. So I tried to brush it off. Told myself: Focus, instead. Just forget about it. Those bad vibes were still there, though, and I started to wonder more and more. Is everybody supposed to be the same on this club? It didn't seem healthy. Everybody's different. Sometimes people pretend, of course. But when they do, they're just hurting themselves and harming the team. Sure, Guardiola had been successful. The club had won a lot under him. I've got to applaud that, and a win is a win.

Looking back now, I think it came at a price. All the big personalities were chased out. It was no accident that he'd had problems with guys like Ronaldinho, Deco, Eto'o, Henry, and me. We're no "ordinary guys." We're threatening to him, and so he tried to get rid of us—nothing more complicated than that—and I hate that sort of thing. If you're not an "ordinary guy" you shouldn't have to become one. Nobody benefits from that in the long run. Hell, if I'd tried to be like the Swedish guys at Malmö FF I wouldn't be where I am today. Listen/Don't listen—that's the reason for my success.

It doesn't work for everybody. But it does for me, and Guardiola didn't understand that at all. He thought he could change me. At his Barça, everybody should be like Xavi, Iniesta, and Messi. Nothing wrong with them, like I said, absolutely nothing at all. It was terrific being on the same team as them. Good players get me fired up, and

I'd watch them the way I'd always done with great talents, thinking, Can I learn something? Can I make even more of an effort?

Just look at their backgrounds. Xavi joined Barça when he was eleven years old. Iniesta was twelve, Messi thirteen. They were molded by the club. They knew of nothing else, and I'm sure that was good for them. That was their thing, but it wasn't mine. I came from outside; I came with my whole personality, and there didn't seem to be space for that, not in Guardiola's little world. Like I said, this was just a feeling, back then in November. Back then, my problems were more basic.

Was I going to get to play, and would I be sharp enough after my time off?

———

The pressure was intense in the lead-up to El Clásico at Camp Nou. Manuel Pellegrini, a Chilean, was the Real Madrid manager then. There was speculation that he might get the ax if Real didn't win. There was talk about me, Kaká, Cristiano Ronaldo, Messi, Pellegrini, and Guardiola. There was a lot of, This guy versus that guy. The city was simmering with anticipation, and I arrived at the stadium in the club's Audi and walked into the locker room. Guardiola was starting with Thierry Henry up front, Messi on the right wing, and Iniesta on the left. It was dark outside. The stadium was floodlit, and camera flashes were going off everywhere up in the stands.

We sensed it right away: Real Madrid was more fired up. They created more chances and, twenty minutes in, Kaká made this incredibly elegant, nimble dribble and played it up to Cristiano Ronaldo, who was completely free. He had a brilliant position, but missed. Víctor Valdés, our goalkeeper, saved it with his foot, and only a minute later Higuaín was on his way through for Real. It was close, very close. There were a lot of chances, and we were playing too stationary and were having trouble with our passing game. Nerves spread through the team, and the home fans booed, especially at Casillas in goal for Real. He was taking his time with his goal kicks. But Real continued to dominate, and we were lucky to hold the score to 0–0 at halftime.

At the start of the second half, Guardiola asked me to warm up, and that was a good feeling, I've got to say. The spectators shouted and cheered. The roar enveloped me, and I returned the applause as thanks, and in the fifty-first minute Thierry Henry came off and I went on. I was desperate to play. I hadn't been away for all that long. It felt like it, though, maybe partly because I'd missed a Champions League match in the group stage against my old team, Inter Milan. Now I was back, and after only a few minutes Daniel Alves, the Brazilian, got the ball over on the right. Alves is quick on the ball, and the attack was swift. There was some confusion in Real's defense and, in those situations, I don't think, I just rush toward the penalty area—and then a cross came. I powered ahead.

I broke free and caught a volley with my left foot—bang, boom!—into the goal, and the stadium erupted like a volcano and I felt it in my whole body: nothing could stop me now. We won 1–0. I was the match winner, and there was praise from all quarters. Now no one was questioning that I'd cost 700 million kronor. I was on fire.

Then came the Christmas break. We headed up to northern Sweden and I drove my snowmobile, like I said, and had fun. It was also the turning point. After New Year's, everything that had been difficult in the autumn got even worse, and I was no longer myself. That's how it felt. I'd become a different, uncertain Zlatan, and every time after Mino had a meeting with the management at Barça I'd ask him, "What do they think of me?"

"That you're the world's best striker!"

"I mean personally. As a person."

I'd never worried about that before. I never used to care about that sort of thing. As long as I got to play, people could say whatever they wanted. Now, it was important all of a sudden, and it showed that I wasn't doing well. My confidence took a nosedive, and I felt inhibited. I hardly celebrated when I scored. I didn't dare to be angry, and that's not a good thing, not at all. I was bottling things up, and I'm really not oversensitive. I'm tough. I've been through a lot. Still, getting looks and comments day after day that I wasn't fitting in or that I was different, it gets under your skin. It was like going back in time, to the years before my career took off. A lot of it isn't worth mentioning, just little things like looks, comments, turns of phrase, stuff I'd never cared about before. I'm used to hard knocks. That's what I'd grown up with. Now I was getting this feeling—like, Am I the foster kid in this family, the guy who doesn't belong? And how messed up was that?

The first time I'd really tried to fit in I was given the cold shoulder, and, as if that wasn't bad enough, there was the thing with Messi. You remember from the first chapter. Messi was the big star. In a way, it was his team. He was shy and polite, definitely. I liked him. But now I was there, and I'd also dominated on the pitch and caused a massive uproar.

It must have been a bit like I'd gone to his place and hopped into his bed. He told Guardiola he didn't want to play on the wing anymore. He wanted to be in the center, and I was locked in up there and didn't get any balls, and the situation from back in the autumn was now reversed. I was no longer the one who scored goals, Messi was, and so I had that conversation with Guardiola. The directors had been pressuring me.

"Speak to him. Sort it out!"

How did it go? It started a war, and I got the silent treatment. He stopped speaking to me. He stopped looking at me. He said good morning to all the others. He didn't say a damn thing to me, and it got uncomfortable, I'm sad to say, it really did. I would've liked to say I didn't care. What do I care about a guy who resorts to bullying? In another situation, I'm sure that would have been my attitude. But I wasn't strong then.

The situation broke me down, and that wasn't easy. Having a boss with such power over you, who consciously ignores you, it ends up getting to you, and now it wasn't just me who noticed it. Others saw it, and they wondered, What's going on? What's this about?

They told me: "You've got to speak to him. This can't go on." No, I'd spoken to that guy enough. I had no intention of crawling to him, so I gritted my teeth and started playing well again, despite my position on the pitch and the disastrous mood on the club. I got into a groove where I scored five, six goals. Guardiola was just as distant— and it was no wonder, I realize now.

It was never about my game. It was about me as a person. Thoughts were whirling in my head, day and night: Is it something I said, something I did? Do I look strange? I went over everything, every little episode, every encounter. I couldn't find anything. I'd kept quiet, been a massive bore. But I kept asking myself, Is it this, is it that? So, no, I didn't just respond with rage.

I was searching for faults with myself just as much. I thought about it all the time. The guy didn't give in, and that wasn't just nasty, it was unprofessional. The whole team suffered as a result, and the management was getting more and more worried. Guardiola was about to wreck the club's biggest investment, and there were important matches coming up in the Champions League. We were going to be facing Arsenal away. Meanwhile, the stalemate between the manager and me continued, and I'm sure he would've preferred to drop me completely. He probably didn't want to go that far, so I started up front with Messi.

Did I get any instructions? Nothing! I just had to go for it on my own. We were at Emirates Stadium. This was big, and, as usual in England, I had the spectators and the journalists against me, and there was a load of crap, like, He never scores against English teams. I gave a press conference. I tried to be myself, in spite of everything. I told them, "Wait and see. I'll show you."

It wasn't easy, though, not with that manager. I stepped onto the pitch and things started off tough. The pace was blinding, and Guardiola vanished from my mind. It was nothing short of magic. Never played a match as good as that, I don't think. It's true, I did miss some chances. I shot right at Arsenal's goalie. I should've made that one, but it didn't happen and we went in at halftime at 0–0.

Guardiola is sure to take me out, I thought. But he let me play on, and the second half had barely started before I got a long ball from Piqué and rushed in deep. I had a defender close on me and the goalkeeper ran out and the ball bounced, and then I lobbed it over him and into the goal. That made it 1–0, and just over ten minutes later I got a nice pass from Xavi and I ran off like an arrow. I didn't lob it this time. I thundered in there. I shot with tremendous force to score 2–0, and we seemed to have the match in the bag. I'd been brilliant. But what did Guardiola do? Was he applauding? He substituted me. Smart move! After that, the team fell apart and Arsenal managed to equalize 2–2 in the final minutes.

I hadn't felt anything during the match. Afterward, though, my calf hurt, and it got worse, and that was shit. I'd regained my form. Now I was going to be out of the return leg at home against Arsenal and the El Clásico that spring, and I didn't get any support from Guardiola. I got more knockbacks. If I went into a room, he'd leave. He didn't even want to be near me, and now, when I look back on it, it feels completely messed up.

Nobody understood what was going on—not the management,

not the players, nobody. There's something strange about that man. Like I said, I don't begrudge him his successes and I'm not saying he's not a good coach in other respects. But he must have some serious problems. He doesn't seem able to handle guys like me. Maybe it's something as simple as a fear of losing his authority. That sort of thing isn't too unusual, is it? Managers who probably have certain qualities but who can't deal with strong personalities and solve it by shutting them out. Cowardly leaders, in other words.

Anyway, he never asked me about my injury. He didn't dare to. Well, actually, he did speak to me before the Champions League semifinal away against Inter Milan. But he was acting strange and it all went wrong, like I said. Mourinho was right. It wasn't us but him who won the Champions League and, afterward, Guardiola treated me as if it was all my fault, and that's when the real storm started brewing.

It was scary in a way, the feeling that everything you've been keeping bottled up needs to come out, and I was happy I had Thierry Henry. He understood me, and we'd joke around, like I said. That eased the pressure, and at some point I stopped letting the whole thing get to me. What else could I do? For the first time, soccer didn't seem so important. I focused on Maxi, Vincent, and Helena, and I became closer to them during that time. I'm grateful for that. My kids mean everything to me. That's the truth.

I still couldn't shake off the atmosphere at the club, and that outburst that had been smoldering inside me finally came out. In the changing room after the match against Villarreal, I screamed at Guardiola. I screamed about his balls and how he'd been shitting himself in front of Mourinho, and you can just imagine. It was war, and it was me against him. Guardiola, the frightened little overthinker who couldn't even look me in the eye or say good morning, and me, who'd been quiet and cautious for such a long time but who finally blew up and became myself again.

This was no game. In another setting, with another person, it wouldn't have been so bad. Outbursts like that are no big deal to me, whether I'm on the giving or the receiving end. They're something I grew up with. They're run-of-the-mill to me, and things like that have often actually turned out well. The outburst clears the air. Vieira and I became friends after an almighty blowup. But with Pep . . . I could tell right away.

He couldn't deal with it. He completely avoided me, and I would often lie awake at night thinking about the whole situation. What's going to happen next? And what should I do? One thing was clear: it was like on the Malmö FF youth squad. I was seen as different. So I had to become an even better player. I had to get so damned good that not even Guardiola could put me on the bench. I had no intention of trying to become a different person anymore—no way. Screw that. "We're like this here. We're ordinary guys here." I was realizing more and more how immature it was. A real manager can deal with different personalities. That's part of his job. A team works well with different types of people. Some are a bit tougher. Others are like Maxwell, or like Messi and the gang.

Guardiola couldn't take that, though, and felt he had to get back at me. I could sense it. It was hanging in the air and, apparently, he didn't really care that it was going to cost the club hundreds of millions. We were going to be playing our last match in the league. He put me on the bench. I hadn't expected anything else. Now, suddenly he wanted to speak to me. He called me into his office at the stadium. That was in the morning, and on the walls in there he had soccer shirts and photos of himself and that sort of thing. The atmosphere was icy. We hadn't spoken since my outburst. He was nervous as well. His eyes were darting around.

That man has no natural authority, no proper charisma. If you didn't know he was the manager of a top team, you'd hardly notice him entering a room. In that office now, he was fidgeting. I'm sure he was waiting for me to say something. I didn't say a thing. I waited.

"So then," he began.

He didn't look me in the eye.

"I'm not really sure what I want to do with you next season."

"Okay."

"It's up to you and Mino what happens. I mean, you're Ibrahimović. You're not a guy who plays in every third match, right?"

He wanted me to say something. I could tell. But I'm not stupid. I know very well: whoever talks the most in these situations comes out worst off. So I kept my mouth shut. I didn't move a muscle. I sat still. Of course, I understood: he had a message; exactly what it was wasn't clear. It sounded like he wanted to get rid of me, and that was no small matter. I was the club's biggest investment ever. Still, I sat there in silence. I did nothing.

Then he repeated, "I don't know what I want to do with you. What do you say to that? What's your comment?"

I had no comment.

"Is that it?" was all I said.

"Yes, but . . ."

"Thanks, then," I said, and left.

I guess I looked cool and hard. That's how I wanted to look, at least. Inside, though, I was fuming, and when I came out I called Mino.

25

Sometimes, maybe, I go too hard on people. I dunno. That's been a thing with me from the very beginning. My dad would go off like an angry bear when he drank, and everybody in the family would be scared and get out of there. But I stood up to him, man to man, and I'd shout things like You have to stop drinking! He'd go crazy: "Goddamn it, this is my home. I'll do what I want. I'll throw you out!"

Sometimes, it was absolute chaos. The whole apartment would shake. We never came to blows, though. He had a big heart. He'd be prepared to die for me. Honestly, though, I was prepared to fight.

I was prepared for anything, and sometimes, sure, I understood there was no point. It'd just lead to confrontation and rage. We wouldn't take a single step in the right direction—quite the opposite. Still, I kept it up. I took those fights, and don't think I'm trying to brag about me being the tough guy in the family. Not at all. I'm just telling it like it was.

That's a trait I had from early on. I stepped up. I didn't run away, and not just with Dad. It was everywhere. My entire childhood was filled with tough people who would go off on a hair-trigger—Mom, my sisters, the guys around the projects—and ever since then I've had it in me, that watchful side: What's happening? Who wants a fight? My body is always ready for battle.

That's the path I chose. The others in our family took on different roles. Sanela was the one you went to with emotional things. I was the fighter. If anybody gave me shit, I'd give them shit back. That was my way to survive, and I learned not to sugarcoat things. I said things straight out, none of this "You're really good, you're great, but . . ." It was straight in there: "You've got to get a fucking grip." Then I'd take the consequences. That's how it was. That was how I grew up, and sure, I'd changed a lot by the time I got to Barcelona. I'd met Helena and had children and calmed down, and said stuff like Please pass me the butter. Most of it was still in there, though. Those days at the club, I clenched my fists and prepared to defend my corner. This was in late spring, early summer 2010. The World Cup was coming up in South Africa, and Joan Laporta was leaving Barça.

They were choosing a new president for the club, and that kind of thing always generates unrest. People get uneasy. A guy called Sandro Rosell was appointed. Rosell had been vice president up until 2005 and he'd been friends with Laporta. But something had happened. Now they were enemies, people said. So, of course, people were concerned. Was Rosell going to dump all the old gang? No one knew. Txiki Begiristain, the sports director, resigned before Rosell could fire him, and naturally I was wondering, What would this mean for my conflict with Guardiola?

Laporta was the one who'd bought me for a record amount, and it wasn't unreasonable to think that Rosell might give him one in the eye by showing it was a stupid investment. Many papers even wrote that Rosell's first task was to sell me. The journalists definitely had no clue about what had happened between me and Guardiola and, in a way, neither did I. But they'd figured that something was wrong, and really, you didn't need to be a soccer expert to understand. I went around with my head hanging, and I didn't react the way I usually did on the pitch. Guardiola had wrecked me, and I remember Mino phoned the new club president. He told him what Guardiola had said in that meeting.

"What the hell did the guy mean?" he asked. "Does he want to get rid of Zlatan?"

"No, no," Rosell replied. "Guardiola believes in him."

"Then why would he say that?"

Rosell couldn't answer. He was new, and nobody seemed to know. The situation was uncertain. We won the league title, and then we went on vacation. I needed a vacation more than I had in a long time. I needed to get away, so Helena and I traveled around to L.A., Vegas, all over, and the World Cup was on then. I barely watched it. I was too disappointed. Sweden wasn't in the tournament, and really, I didn't want to think about soccer at all. I tried to block out the whole mess with Barça. It couldn't last forever, of course. The days went by. I'd be going back soon, and no matter how much I tried to stop them, all the questions came back. What's going to happen? What should I do? My mind was buzzing, and I realized there was an obvious solution. I could make sure I got sold. I didn't want to let go of my dream that easily, though. Never, ever. I decided to work like a dog in practice and get better than ever.

Nobody was going to crack me. I'd show them all. But what do you think happened? I didn't get a chance to show anybody anything. I hadn't even put my shoes on when Guardiola called me in again. This was on July 19, I think. Most of them hadn't come back from the World Cup yet. It was pretty quiet around us, and Pep attempted some small talk. He clearly had an agenda. He was nervous and awkward. He probably wanted to be a bit pleasant at first, for the sake of things.

"How was your vacation?"

"Good, good!"

"And how do you feel, ahead of the new season?"

"Fine. I'm up for it. I'm going to give a hundred percent."

"Look . . ."

"Yeah."

"You should be prepared to sit on the bench," he said, and, like I said, this was the first day. The preseason hadn't even gotten under way yet. Guardiola hadn't even seen me play, not even for a minute. There was no way to interpret his words other than as a new personal attack.

"Okay" was all I said. "I understand."

"And, as you know, we've acquired David Villa from Valencia." David Villa was a hot property, no doubt about it. He was one of the stars of the Spanish national team, who were down there winning the World Cup, but still, he was a winger. I played in the center. He had nothing to do with me, not really.

"And what do you say to that?" he continued.

Nothing, I thought at first, beyond "Congratulations." But then it struck me: Why not test Guardiola? Why not check whether this has anything at all to do with soccer, or whether it's all just about driving me out of the club?

"What do I say to that?" I began.

"Yes."

"Well, that I'll work harder. I'll work like a madman to earn my place on the team. I'll convince you I'm good enough." To be honest, I could hardly believe it myself.

I'd never sucked up to a coach like that before. My philosophy had always been to let my playing do the talking. It's just ridiculous to go around saying you're going to give a hundred percent. You're paid to give a hundred percent. But this was my way of trying to understand. I wanted to hear what he'd say. If he said, Okay, then we'll see if you make it, that would mean something. But now he just looked at me.

"I know that. But how are we going to continue?" he asked.

"Just like that," I replied. "I'll work hard, and if you think I'm good enough, I'll play in whatever position you want, behind or in front of or underneath Messi. Wherever. You decide."

"I know that. But how are we going to continue?"

He kept repeating the same thing, and not once did he say anything that made sense. He has no aptitude for that. It wasn't necessary, though. I understood. This had nothing to do with whether I earned a place or not. This was personal, and instead of coming out and saying he didn't like my personality, he was trying to sugarcoat it in a single, obscure phrase:

"How are we going to continue?"

"I'll do like everybody else, I'll play for Messi," I said.

"I know that. But how are we going to continue?"

It was ridiculous, and I suppose he wanted me to lose control and shout, I won't accept this, I'm leaving the club. Then he'd be able to come out and say, Zlatan was the one who wanted to leave, it wasn't my decision. Maybe I'm a savage, a guy who goes in for confrontations too often. But I also know when I need to restrain myself. I had nothing to gain by announcing I was for sale, so I thanked him calmly for speaking to me and got out of there.

Of course, I was furious. I was seething. Still, the meeting had been productive. I understood where things stood. He had no intention of letting me play, even if I learned to fly, and the real question now was: Would I be able to cope with that, go to practice every day and have that guy standing in front of me? I doubted it. Maybe I needed to change tack. I thought about it. I thought about it all the time.

We headed to South Korea and China for preseason training, and I got to play a few matches out there. It meant nothing. The key players hadn't returned from the World Cup yet. I was still the black sheep, and Guardiola was keeping his distance. If he wanted anything, he'd send others to speak to me, and the media was completely out of control. It had been like that all summer: What's happening with Zlatan? Will he be transferred? Will he stay? They were constantly after me, and it was the same for Guardiola. He got questions about it all the time, and what do you think he told them? Nice and straight, like, I don't like Zlatan, I want to get rid of him? Not exactly. He looked uncomfortable, and came out with his waffle:

"Zlatan will decide his own future."

What crap. Something started ticking inside me. I felt under fire, and I was furious. I wanted to do something explosive. But also—how can I put it? Something was sparked off inside me as well. I understood that things had entered a new phase. Now it wasn't just war. Now the fight on the transfer market had begun, and I like that game, and I had the guy who's the best of them all at that on my side—Mino. He and I talked all the time, and we decided to play tough and hard. Guardiola deserved nothing else.

In South Korea, I had a meeting with Josep Maria Bartomeu, the club's new vice president. We sat in the hotel and talked, and at least that guy was clear.

"Zlatan, if you've got any offers, think them over," he said.

"I'm not going anywhere," I replied. "I'm a Barcelona player. I'm staying at Barça."

Josep Maria Bartomeu looked surprised.

"But how are we going to resolve this?"

"I've got an idea," I replied.

"Have you?"

"You can phone Real Madrid."

"Why should we phone them?"

"Because if I really have to leave Barça, I want to go to Real. You can make sure I get sold to them."

Josep Maria Bartomeu was horrified.

"You're joking," he said. I looked deadly serious.

"Not at all. We've got a problem," I continued. "We have a coach who isn't man enough to say he doesn't want me here. I want to stay. But if he wants to sell me, he'll have to come out and say so himself, loud and clear. And the only club I want to go to is Real Madrid, just so you know."

I left the room, and now there was no more messing about. It was game on. Real Madrid, I'd said. Of course, that was just the kickoff, a provocation, a strategic bluff. In reality, we had Manchester City and AC Milan in the works.

Sure, I knew all about the incredible things that had happened at Man City and all the money that seemed to be there since the bunch from the United Arab Emirates had taken over. City could surely become a big club within a few years. But I'd soon turn twenty-nine. I didn't have time for long-term plans, and money was never the key thing. I wanted to go to a team that could be good now, and there was no club with a history like AC Milan.

"Let's go for Milan," I said.

———

Now, when I look back on it, it's really incredible. Ever since that day Guardiola called me in and told me I'd be sitting on the bench, we'd played a tough game, and, of course, we realized we were stressing Guardiola and the management out. That was entirely according to plan. The idea was that those guys would become so demoralized, they'd have to let me go cheap, which would help us get a good personal contract. We had a meeting with Sandro Rosell, the new president, and we could sense it right away: Sandro Rosell was in a tight spot.

He hadn't understood what the problem was between me and Guardiola either. He only realized that the situation was untenable and he was going to have to sell me at any price, unless he was going to fire the manager. But he couldn't do that. Not after all the successes the club had had. Rosell had no choice. Regardless of whether he loved me or hated me, he had to get rid of me.

"I'm sorry about this," he said. "But things are the way they are. Do you have a particular club you want to go to?"

Mino and I gave him the same line we'd played against Bartomeu.

"Yes, as a matter of fact," I said, "I do."

"Good, very good." Sandro Rosell's face brightened. "Which club?"

"Real Madrid."

He went pale. Letting a Barça star go to Real is tantamount to high treason.

"Not possible," he replied. "Anything but that."

He was shaken, and both Mino and I could tell: now we're playing our game. I continued calmly, "Well, you asked a question and I gave you an answer, and I'm happy to say it again: Real Madrid is the only club I can see myself going to. I like Mourinho. But you've got to phone them up and tell them yourselves. Is that okay?"

It was not okay. There was nothing in the world that was less okay, and of course we knew that, and now Sandro Rosell was starting to panic. The club had purchased me for the equivalent of £40 million ($60 million). The guy was under pressure to get the money back, but if he sold me to Real, which was Mourinho's new club, Rosell would basically get lynched by the fans. This wasn't easy for him, to put it mildly. He couldn't keep me because of the manager. He couldn't sell me to their archenemy. The guy had lost the upper hand, and we kept up the pressure.

"Just think how smoothly it'll go. Mourinho's said himself how much he wants me."

We knew no such thing. That was the line we took, though.

"No," he said.

"That's a shame. Really! Real Madrid is the only club we have in mind."

We left the room, smiling. We'd gone on and on about Real Madrid. That was our official line. But we had AC Milan dangling, and we were working on them. If Rosell was desperate, that was no good for Barça. However, it was good for Milan. The more desperate Rosell was to sell, the cheaper it would be to buy me, and that would benefit us in the end. It was a game, and it was being played on two levels: one in public and one behind the scenes. Still, the clock was ticking. The transfer window was closing on August 31, and on the twenty-sixth we had an exhibition match against none other than AC Milan at Camp Nou. Nothing was set yet. But the matter was out in the media anyway. There was speculation everywhere, and Galliani, vice president of AC Milan, formally announced that he was not leaving Barcelona without Ibrahimović.

In the stadium, supporters waved signs saying, "Ibra, stay!"

There was a lot of attention on me, of course. It was mostly Ronaldinho's match, though. Ronaldinho is like a god at Barcelona. He played for AC Milan, but he'd been at Barça before, and he'd been voted World Player of the Year two years in a row. Before the match, we were going to be shown clips of his best moments on the big screen, and he was supposed to run a lap of honor around the pitch. But, that guy . . . well, he just does what he wants.

We were sitting in the locker room, waiting to run out onto the pitch. It felt odd. I could hear the roar of the crowd outside. Obviously, Guardiola wasn't looking at me, and of course I was wondering, Is this my last match with the team? What's going to happen? I didn't have a clue. Then everybody sat up. Ronaldinho looked in through the doorway—and Ronaldinho, he's got charisma. He's one of the true greats. Everybody was staring at him.

"Ibra!" he shouted, grinning.

"Yeah," I replied.

"Have you packed your bags? I'm here to take you along with me to Milan!" he said, and everybody laughed, thinking, Typical Ronaldinho, sneaking into our locker room like that, and people looked at me.

Of course, everybody'd had their suspicions. Nobody'd heard it straight out like that before. Now it was being repeated over and over again. I got to play from the start. The match didn't really mean anything, and just before kickoff Ronaldinho and I carried on joking about it, saying, Are you mad? Photos of us laughing on the pitch appeared everywhere. The worst thing was in the players' tunnel on our way out after halftime. All the big names were calling to me: Pirlo, Gattuso, Nesta, and Ambrosini.

"You have to come, Ibra. We need you!"

AC Milan hadn't been having an easy time recently. Inter had dominated the Italian League in recent years, and of course everyone at AC Milan was longing for a new era of glory, and I know now that many of the players, especially Gattuso, had put pressure on the club's management:

"For Christ's sake, buy Ibra. We need somebody with a real winner's mind-set on the team."

It wasn't that simple. AC Milan didn't have as much money as they used to, and no matter how desperate Sandro Rosell was, he kept trying to extract as much money for me as possible. He wanted 50, 40 million euros. But Mino continued to play hardball.

"You won't get a damn thing. Ibra's going to Real Madrid. We don't want to go to Milan."

"How about thirty million?"

Time was getting short, and Rosell lowered his price again and again. Things were looking more and more promising, and Galliani came to visit Helena and me in our house in the hills. Galliani is a real heavyweight, and an old friend and business partner of Berlusconi. He's a bastard of a negotiator.

I'd had dealings with him before. That was when I was leaving Juventus, and that time he'd said, "I'll offer you this, or nothing!" Juventus was in crisis then, and he had the upper hand. Now the tables were turned. He was the one under pressure. He couldn't go home without me, not after the promises he'd made and the pressure from the players and fans. Besides, we'd helped him. We'd made sure we got the transfer fee down. It was like he was getting me on sale.

"These are my conditions," I said. "It's this, or nothing," and I could see how he was thinking things over and sweating.

They were some pretty tough terms.

"Okay," he said.

"Okay."

We shook hands, and then the negotiations for my transfer fee continued. That was between the clubs, and I wasn't bothered, not really. It was quite a drama, and there were a number of factors involved. Time was one. The clock was ticking. The seller's unease was another. The fact that the manager couldn't deal with me was another. With every hour, Sandro Rosell got more nervous, and my fee kept going down. Finally, I was sold for 20 million euros. Twenty million! Thanks to a single person, my price tag had gone down by 50 million euros.

Because of Guardiola's problem, the club was forced to do a disastrous deal—it was crazy, and I said all this to Sandro Rosell as well. Not that I really needed to. He knew it, and I'm sure he'd been kept awake at night, cursing the situation. I mean, I'd scored twenty-two goals and fifteen assists during my season at Barcelona. Yet I'd lost nearly 70 percent of my value. Whose fault was that? Sandro Rosell knew all too well, and I remember how we were all standing there in the office at Camp Nou: him, Mino, me, Galliani, my lawyer, and Josep Maria Bartomeu. The contract was lying there in front of us. The only thing remaining was to sign it and then say thanks and goodbye.

"I want you to know . . ." Rosell faltered.

"Yes?"

"I'm doing the worst deal in my entire life here," he continued. "I'm selling you off dirt cheap, Ibra!"

"You see how much rotten leadership can cost."

"I know it wasn't handled well," he said, and then he signed. Then it was my turn. I took hold of that pen, and everybody was watching me, and I felt I ought to say something. Then again, maybe not. Maybe I should have kept quiet. But I had a few things I wanted to get off my chest.

"I've got a message for Guardiola," I announced, and of course that made everybody nervous. What's happening now? Hasn't there been enough arguing? Can't the guy just sign?

"Do you have to?"

"Yes. I want you to tell him . . ." I began, and then I told them exactly what I wanted them to say to him.

Everyone in the room gulped, and I could tell they were thinking, How come he's coming out with this stuff now? Believe me, I needed to say it. Something happened in my head then. I got my motivation back. Just the thought of being able to do my thing again got me fired up—that's the truth.

When I'd put my signature on that document and said those words, I became myself again. It was like waking up from a nightmare, and, for the first time in a long while, I was itching to play soccer. All those thoughts of quitting were gone, and after that I entered a phase when I played out of sheer joy. Or rather, I played out of sheer joy and sheer rage—joy at having escaped from Barça, and rage that a single person had destroyed my dream.

It was as if I'd been set free, and I also began to see the whole thing more clearly. When I was caught up in the middle of it, I'd mainly tried to buck myself up: It's not that bad, I'll get back in, I'll show them. I kept that up all the time. Then, when it really was over, I realized it had been tough. It had been hard. The person who was supposed to mean the most to me as a soccer player had given me the cold shoulder completely, and that was worse than most stuff I'd been through. I'd been under immense pressure, and in situations like that you need your coach.

What did I have? A guy who avoided me. A guy who tried to treat me as if I didn't exist. I was supposed to be a huge star. Instead, I'd spent my time there feeling unwelcome. I'd been with Mourinho and Capello, the two most disciplined managers in the world, and I'd never had any problems with them. But then this Guardiola . . . I was seething when I thought about it, and I'll never forget when I told Mino: "He wrecked everything."

"Zlatan," he replied.

"Yeah?"

"Dreams can come true and make you happy."

"Yeah."

"But dreams can also come true and kill you," he went on, and I realized immediately he was right.

A dream had both come true and been crushed at Barça, and I continued down the stairs toward the sea of journalists waiting outside. That's when it came to me: I didn't want to call that guy by his real name. I needed something else, and I remembered all the drivel he'd spouted, and, suddenly, there outside Camp Nou in Barcelona, it came to me. The Philosopher!

I would call him "the Philosopher."

"Ask the Philosopher what the problem is," I said, with every scrap of pride and rage inside my being.

26

There was a huge uproar, and I remember something Maxi said afterward—or two things, actually. The first thing was just funny. He asked, "Why is everybody looking at me, Daddy?" and I tried to explain the situation: "Daddy plays soccer. People see me on TV and they think I'm good," and I felt proud afterward—Daddy's pretty cool. Then things took a different turn. It was our nanny who told us.

Maxi had asked why everybody was looking at *him,* because, of course, that was something he got a lot during those days, especially when he arrived with me in Milan—and, worst of all, he added, "I don't like it when they look at me like that." I'm sensitive to stuff like that. Was he going to start feeling different now too? I hate it when children feel they're being singled out, also because it brings back so much of my own childhood: Zlatan doesn't belong here. He's this. He's that. All that's still inside me.

I tried to spend a lot of time with Maxi and Vincent during that time. They're terrific, wild kids. It wasn't easy. Things were going crazy. After I spoke to the journalists outside Camp Nou, I drove home to Helena.

She probably hadn't been expecting to have to move again so soon, and I bet she would've liked to stay. But she knew better than anyone that if I'm not doing well on the soccer pitch, I just wilt. It affects everybody in the family, so I told Galliani, I want to go to Milan with the whole gang—Helena, the boys, the dog, and Mino. Galliani nodded: *si, si.* Everybody come along! He'd clearly organized something really special, so we all hopped on one of the club's private planes and left Barcelona. I remember when we landed at Milan Linate airport. It was like Obama was coming or something. There were eight black Audis lined up in front of us and a red carpet was rolled out, and I went out carrying Vincent in my arms.

For a couple of minutes I was interviewed by a few selected journalists, guys from Milan Channel and Sky and some others, and on the other side of the fence there were hundreds of screaming fans. It was great. I could feel it in the air. The club had been waiting a long time for this. Five years earlier, when Berlusconi had booked a table for me and him at Ristorante Giannino, people had thought everything was done and dusted, and they'd made all sorts of preparations, including putting something on the club's website, an elaborate thing that first was black, and then there was a light in the center, and it went boom, boom! like serious sound effects, just before my name appeared—Ibrahimović, like a flashing, thundering streamer—and then the words "Finally ours."

It was crazy, and they put that thing up now, and clearly nobody was prepared for the level of interest. The website crashed. It totally went down, and I remember walking past the fences at the airport where the fans stood shouting my name, "Ibra, Ibra!"

Then I got into one of the Audis and we drove through the city. It was chaos, I'm telling you. It was like, Zlatan has landed. There were cars and scooters and TV cameras after us, and sure, I got a buzz out of it. The adrenaline was pumping, and I realized even more the kind of black hole I'd been living in at Barça. It was as if I'd been locked up in jail and then greeted by a festival outside the prison walls, and everywhere I sensed one thing: all of Milan had been waiting for me, and they wanted me to take charge. I was going to lead them to trophies again and, to tell you the truth, I liked it.

The street outside the Boscolo Hotel, where we were going to be staying, was cordoned off. All around Milan, residents were shouting and waving, and inside the hotel the management stood in a row and bowed. In Italy, soccer players are like gods, and we were given the deluxe suite. We could tell right off everything was really well organized. This was a solid club with traditions, and honestly, my body was trembling. I wanted to play soccer. That same day, AC Milan was playing against Lecce in the Serie A season opener, and I asked Galliani if I could play.

It wasn't possible. My papers hadn't been finalized. I still went to the stadium. I was going to be introduced at halftime, and I'll never forget that feeling. I didn't want to go into the locker room. I didn't want to disturb the players as they regrouped. But there was a lounge just next door, so I sat in there with Galliani and Berlusconi and some other bigwigs.

"You remind me of a player I used to have," Berlusconi said.

Of course, I could guess who he was talking about, but I wanted to be polite.

"Who's that?" I said.

"A guy who could take care of situations on his own."

He was talking about van Basten, of course, and then he welcomed me into the club—"It's a great honor" and all that stuff—and then we went up into the stands. I had to sit two places away from him, for some political reason or other. There's always loads going on around that guy. It was pretty calm then—at least compared to what followed. Two months later, the whole circus surrounding Berlusconi blew up, with rumors about young girls and court cases. Now, though, he sat there and seemed pleased, and I started to feel the vibes. People were screaming my name again, and I went down onto the pitch. They rolled out a red carpet and put up a little stage down there, and I waited on the sideline for a long time—at least that's what it felt like. The stadium was at the boiling point. San Siro was full to capacity, even though it was August and the holiday season, and I stepped out onto the pitch. There was a roar all around me, and I was like a little boy again. It wasn't long since I'd stood in Camp Nou in the same situation, and then I went out to all the cheering and applause, and there was a load of kids standing by the red carpet. I gave them all high-fives and stepped up onto the stage.

"Now we're going to win everything," I said in Italian, and the roar got even louder.

The stadium was shaking, and afterward I got a match shirt. It had my name on it, but no number. I didn't have a number yet. I'd been given a few to choose from, but none of them was any good, and there was a chance I could get the eleven, which Klaas-Jan Huntelaar currently had. Huntelaar was on the transfer list but, because he hadn't been sold yet, I'd have to wait. In any case, it was starting now. Now I was going to make sure AC Milan won their first Scudetto in seven years. A new era of glory was about to begin. That's what I promised.

Both me and Helena had bodyguards, and some people might think, What kind of luxury is that? It's no luxury, though. In Italy, soccer stars are surrounded by hysteria, the pressure is terrible and some bad things had happened—not just that fire outside our door in

Turin. When I was at Inter and was going to play a match at San Siro, Sanela came to visit us. She and Helena drove to the stadium in our big new Mercedes. There was chaos and there were traffic jams outside the stadium. Helena could only inch forward in the car, and people around her had plenty of time to gawp and see who she was. Then a guy on a Vespa drove past a little too fast and a little too close and clipped her side mirror.

In that situation, Helena couldn't tell whether it was intentional or not. It was more like, Oh no, what's he done? She opened the window to adjust the mirror and saw something out of the corner of her eye: another guy in a cycle helmet was rushing toward her and then she realized, This is something wrong—a trap. She tried to close the window, but it was a new car and she wasn't familiar with all the controls so she didn't manage to get the window up in time. The guy came up and punched her in the face.

It turned into a vicious scuffle, and the Merc crashed into the car in front, and the guy tried to pull her out through the window. Fortunately, Sanela was there. She grabbed hold of Helena and held her in. It was completely crazy. It was a tug-of-war for life or death—that's what it felt like. Finally, Sanela was able to drag Helena back inside the car, and then Helena managed to turn herself around somehow.

She landed a kick in the bastard's face from an impossible angle, and she had on four-inch heels. That must have hurt like hell, and the guy ran off. People had started to gather around the car. It was absolute chaos, and Helena was bruised.

It could have ended really badly. There have been a few things like that, unfortunately. That's the truth. We needed protection. Anyway, my bodyguard, a good guy, drove me out to Milanello, the club's training facility, on the first day.

———

I was getting all the usual medical exams. Milanello is nearly an hour's drive from Milan, and of course there were fans waiting down by the gates when we drove in. I felt the weight of all the traditions at Milan, and I greeted all the legends on the squad: Zambrotta, Nesta, Ambrosini, Gattuso, Pirlo, Abbiati, Seedorf, Inzaghi, Pato, the young Brazilian, and Allegri, the coach, who'd just arrived from Cagliari and didn't have much experience but who seemed good. Sometimes, when you're new in the gang, you're called into question. There's a fight for your place in the pecking order, as if people are saying, You think you're the star here? Here, though, I could sense it immediately. I got respect straight away. Actually, maybe I shouldn't say this, but a number of players told me afterward: We got a 20 percent boost when you came. You brought us out of the shadows. AC Milan hadn't just been having a tough time in the league the last few years. The club hadn't been the best team in the city for a long time, either.

Inter had dominated. Inter had dominated ever since I arrived at the club in 2006, with all that attitude I'd got from Capello which somehow said, Practice sessions are just as important as matches. You can't train soft and play aggressive. You've got to do battle every minute, otherwise I'll come after you. I went around trying to give encouragement and joke around with the guys, everything that had come naturally to me everywhere except at Barcelona. In a way, it reminded me of my early days at Inter. Lead us, lead us, the guys seemed to be saying, and I thought, Now the balance of power is going to wobble a little again. I went into every practice incredibly fired up and, just like I'd done before Barcelona, I screamed at people. I made noise and I yelled. I made fun of the ones who lost, and people said to me, What's going on? We haven't seen the guys this fired up in ages.

———

There was another new guy on the team. His name was Robson de Souza, but people called him Robinho. I'd been involved in that transaction. Galliani had asked me while I was still at Barcelona, "What do you think of Robinho? Can you play with him?"

"A brilliant player, just bring him here. The rest will work itself out."

The club paid 18 million euros for him, which was seen as cheap, and Galliani gained a lot of prestige for that as well. He'd managed to buy both me and Robinho at bargain prices. Not long ago, Manchester City had paid far more than twice that for Robinho. The purchase had been something of a risk. Robinho was a prodigy who'd lost his way a bit. There's no greater god in Brazil than Pelé, and in the nineties he was in charge of the Santos youth organization— Santos FC had been Pelé's home club, and they'd been going through a rough patch for many years. People dreamed that he'd discover a new super-talent, though not many believed it would really happen. A new Pelé! A new Ronaldo, the kind of player that only comes along a few times in a hundred years. Even in the first practice session, Pelé just stood there, totally blown away. He called time out, so the story goes, and went over to a skinny, impoverished kid on the pitch.

"I'm about ready to cry," he said. "You remind me of myself." That was Robinho, a guy who grew up and became the big star everybody was waiting for—at least at first. He was sold to Real Madrid and later to Manchester City, but more recently he'd had quite a bit of negative publicity. There had been a lot of drama surrounding him. We became close at AC Milan. We were two guys who'd grown up in difficult circumstances, and there were parallels in our lives. We'd both been chewed out because we dribbled too much, and I loved his technique. He was a little too unfocused on the pitch, though, and did too many tricks on his own over near the sideline.

I was on him a lot about that. I was on everybody on the team, and before my first match away at Cesena I was sizzling with energy, and you can imagine the hype surrounding me. The papers wrote page after page: now I was going to show what I meant for my new club.

It was me, Pato, and Ronaldinho in front, and that seemed strong. Robinho started on the bench. But it was useless. I was in overdrive, just like in my early days at Ajax. I wanted too much, so we ended up with too little, and at halftime we were behind Cesena 2–0. Losing to Cesena, when we were AC Milan! That was unbearable, and I was angry and completely crazy on the pitch. Damn it, nothing worked. I worked like a dog and, toward the end, we got a penalty. Who knows, maybe we could turn it around? I was going to take the penalty, and I stepped up and shot—into the goalpost. We lost, and how do you think I felt? I had to do a doping test after the match, and I came into the room so furious that I trashed a table, and the doping guy in there was totally terrified.

"Calm down, calm down."

"Listen," I said. "You don't tell me what to do. Otherwise you could end up like that table down there."

That wasn't a nice thing to do; he was an innocent doping tester. That's the attitude I brought to Milan, though, and when we lost, the red mist descended. That's when you need to leave me to wreck stuff in peace. I was boiling with rage, and was just happy when the papers went at me the next day and gave me miserable reviews. I deserved it, and I clenched my fists. Things didn't loosen up in the next match either, or the one after that, even though I scored my first goal away against Lazio and it looked as if we were going to win. Then, in the final minutes, we let in an equalizer, and this time there was no doping check.

I went straight into the locker room, where there was a whiteboard that the manager writes the game plans on, and I kicked it with all my strength. The board went flying like a missile and struck a player.

"Don't play with fire. It's dangerous," I roared, and the room went silent, because I guess everybody understood exactly what I meant: we were supposed to win, nothing else, and we damn well shouldn't let in any unnecessary goals at the end. We couldn't continue like that.

After four matches, we had only five points, and Inter was at the top of the league standings, same as always, and I was feeling more and more pressure on my shoulders. We were still living in the Boscolo Hotel, and we'd managed to settle in a bit. Helena, who had been staying out of the public eye, gave her first interview. It was for a magazine, and that became a complete circus. Every word about us made headlines. I could say totally meaningless stuff, like There's been less meatballs and noodles since I met Helena. In the papers, that became Zlatan's great declaration of love for Helena, and it felt more and more like I was changing. Me, who always got a buzz from being the center of attention—I was starting to become more shy and retiring.

I didn't like having too many people around me, and we led a quiet life. I stayed indoors, and after a few months we moved into an apartment the club had arranged for us in the city center. That was nice, of course, but it didn't have our furniture and our things—it was nice, as I say, but really impersonal. In the mornings, the bodyguard would be waiting for me down in the lobby and we'd drive out to Milanello. I'd get breakfast before training and lunch afterward, and then there'd often be a load of PR stuff, having photos taken and things, and, as always in Italy, I was away from the family a lot. We stayed in hotels ahead of our away matches, and we'd be shut up at Milanello before our home battles, and that's when I started to get that feeling.

I was missing out on a lot at home, Vincent was getting bigger; he was talking more and more. It was crazy, really. Maxi and Vincent had moved around so much they spoke three languages fluently: Swedish, Italian, and English.

Life was entering a new phase, and I often thought, What will I do when my career is over and Helena starts hers up again? I had some thoughts like that. Sometimes I longed for the time after soccer. Sometimes I didn't.

Still, I was no less fired up, and very soon things also loosened up on the pitch. I decided seven, eight matches in a row, and the old ecstasy and hysteria returned. It was "Ibra, Ibra!" everywhere. The papers made this photo montage. There was me, and then the whole team above, as if I was carrying all of AC Milan on my shoulders. It was that sort of talk. I was hotter than ever.

There was one thing I knew better than most at this point: in soccer you can be a god one day and completely worthless the next; and our biggest league match that autumn was approaching: the Milan Derby against Inter at San Siro. There wasn't exactly any doubt that the Ultra fans were going to hate me. The pressure was going to get even greater. On top of that, I had issues with a guy on the team. His name was Oguchi Onyewu, he was an American the size of a house, and I told a friend on the squad, "Something serious is gonna happen. I just feel it."

27

People said he was the nicest guy in the world. Oguchi Onyewu resembled a heavyweight boxer. He was nearly six foot five and weighed 220 pounds. Even though he didn't gain a place on the starting team, he'd previously been voted Best Foreign Player of the Year in the Belgian First Division and the U.S. soccer player of the year. But he couldn't deal with me. He wanted to get it on with me.

"I'm not like the other defenders," he said.

"Okay, good for you then."

"I'm not gonna be psyched out by your trash-talking. By your mouth that's going all the time."

"What are you talking about?"

"You. I've seen you in matches, you do nothing but trash-talk," he continued, and that annoyed me.

Not just because I was sick of all the defenders who want to provoke me. I'm not the one who trash-talks, either. I get my revenge on the pitch. I've heard so much shit over the years: "Fucking Gypsy," stuff about my mom—all that stuff. The worst is "I'll see you after the match!" What the hell is that? Are we going to settle it in the parking lot? It's ridiculous. I remember Giorgio Chiellini, a center back at Juventus. We'd played together and, later on, when I was at Inter Milan, we met on the pitch and he was on me all the time: "Come on now, it's not like it was before, is it?" He tried to provoke me, and then he tackled me from behind. You realize, that's a cowardly thing to do. You don't see the guy coming, and I went down in pain. I was in a lot of pain. Still, I didn't say anything. I don't in those situations. I think, I'll get you back in our next encounter. Then I'll go at him so hard he doesn't get up for a long time. So no way, I'm not the one who trash-talks. I tackle instead. I go off like a bomb in encounters. I didn't get an opportunity that time, though, so after the final whistle I went up to him and took hold of his head and dragged him like a disobedient dog, and Chiellini got scared, I could see it.

"You wanted to fight. So how come you're shitting yourself now?" I hissed, and headed off to the locker room.

No, I retaliate with my body, not with words, and I said that to Oguchi Onyewu as well. He just kept on, and once when I yelled, "That was no free kick!," he shushed me with his finger, as if to say, See, you're just talking shit, and I thought, I've had enough, that's it.

"You, pass it," I said.

He shushed me again, and I saw red. I didn't say anything, not a word. That bastard was going to find out how I trash-talk in these situations, and the next time he got the ball I rushed toward him and jumped up with my feet and studs out in front—the worst type of tackle. But he saw me. He leapt out of the way and we both crashed to the ground, and my first thought was, Shit! I've missed. I'll get him next time. Then as I got up and walked away I felt a blow to my shoulder. Not a good idea, Oguchi Onyewu.

I headbutted him, and then we flew at each other. I'm not talking about a little scrap. We wanted to tear each other limb from limb. It was brutal. We were two guys who each weighed over two hundred pounds, and we were rolling around, punching and kneeing each other, and, of course, the whole team rushed over and tried to separate us. That wasn't easy, not at all. We were crazy and furious, and sure, of course, I admit you need adrenaline on the pitch, you've got to do battle. But this crossed the line. It was like life and death. And the weirdest thing happened afterward.

Oguchi Onyewu started praying to God with tears in his eyes. He made the sign of the cross, and I thought, What is this? I got even more furious. It felt like a provocation, and at that point Allegri, the manager, came up and said, "Calm down, Ibra." It didn't do any good. I just pushed him out of the way and ran toward Oguchi again. I was stopped by my teammates, and I suppose that was a good thing. It could have turned out nasty. Afterward, Allegri summoned us both in. We shook hands and apologized. But Oguchi was cold as a fish, and that was fine by me. If he's cold, I'll be cold back, no problem, and afterward I was driven home. I phoned Galliani, the boss—and there's one thing you should know, which is that I don't like to blame other people. It's unmanly. It's a shitty thing to do, especially on a team where you've taken on the role of a leader.

"Listen," I told Galliani. "An unfortunate thing happened in practice. It was my fault, and I take responsibility. I want to apologize, and you can give me whatever punishment you want."

"Ibra," he said. "This is Milan. We don't work like that. You've apologized. Now we move on."

It wasn't over, though—not yet. There had been supporters along the sideline, and the whole thing was in all the papers. Nobody knew the background story. But the fight became public knowledge. It took ten people to pull us apart, they wrote, and there was talk of unrest on the team and Ibra the bad boy and all the usual stuff. I didn't care.

Write what you want! Even so, I was thinking, Shit, my chest hurts, so we had it checked out. I'd broken a rib in the fight, and there's nothing you can do about a broken rib. The doctors just bandaged me up.

That was hardly the best thing that could have happened. Things were gearing up for the Derby against Inter. We had Pato and Inzaghi injured, and of course the papers wrote pages and pages about it, not least of all about the duel between me and Materazzi. It was going to be particularly vicious, they said. Not just because Materazzi was a tough guy and we'd fought in the past and played on the same team. Materazzi had mocked me for kissing my Barça badge at Camp Nou. It was this and it was that. Most of it was just talk, but one thing was certain: Materazzi was going to go after me hard, because that was his job. It was important that the team stopped me, and in those situations there's only one way to respond. You've got to hit back just as hard. Otherwise, you lose the upper hand and risk getting hurt.

No supporters are worse than Inter Milan's Ultras. They're not forgiving types, believe me, and to them I was Public Enemy Number One. Nobody had forgotten our fight from the Lazio match, and of course I knew there would be boos and trash talk. But hell, that stuff is part of it.

I wasn't the first Inter player who'd signed for AC Milan, either. I was in good company. Ronaldo joined Milan in 2007, and then the Inter fans handed out whistles to put him off his game. The matches between Inter and AC Milan, known as the Derby della Madonnina, always stir up a lot of emotions, and there's politics and shit involved as well. It's a huge rivalry.

It's like Real Madrid and Barça in Spain, and I remember the players in the stadium. You could see it in their faces. This was big. This was important. We were at the top of the standings then, and a win would mean a lot. AC Milan hadn't won a Derby in several years. Inter had also brought home the Champions League trophy that year. It was Inter who dominated. But if . . . if we won, that would signal a shift in power, and I could hear the roar of the crowd in the stadium and music blaring from the loudspeakers. There was an atmosphere of hate and carnival at the same time, and I wasn't nervous, exactly.

I was just fired up. I sat and hoped I'd get to run in and do battle. Of course, I knew you can be bursting with adrenaline. You can still end up completely outside the game and not get a thing out of it. You never know, and I clearly remember the start of the match and the roar in there at San Siro. You never really get used to it. The place is at the boiling point all around you, and Seedorf headed over the bar almost immediately. The game surged back and forth.

In the fifth minute, I got a ball from the right side. I dribbled and got into the penalty area, and I had Materazzi on me. Of course, Materazzi wanted to come right out and say, You're not gonna get away, just you wait! But he made a mistake. He brought me down and I crashed onto the ground, and, obviously, I thought, Is that a penalty? Is that a penalty?

It should've been. But I didn't know. There was a horrible racket, and, naturally, all the Inter players thrust out their arms, as if to say, What the hell? The referee ran toward the penalty spot and I took a deep breath. I was the one who was going to take it, and you can just imagine. My team was behind me, and you don't have to wonder what they were thinking: Don't miss, Ibra! For God's sake, don't miss this one!

In front of me were the goal and the goalkeeper, and behind them were Inter's Ultra fans. They were insane. They were booing and screaming. They were doing everything they could to rattle me, and some of them had laser pointers. I got a green light right in my face, and Zambrotta blew up. He went to the referee.

"Goddamn it, they're interfering with Ibra. They're blinding him!"

What could they do, though? Search through the whole stadium? That wouldn't work, and I was totally focused. They could've put me under headlights and spotlights. I just wanted to go up and shoot, and this time I knew exactly how it would go: the ball would go into the goal's right corner. I stood still for a couple of seconds, and sure, it was like a little twinge inside me: I had to score. I'd started my season by missing a penalty. It couldn't happen again. But I couldn't think about that. You can never think too much on the pitch. You just have to play, and I ran up and shot.

I shot exactly as I'd imagined, and it went in, and I raised my arms up and looked the Ultra fans straight in the eyes, thinking, Your damned tricks don't work. I'm stronger than that, and I've got to say, when the entire stadium roared and I saw up on the big screen, "Inter—AC Milan, 0–1, Ibrahimović," that felt good. I was back in Italy.

Even so, we were just a few minutes into the match, and the fight was intensifying. In the sixtieth minute we had Abate sent off, and it's no fun playing with ten men against Inter Milan. We were working like dogs. Materazzi was on me like a leech, and in one encounter a few minutes later I rushed toward the ball and slammed into him and totally floored him. It was unintentional, of course. But he was still lying on the ground, and the doctor and all the Inter subs ran out, and the hatred from the Ultra fans just grew, especially when Materazzi was taken off on a stretcher.

In the final twenty minutes, the pressure on us was terrible, and I was completely worn out. I was ready to vomit from exhaustion. But we made it. We held on to our lead and won. The next day, I was due to receive my fifth Guldbollen award in Sweden. I'd found out about it in advance, and I really wanted to get to bed early, as early as it's possible to do when you've got a match like that spinning around in your head. However, we decided we'd go out and party at the Cavalli nightclub. Helena came along. We sat pretty quietly in a corner with Gattuso while Pirlo, Ambrosini, and all the rest partied like madmen. There was such a sense of relief everywhere, and really crazy joy, and we didn't get home until four in the morning.

———

In December 2010, AC Milan purchased Antonio Cassano. Cassano has something of a reputation as a bad boy like me—he likes to be seen and to talk about what a brilliant player he is. The guy's been through a lot and has often got into fights with players and managers, including Capello at Roma. Capello even coined a new term, *"cassanata,"* which means sort of irrational and crazy. Cassano has a brilliant quality to his playing. I really liked him, and we got better and better as a team.

There was a problem, though. The feeling crept up on me. I was starting to feel burnt out. I'd given a hundred percent in every match, and I don't think I'd ever felt such pressure before. That might sound strange when you think of everything I'd been through. It'd been tough, joining Barça. It hadn't been easy at Inter, either. I was feeling it here more than ever before: we had to win the league title, and I was the one who was supposed to lead the team. I was playing every match basically as if it were a World Cup final, and I was paying the price. I was getting worn out.

Eventually, I wasn't able to follow through on my ideas and images on the pitch. My body was a step behind, and I'm sure I should have sat out a match or two. Allegri was new. He wanted to win at any price too. He needed his Zlatan, and he was squeezing every drop out of me. Not that I blame him for a second.

He was just doing his job, and I wanted to play. I'd found my flow.

I had a rhythm. I would've wanted to play even with a broken leg, and Allegri got me going. We had respect for each other. But I was paying a price, and I wasn't as young as I used to be.

I was physically big—not like in my second season at Juventus, not at all. There was no junk food, no excess weight. I was careful about what I ate. It was all muscle, but I was older and a different player from what I'd been at the start of my career. I was no longer a dribbler, no Ajax guy. I was a heavy, explosive striker, and I was forced to play smarter in order to last the whole match, and in February I was starting to feel tired.

It was supposed to be a secret within the club, but it got out to the press and there was a lot of talk about it. Will he last? Can he cope? We also started losing late in a number of matches. We couldn't go the distance, and we conceded a whole load of unnecessary goals, and I went a whole month without scoring at all. My body was missing that real explosiveness, and we crashed out of the Champions League against Tottenham. Of course, that was hard—I thought we were the better team. But we lost our initiative in the Italian League as well, and Inter was in top form again.

Were they going to overtake us? Would we lose the grip we'd had on the league? There was some talk of that. The papers wrote about every possible scenario, and my red cards didn't help anything. The first one was against Bari, one of the bottom teams. We were trailing 1–0, and I was standing in the penalty area; a defender was holding me and I felt trapped. I reacted instinctively. I lashed out with my open hand and smacked him in the stomach, and he went down. It was completely idiotic of me. I admit it.

It was a reflex reaction, though, nothing more, and I wish I had a better explanation. I didn't. Soccer is a fight. You come under attack and you strike back, and sometimes you go too far without knowing why. I've done that many times. Over the years, I've learned a lot.

I'm not the crazy kid at Malmö FF any longer, but that stuff will never leave me entirely. My winner's mind-set has a downside. I go ballistic, and that time against Bari I got a red card. A red card can make anybody lose it. I just left the pitch immediately, without saying a word. Cassano tied not long after. That was reassuring. Goddamn it, though, I got a ban—and not just for the next match against Palermo but for the next Derby against Inter Milan as well.

The AC Milan management tried to protest. There was a huge fuss about it. It didn't work, and that was a disgrace, of course. I didn't take it as hard as I would have in the past, though. That's the truth. My family helped there. It doesn't work to get too down anymore. I have to be there for my kids. Still, my rage continued. I played again against Fiorentina, and it looked as if I was going to behave. We were ahead, with just a few minutes remaining. Then I got a throw-in against me. I was furious and screamed, *"Vaffan-culo!,"* which sort of means "Go to hell," at the referee, and sure, that wasn't good, especially with regard to what had happened against Bari. But come on! Have you been there on the pitch? People say *"Vaffanculo!"* and things like that all the time. They don't get sent off because of it. They don't get a ban for several matches. The referees let it pass, at least most of the time.

People yell harsh things all the time out there. But I was Ibra. Milan was Milan. We were leading the league. There was politics involved. They saw an opportunity to punish us. That's what I believe. I got a three-match ban. This stupid thing looked as if it was going to cost us the Scudetto, and the club was doing everything to salvage the situation. We came up with an explanation. We said I'd been swearing at myself. I mean, we had to fight back.

"He was angry about his mistakes on the pitch. He was talking to himself."

But, honestly, that was bullshit—sorry about that! On the other hand, the punishment was ridiculously harsh. *"Vaffanculo!"*? That was stupid of me. But it was nothing. As a swear word, *"Vaffanculo!"* isn't even particularly strong. I've heard worse. Still, things were the way they were. I just had to lump it and take the mocking and scolding, and I was awarded some booby prize by a TV channel, the Tapiro d'Oro, or "Golden Tapir." That's the game. They build you up. They knock you down. I was used to it.

Meanwhile, Napoli had shot up to second place in the league standings, just ahead of Inter. Napoli had had their glory days in the eighties when Maradona played for them, but in more recent years they'd had all sorts of difficulties, and they were only just back in top form.

We were leading by three points, but there were six matches left to play and I was banned for three of them. That was shit, but I did get a chance to rest and think about my life. I was working on this book. It forced me to remember things, and it struck me—I haven't always been the nicest guy. I haven't always said the right things, and, of course, I take full responsibility for all that. I'm not going to blame anybody else.

Still, there are a lot of people like me out there, young guys and girls who get told off because they're not like everybody else, and sometimes, sure, they need to get told off. I believe in discipline. What makes me so angry, though, is all those coaches who've never fought their way to the top themselves and yet are so sure: This is how we're going to do it, and no other way. That's so narrow-minded. So stupid.

There are a thousand paths to go down, and the one that's a little different and a little awkward is often the best one. I hate it when people who stand out get put down. If I hadn't been different, I wouldn't be sitting here now, and, obviously, I don't mean: Be like me; try to be like Zlatan. Not at all! I'm talking about going your

own way, whatever that way is, and there shouldn't be any damn petitions and nobody should get the cold shoulder just because they're
not like the others.

It has to be said, though, it's not good to ruin the Scudetto you've
promised your club just because you've got a terrible temper.

28

Adriano Galliani was sitting up in the Stadio Olimpico in Rome with his eyes closed, begging, Please let us win, please let us win, and I can really understand him. This was May 7, 2011. It was half past ten at night, and the minutes were ticking by. They were going too slowly, and Allegri and the guys were fidgeting on the bench. Whether you believed in God or not, it was time to pray. We were facing Roma, and if we managed just one point the Scudetto would be ours, the first in seven years.

I was back on the pitch. How great that felt! I'd been away for a while because of my ban. Now, though, I could be there and decide the league title—not that I thought it was going to be easy. Roma and AC Milan were at war as well, not just because it was two major cities facing each other. This was a crucial match for both teams.

We were fighting for the league title, and Roma was fighting to claim fourth place. A fourth-place finish is a big deal, because as number four you get to be in the Champions League, and that means a lot of money for the TV rights. But something had happened back in 1989, and people have long memories in Italian soccer. Things cast a long shadow, like I said. They keep hanging around. Everybody remembers Ronaldo, who didn't get his penalty that time. But this was something far worse. It was Antonio De Falchi, a young Roma supporter who'd traveled to Milan to watch the away match against AC Milan. His mother was worried, and told him, "Don't wear anything red and gold. Don't reveal you're a Roma supporter." And he obeyed.

He was dressed so as not to attract attention. He could've been a guy with any club at all, but when one of Milan's hard-core supporters went up and asked him for a cigarette, his accent gave him away, and they said, "Are you a Roma fan, you bastard?" and he was surrounded. He was kicked and beaten to death. It was a terrible tragedy, and before our match a *tifo* was held for him.

A *tifo* is a tribute from the stands, and Antonio De Falchi's name was lit up in yellow and red in the stadium. That was a nice gesture, of course, but it also affected the mood in there. It was a big, tense day. Totti is the big star at Roma. He's played for the club since he was thirteen years old. He's like a god in that city. He's won the World Cup, the Capocannoniere, the Golden Boot, everything, and even though he wasn't exactly young anymore he'd been in top form recently, so, of course, there were Totti posters everywhere and Roma signs, but there were AC Milan and Ibra banners as well. We had a lot of fans who'd traveled to watch us and were hoping to be able to celebrate the league title, and smoke from all the flares hung over the stands.

The match got under way at a quarter to nine, as usual. It was me and Robinho in front. Cassano and Pato were on the bench, and we got off to a good start. But in the fourteenth minute, Vučinić broke free. It felt like a goal, like he was going to score it. But Abbiati, our goalkeeper, made a spectacular save. It was pure reflex, and things started to feel tense. Roma had beaten us the last time we'd met at San Siro, and we started working even harder. We were chasing the ball up there, and I had several chances, and Robinho struck the post. Prince Boateng had a brilliant position, but we didn't score, and time was ticking away. A 0–0 draw would be enough, and the clock kept on ticking and, finally, ninety minutes had passed. It should have been over.

Then the goddamn referee said, "Five added minutes!" Five minutes, and we kept playing—honestly, I bet there were others besides Galliani who were praying. Seven years without a Scudetto is a long time for a club like Milan, and now it was close, and remember? I'd promised we would win. That was the first thing I'd said when I was introduced at San Siro, and sure, athletes say all kinds of things. They'll promise the moon, and nothing comes of it. But some, like Muhammad Ali, kept their promises, and I wanted to be one of them. I wanted to talk the talk and walk the walk. I'd come to Milan with my whole winner's mind-set and sworn and promised and fought and worked, and now . . . now, the seconds were counting down: 10, 9, 8, 7 . . . and there it was.

The referee blew his whistle, and victory was ours. Everybody rushed onto the pitch and smoke rose from the stadium. People were yelling and singing. It was beautiful and hysterical. It was absolutely fantastic, and Allegri got thrown up into the air and Gattuso ran around with a magnum bottle of champagne, spraying everybody. Cassano was interviewed on TV, and everybody around me was completely nuts. There was a lot of "Thank you, Ibra, you delivered on your promise," but there were some crazy things too.

We were all high on adrenaline, and Cassano was a cool guy. Maybe he needed a kick. I walked past him and the TV reporter and brought my foot up against Cassano's head—not hard, of course, but not really gentle either, and the guy flinched.

"What's he doing?" the reporter asked.

"He's crazy."

"Seems that way!"

"A player who helps us to win the league trophy can do whatever he wants," Cassano said, laughing.

But he was in pain. He went around with an ice pack on his head afterward. There was a bit of roughhousing, and then the party started. I didn't end up asleep in the bathtub that night. It was pretty wild, though, and honestly, when I stopped to think about it, it was big. I'd been in Italy six years and had won the Scudetto every year. Has anybody else done anything like it? I doubt it, and we didn't just win the league title either. We brought home the Super Cup, the match between the league champions and the Cup winners. We went to China. There was hysteria around me out there as well, and I scored and was named Man of the Match and got my eighteenth title trophy—my!—and I was happy, I really was.

Something had also happened to me. Soccer was no longer everything. I had my family, and I'd said no to the Swedish national team. I liked Lars Lagerbäck. But I hadn't forgotten that business from Gothenburg. I have a long memory, and I wanted more time with Helena and the boys. So I didn't play for Sweden for a while, but still, it came up during that last summer at Barça when everything was hard and I felt like that annoying, different guy from the housing projects again, the one who didn't really fit in.

That summer, many of my teammates from Barcelona played in the World Cup and won the tournament, and I was feeling more and more like, I miss that—not that I wanted to be on the national team. It took up too much time. I was hardly ever at home with the kids already. I was missing out on so much. Then, around that time, Lars Lagerbäck quit. Erik Hamrén became the new coach for the Swedish team. He phoned.

"Hi. I'm the new coach."

"I've gotta say right off," I said, "I have no plans to come back."

"Huh?"

"I don't know what people have told you. You might have gotten some false hopes, but I'm not playing."

"Shit, Zlatan. You're pulling the rug out from under me. I had no idea about that." He was a stubborn bastard, though. I like stubborn bastards. He kept on talking. It's gonna be awesome. It'll be great, all that stuff, and I invited him over to our house in Malmö, and I sensed, This guy is cool. We hit it off. He was no regular Swedish coach. He was willing to cross some boundaries, and those guys are always the best. I don't believe in sticklers for rules, you know that. Sometimes you've got to break the rules. That's how you make progress. I mean, what happened to the guys in the Malmö FF youth squad who always behaved? Are there any books written about their lives?

In the end, I said yes, and we agreed he'd make me captain and I'd be a leader on the national team as well. I liked that. I even liked the fact that I was the one who'd be taking the crap in the media if we lost. It got me buzzing, and when we met the guys on the team, I looked at them. They were thinking, What the hell is this? Normally, a handful of fans turn up to check out our practice sessions. Now there were six thousand for one little team session in Malmö.

I said very calmly: "Welcome to my world."

It's always something special to come to Malmö. Sure, I'm there pretty often. Malmö is our home. But we usually stick around at home. It's something else to play there. That's when the memories come back. The summer after the Scudetto and the Super Cup victory, Malmö FF and AC Milan were going to play an exhibition match. The negotiations between the clubs and the sponsors had gone on for a long time, but when the tickets went on sale people came streaming to the stadium. It was raining, I heard. People stood in long lines with their umbrellas, and the tickets sold out in twenty minutes. The demand was insane, and the lines snaked all the way back to Pildamm Park.

I've said a lot of stuff about Malmö FF over the years. I haven't forgotten what Hasse Borg and Bengt Madsen did, but I love the club too, and I'll never forget when we arrived in Malmö that day. The whole city embraced me. It felt like a carnival. Everything was chaotic, with streets cordoned off, and hysteria, and crowds of people. People jumped up and down, waved and shouted when they saw me. A lot of them had stood there for hours just to get a glimpse of me. All of Malmö was having a party. Everybody was waiting for Zlatan, and I've gone into a lot of roaring stadiums. But this was special: it was the past and the present all at once.

It was my life all over again, and the entire stadium was singing and screaming my name. There's a scene in *Blådårar,* that old documentary, where I'm sitting on a train, just talking to nobody in particular.

"There's one thing I've decided," I say. "I'm gonna have a purple Diablo, a car, Diablo, that's a Lamborghini. And it'll say 'TOYS' in English on the license plate."

It was kind of childish. I was young. I was eighteen, and an awesome car was the coolest thing a kid like me could imagine; and the world was my oyster. Those words got repeated everywhere: Have you heard what that whippersnapper Zlatan said? That was a long time ago. It was far away, but still near somehow, and that night in the stadium in Malmö, the fans unrolled a gigantic banner across the front of the whole stand. I stared at it, and it took a second. Then I got it. It was a drawing of me, next to that car with the TOYS license plate.

"Zlatan, come home. We'll get you the dream car," it said.

That touched my heart—or, as one of my friends once put it, The whole thing is a fairy tale. It's a journey from the projects to a dream. Not long ago, somebody sent me a picture, a photo of the Annelund bridge. That bridge is just outside Rosengård, and somebody had put a sign on it: *You can take a guy out of Rosengård but you can never take Rosengård out of the guy,* it said, signed *Zlatan.*

I hadn't known anything about it. That was news to me. I was injured at the time. I'd sprained my foot and I went home to Malmö for a few days for some physiotherapy. I had a physio guy from Milan with me, and one afternoon we headed out to the bridge to check out that quote. It was a strange feeling. It was summer and the weather was warm, and I got out of the car and checked out the sign and sensed something really happening in me. That place was special.

My dad had been mugged and got a punctured lung under that bridge. Not far away is the tunnel where I used to run home in the dark, terrified, to Mom's place on Cronmans Väg, using the lampposts to guide me. This was the neighborhood of my childhood. These were the streets where everything had started, and I felt—how can I put it? Big and small at the same time.

I was the hero who returned. I was the soccer star, but also the frightened kid in the tunnel again, the one who thought he'd make it if he just ran fast enough. I was everything all at once, and, I'm telling you, a hundred memories came flooding back.

I remembered Dad in his headphones and his workman's dungarees, and the empty fridge and the beer cans, but also how he carried my bed on his back, mile after mile, and watched over me in the hospital. I remembered Mom's face when she came home from her cleaning jobs, and her hug when we headed off to the World Cup in Japan. I remembered my first soccer shoes, the ones I'd bought for 59.90 kronor from next to the tomatoes and the vegetables in the discount supermarket, and I remembered my dreams of becoming the best all-round soccer player I could, and I thought: I made that dream come true, and it wouldn't have happened without all the great players and coaches I'd played with; and I felt grateful. There was Rosengård. There was the tunnel. In the distance, I heard a train going over the bridge. Somebody was pointing at me.

A woman in a headscarf came up and wanted to have her picture taken with me, and I smiled at her. People started to gather around me. It was a fairy tale, and I was Zlatan Ibrahimović.

CAREER TIMELINE

1999

Taken up onto Malmö FF's first squad. Allsvenskan League debut, scores one goal. Malmö FF relegated to Superettan.

2000–2001

Scores twelve goals for Malmö FF in the Superettan. Debut with Swedish national team. Purchased by Ajax. Returns to Allsvenskan with Malmö FF, scores three goals.

2001–2002

Debut with Ajax, scores six goals in league. Scores two goals in UEFA Cup. Scores one goal in Dutch Cup. Wins league title with Ajax. Wins Dutch Cup with Ajax. Second round of World Cup.

2002–2003

Wins Super Cup with Ajax. Scores thirteen goals for Ajax in league. Scores five goals in Champions League. Scores three goals in Dutch Cup.

2003–2004

Scores thirteen goals for Ajax in league. Scores one goal in Champions League qualifier. Scores one goal in Champions League. Wins league title with Ajax. Euro 2004 quarterfinal.

2004–2005

Scores three goals for Ajax in league. Scores goal of the year, as chosen by Eurosport viewers. Sold to Juventus. Scores sixteen goals for Juventus in league. Wins Scudetto with Juventus. Voted Player of the Year at Juventus. Voted Best Foreign Player in Italian League. Voted Best Forward in Sweden. Wins Swedish Guldbollen award.

2005–2006

Scores seven goals for Juventus in league. Scores three goals in Champions League. Wins Scudetto with Juventus. Second round of World Cup.

2006–2007

Sold to Inter Milan. Wins Super Cup with Inter. Scores fifteen goals for Inter in league. Wins Scudetto with Inter. Voted Best Forward in Sweden. Wins Swedish Guldbollen award.

2007–2008

Scores seventeen goals for Inter Milan in league. Scores five goals in Champions League. Wins Scudetto with Inter. Selected for UEFA team. Voted Best Foreign Player in Italian League. Voted Player of the Year in Italian League. Voted Male Sports Personality of the Year in Sweden. Wins Jerring Prize in Sweden. Voted Best Forward in Sweden. Wins Swedish Guldbollen award.

2008–2009

Wins the Super Cup with Inter Milan. Scores twenty-five goals for Inter in league. Scores one goal in Champions League. Scores three goals in Italian

Cup. Wins Scudetto with Inter. Wins Italian goal-scoring title. Scores the best goal of the year in Italian League. Voted Best Foreign Player in Italian League. Voted Player of the Year in Italian League. Voted Best Forward in Sweden. Wins Swedish Guldbollen award.

2009–2010

Sold to Barcelona. Wins Super Cup with Barcelona. Wins UEFA Super Cup. World champion club team with Barcelona. Scores sixteen goals for Barcelona in league. Scores four goals in Champions League. Scores one goal in Spanish Cup. Wins league title with Barcelona. Selected for UEFA team. Voted Male Sports Personality of the Year in Sweden. Voted Best Forward in Sweden. Wins Swedish Guldbollen award.

2010–2011

Scores one goal and wins the Super Cup with Barcelona. Sold to AC Milan. Scores fourteen goals for Milan in league. Scores four goals in Champions League. Scores three goals in Italian Cup. Wins Scudetto with Milan. Scores one goal and wins the Super Cup with Milan in August 2011.

2011–2012

Scores twenty-eight goals in thirty-two matches for AC Milan in the league. Scores five goals in eight matches in Champions League. Voted Best Foreign Player in Italian League. Wins Swedish Guldbollen award. Sold to Paris Saint-Germain at the end of the season.

SWEDISH NATIONAL TEAM

Eighty-six international matches and thirty-nine goals. In an international exhibition match for Sweden in November 2012, scores all four goals, including one of the best goals of all time, in a 4–2 win over England.

To be continued . . .

ABOUT THE AUTHORS

ZLATAN IBRAHIMOVIĆ is a professional soccer player, one of the world's most prolific strikers. Captain of the national team in his native Sweden, he has played for all of Europe's top teams, including Ajax, Juventus, Internazionale, Barcelona, Milan, and, most recently, Paris Saint-Germain, where he is the league's top goal-scorer. Widely regarded as one of the best soccer players of his generation, he is also the most highly valued soccer player of all time, having received approximately $205 million in transfer fees over the course of his career. His bicycle kick for Sweden against England won the 2013 FIFA Award for Goal of the Year.

DAVID LAGERCRANTZ made his debut as an author with *Ultimate High: My Everest Odyssey,* about the Swedish mountaineer Göran Kropp, which became an international bestseller. Since then he has devoted his career to writing about geniuses and exceptional people who go against the flow and blaze their own trails. He achieved critical and commercial success with a novel based on the life of the computer pioneer Alan Turing. He has written several other works of fiction and nonfiction, and he also lectures on creative writing.

ABOUT THE TYPE

This book was set in Times Roman, designed by Stanley Morison specifically for *The Times* of London. The typeface was introduced in the newspaper in 1932. Times Roman had its greatest success in the United States as a book and commercial typeface, rather than one used in newspapers.